C000170810

In Search of
Shambhala

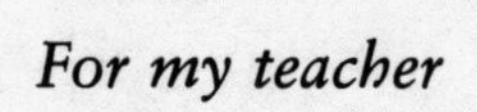

For my teacher

In Search of Shambhala

❖

Elaine Brook

Foreword by
His Holiness the Dalai Lama

JONATHAN CAPE
LONDON

by the same author

THE WINDHORSE
(with Julie Donnelly)
LAND OF THE SNOW LION

First published 1996

1 3 5 7 9 10 8 6 4 2

First published in the United Kingdom in 1996 by Jonathan Cape,
Random House, 20 Vauxhall Bridge Road, London SW1V 2SA

Random House Australia (Pty) Limited
20 Alfred Street, Milsons Point, Sydney,
New South Wales 2061, Australia

Random House New Zealand Limited
18 Poland Road, Glenfield,
Auckland 10, New Zealand

Random House South Africa (Pty) Limited
PO Box 337, Bergvlei, 2012 South Africa

Random House UK Limited Reg. No. 954009

A CIP catalogue record for this book
is available from the British Library

ISBN 0-224-03650-5

Typeset by Intype London, Ltd
Printed and bound in Great Britain by
Mackays of Chatham PLC

Contents

THE DALAI LAMA

FOREWORD

In Search of Shambhala describes a physical journey, in part through areas where a culture and traditions closely associated with those of Tibet still exist. Whereas in Tibet these traditions have been forcibly destroyed, in the regions through which the author travelled they remain an important feature of everyday life. However, even there she notes how they are gradually being eroded by urban values.

In its deepest sense the quest for Shambhala represents the search for spiritual attainment. Originally the kingdom of Shambhala represented an entire community living according to the peaceful principles of Buddhism. Nowadays, no one knows where Shambhala is. Although it is said to exist, people cannot see it or communicate with it in an ordinary way. Some people suggest that it is located on another planet, others that it is like a pure land. Whatever the answer may be, the search for it traditionally begins as an outer journey that slowly becomes a journey of inner exploration and discovery.

May 10, 1996

INTRODUCTION

The Legend

།ལར་རང་ཤོང་རྡོ་ཡི་ཁང་ཆུང་དུ།

It had been snowing all day, a soft heavy snow that whitened the winter trees and muffled footsteps in its soft blanket. At almost 13,000 feet the Himalayan air was thin and rasped dry on my gasping lungs. As I climbed higher the trees gave way to stunted juniper and the slope steepened, rocky now with clumps of spiny grass bristling through the new snow. Slowly, the clouds began to break up and a watery sun filtered through, touching the snow peaks above the valley and silvering the wings of the raven that floated below, iridescent against the deep blue space beneath.

The first sign of the cave was the cluster of prayer flags fluttering Tibetan mantras to the cold wind on top of a mossy boulder outside the entrance. Inside, stumbling in the gloom, I waited for my eyes to focus in the dim light. The hermit sat on a low cushioned bench in the corner, a vision like a sombre coloured Rembrandt painting: an archetypal sage with his high cheekbones and long wispy white hair and beard, and eyes that seemed to see right through you to an eternity beyond this world. He took the white silk scarf I offered and as his hands briefly brushed against my own I felt a strange sensation as if I had touched upon a hidden source of energy that resonated with something lying dormant within myself. Shaken, I sat down on a piece of thread-bare Tibetan carpet in front of him.

I wanted to ask him about Shambhala, the mystical kingdom which is said to lie hidden somewhere beyond the ice walls of the Himalaya and the barren deserts and mountains of Tibet.

There was a pause, then the hermit laughed softly.

'There is an old Tibetan story about a young man who set off, alone, seeking Shambhala. He crossed many snowy mountains until at last he came to the cave of a wise yogi who asked him where he was going in such a wilderness. "To find Shambhala," was the answer. "Then you need not journey much further," said the yogi, "because the Kingdom of Shambhala is in your own heart." '

I was puzzled. 'So Shambhala does not exist as an actual country in reality?'

The hermit smiled again. 'I did not say that. I am simply reminding you that the reality to which you cling is not the only one, nor is it the most valid of possible perceptions. If you want to find Shambhala you must first discover within yourself the clarity with which to see.'

As I slithered and stumbled down the mountainside the snow was glazing into ice as the sun dipped and the peaks faded from dusty pink to deep purple. The hermit's answer remained an enigma, forcing me to recognise that Shambhala, provocative in its very elusiveness, could not be defined in simple terms. I was determined to find out more about the legend.

According to Tibetan legend, Shambhala is a land of peace and harmony, where a dynasty of enlightened kings protect the most secret teachings of Buddhism against the time when all civilisation and culture in the outside world is destroyed through the ravages of war. Then, so the prophecy goes, the King of Shambhala will ride out, defeat the forces of evil and establish a Golden Age.

The date of this Armageddon varies, according to different sources, from a few years to a few hundred years hence. Some of the descriptions of conditions leading up to the final conflict sound chillingly contemporary:

> . . . the world will be wholly depraved. Then property alone will confer rank; wealth will be the only source of devotion; passion the sole bond of union between the sexes; falsehood the only means of success in litigation; and women will be objects merely of sensual gratification. Earth will be venerated but for its mineral resources. . .

Shambhala itself is surrounded by a protective ring of snow mountains, within which lie eight principalities 'like the petals of a lotus'. In the centre, ice mountains surround the jewelled palace of the King of Shambhala.

The golden pagodas of the cities of the kingdom glow among fertile fields, lush forests and beautiful parks. The inhabitants live long and happy lives, free from hunger or sickness. They are intelligent and beautiful, and wear long flowing white robes. Each has great wealth, but never needs to use it. Yet, this is no mere pleasure-garden of the gods. Rather than becoming mindlessly absorbed in hedonistic pursuits, the inhabitants of Shambhala are using their lives and pleasures on the path to spiritual enlightenment by practising the highest of the Buddhist Tantras, the Kalachakra. Ancient texts tell how the Buddha taught the Kalachakra to the first of the lineage of the Kings of Shambhala. The wisdom of these teachings has been passed on by each King, who, in turn, guides his subjects through the practices.

The legend of Shambhala, or part of it, became the inspiration for James Hilton's 'Shangri-La', whose story reached people across the world to the point where Shangri-La has become almost a household word symbolising utopia. This is by no means the only influence the Shambhala legend has had on the West. In 1819 Alexander Csoma de Koros, a Hungarian scholar, set off alone to search for the origins of the Hungarian people. Eventually he reached Tibet, where he spent the rest of his life studying in monasteries, translating texts on both the Kalachakra and Shambhala. So the first news of Shambhala came to the West.

The mystical ideas of the Theosophists sprang from Buddhist teachings, especially those most closely linked to Shambhala; many Theosophists regarded Shambhala as the centre of the spiritual world. One of them, Nicholas Roerich, even led a scientific expedition across central Asia in search of the mystical kingdom. Roerich's ideas influenced American politics in the time of Roosevelt, culminating in the Roerich Pact and Banner of Peace, a treaty by which nations would respect and preserve cultural and scientific treasures in time of war. Roerich's excitement on hearing of the prophecies of Shambhala comes through clearly in his accounts of his expedition in *Altai Himalaya*, published in 1924:

> From hand to hand among the local inhabitants the prophecies and new commands are travelling. With excitement they are comparing the dates which have already been fulfilled. And they prepare and await, await, await. . .

Someone comes in the evening and whispers about a new manuscript of Shambhala. We ask him to bring it. . . One must be in these places to understand what occurs! One must look in the eyes of these coming ones, in order to realise how vitally important for them is the meaning of Shambhala. And the dates of events are not a curious oddity but are connected with the structures of the future. Though these structures are sometimes dust-ridden and perverted, their substance is vital and stirs the thought.

It is told in the prophecies how the new era shall manifest itself; first will begin an unprecedented war of all nations. Afterward brother shall rise against brother. Oceans of blood shall flow. And the people shall cease to understand one another. They shall forget the meaning of the word Teacher. But just then shall the Teachers appear and in all corners of the world shall be heard the true teaching. . . And one can already perceive unusual manifestations and encounter unusual people.

Although Roerich did not find any material traces of Shambhala, there are several Tibetan lamas who claim to have gone there, albeit in meditation or in dreams. There are even guide books, ancient Tibetan texts which give descriptions of the long and difficult journey that leads to Shambhala. Most sources give Bodhgaya in India, the place of Buddha's enlightenment, as the starting point and from there the journey leads northwards through the Himalayan range. Gradually the descriptions become more and more mystical and difficult to understand, let alone try to follow. The lamas say this is because ordinary people are not yet ready to go to Shambhala. Only those who have heightened awareness through meditation – or, in Buddhist terms, have developed the 'Wisdom Eye' – would be able to perceive the hidden kingdom for what it really is, and be able to understand the twilight language of the guides. Only such yogis could make the spiritual as well as the physical journey; others might succeed in arriving at the correct geographical location but would see only icy mountains or empty desert.

The legend had inspired others beside Csoma de Koros and the Theosophists. I was by no means the first to feel the lure of Shambhala and the intriguing concept of an inner, spiritual journey beneath the surface of the outer. But Shambhala is so remote as to be almost a symbol of the unattainable. Even the

Dalai Lama, who has given the Kalachakra initiation to thousands, from Bodhgaya to Los Angeles, professes (publicly at least) to be unsure of where Shambhala lies.

It was not until my explorations led me to some of the remote corners of the Himalaya that I first began to hear rumours of other Hidden Valleys, like tiny Shambhalas, which lay concealed within the icy fastness of the highest mountains on earth. Trulzhig Rinpoche, the High Lama of the Sherpa region of Khumbu, has remains of an old guide to Khembalung, the 'Valley of Incense Plants' which lies somewhere east of Khumbu. Although the lamas maintain that, like Shambhala, these Valleys can only be reached by great yogis, here at last were places which seemed almost within reach. Some inhabited valleys are said to have originated as Hidden Valleys which were discovered and 'opened' by those who had, apparently, the right karma, physical strength, and yogic perceptions to succeed in their quest. Others had been able to follow and colonise the Valleys. Some Sherpas say that Khumbu itself was once a Hidden Valley, concealed by the saint Padmasambhava, 'the Guru Rinpoche' of the Tibetans, for the time when it would provide Tibetans with a sanctuary. Five centuries ago the first Sherpas crossed the Himalaya from Tibet and discovered the beautiful uninhabited valley south of Chomolungma, their 'Mother Goddess of the World', which we call Mount Everest. Even today, with the invasion of foreign tourists and attendant problems, Khumbu still possesses a magical quality that uplifts the spirit, easily perceived as the echo of a past paradise on earth.

The Hidden Valleys are said to have an outer, an inner, and a secret part, so that even if the outer part has been 'opened' and colonised, the inner and secret parts may still remain hidden, accessible only to the great yogis and mystics.

For most of us with 'impure karma', even to hear about Shambhala and other Hidden Valleys is said to be a rare piece of good fortune. To reach their innermost essence without the wisdom eye of a great yogini would seem impossible, or so I thought. Yet to tramp through the Himalaya and perhaps catch a glimpse of the outer reaches of these Valleys was a temptation impossible to resist, in spite of the warnings in the guidebooks that to try to reach a Hidden Valley before your time is right is to court great danger, even death.

❖

The path contoured round, clinging to the cliff at mid-height and leading into a vast amphitheatre of grey rock. I could see the storm coming towards us up the valley and felt relieved that we would have time to cross the precarious trail through the amphitheatre before it hit. Suddenly I realised that the storm had gathered speed, rushing towards us as the wind funnelled into the narrow chasm. We were caught in the middle of the cliff as the first blast of windborne hail threw me against the rock wall and black clouds blotted out the sun. Within seconds rocks were dislodged above and crashed on to the path in front and behind us on the concave rock wall.

We started running, oblivious of the sheer drop below and the slick mud that had formed on the narrow path. We had to get out of this barrage of rocks, but the amphitheatre was enormous and there was no immediate escape. It was insane, this reckless, mindless flight from danger into danger. Any second now, one of us would slip and plunge into the depths below.

'Stop!' I screamed above the bedlam.

The others stopped abruptly and looked back. I waved frantically towards an overhang near the base of the cliff above, with a funnel of steep grass leading up to it.

'Up there!'

I was already scrambling and scrabbling up the grass and rubble to the overhang. The others followed. We huddled under the bulge of rock as the boulders continued to crash around us. The protection was minimal; the overhang was far shallower than it had appeared from the trail. A rock smashed down a few feet away and exploded, spraying us with shrapnel. My knuckles were scraped and bleeding but I hardly noticed as another rock hit the lip of the bulge and bounced off, inspiring us to cower further back under its inadequate shelter.

What the hell was I doing here? Why had I left behind home, friends and creature comforts for this howling hell-hole of hailstones and flying rocks? Curiosity about a hidden 'Shangri-la' somewhere deep in the mountains could really get you into some unpleasant places. Maybe 'paradise' was an allegory for the relief you felt if you succeeded in extricating yourself.

PART ONE

Behind the Ranges

Something hidden. Go and find it. Go and look
behind the Ranges –
Something lost behind the Ranges. Lost and waiting
for you. Go!

Rudyard Kipling

I

The Reality Perceived by Those with Impure Karma

།སྣང་རིགས་གཉིས་གཡུལ་ངོ་འགྱེད་པའི་ཚོ།

The night bus rattled and roared over the flat plains of the Nepal Terai, jarring bones into their sockets and making me wish I had brought some cotton wool to stuff in my ears. I looked across at my companion. She was staring silently out of the darkened window, the tension in her pale features accentuated by the cropped dark hair and the red glow of her cigarette. Ang was asleep, heavily, against my left shoulder. I envied him his oblivion. For me, sleep was impossible in this clanking torture chamber, and no doubt would remain so until morning. The rest of the tightly-packed occupants were all male, all chain-smoking *biris* (tobacco rolled in eucalyptus) and all suffering from the resulting chronic bronchial problems.

I tried once more to prise Ang off my cramped shoulder, but gave up when he almost fell into the aisle. I wondered what he thought of being assigned to a journey like this as part of his job. If the Sikkimese trek permits came through in time to fit the schedule, he would help to organise supplies and porters.

The bus groaned to a halt at the Indian border as grey dawn light forced its way through a damp mist. I bade a silent and thankful farewell to my fellow-prisoners as their coughing and wheezing faded into the fog, leaving just the memory of their thousand cigarettes as a stale cloud in the morning air.

Two Indian customs officers emerged from a dilapidated shed and spent twenty minutes searching every corner of our three large backpacks and listing every item of camera equipment. Fifty yards into a dusty no-man's-land, a canvas awning lurched above a rickety wooden table at which sat a bored bureaucrat who peered suspiciously at our passports and demanded to see our permits for Darjeeling. Similar bureaucrats in Delhi had given instructions to collect the delayed Sikkim permits in Darjeeling, but had failed to mention any permits for Darjeeling itself.

Immigration handed back the passports. 'You will have to return to Kathmandu and obtain a special permit from the Embassy there.'

Ten minutes of bleating and wheedling elicited little more than a polite offer to throw us in jail. Then he suddenly relented.

'You can cross the border at Galgalia in Bihar, outside the Restricted Area. After that, it is not my affair.'

I thanked him and retreated before he could change his mind. Customs spent another twenty minutes painstakingly checking that we had not sold our cameras while we had been in India, then left us to bargain for a taxi to Galgalia. Even at an extortionate two hundred rupees, it was worth every *paise** not to be back on the bus. Half an hour and thirty-six body-crunching kilometres later, the taxi slithered to a halt in a bunker of soft white sand. Only a few plank and corrugated iron shacks broke the monotony of the flat brown farmland. 'Customs' here were sitting round a table under a shady pipal tree, playing cards. With a perfunctory glance at our bags, they waved us through.

'You pay taxi here. Taxi no going. There is one river. No bridge.'

They enjoyed my look of alarm and offered diverse opinions as to how deep the water actually was.

Half a mile through the sand and there it was, considerably wide and of uncertain depth. I peeled off sweaty shoes and socks and waded in, feeling the mud slithering between bare toes and trying not to think about the slimy wriggly things that burrow into unprotected flesh. I turned to Ang, thigh-deep in the current, dwarfed by his pack.

'You like trekking? No sleep, no food, just swimming!'

He smiled, plodded to the far bank, and began drying off his toes with the end of a sock. There was no response from my companion. It had been one of her silent days and I had learned to leave her alone when she felt like this.

At the top of the river bank was a line of bicycle rickshaws

---

* 100 paise = 1 rupee

awaiting customers. We piled ourselves and our luggage into two of these dilapidated contraptions and were pedalled along the raised dirt road through the flat winter farmland of tropical Bihar.

Ahead stood a small thatched hut, alone in the wide expanse of barren paddy fields. Outside, a group of men were seated in a circle on a battered piece of rice straw mat, gambling.

'Immigration,' intoned the rickshaw driver.

Immigration looked up and wiped a sweaty palm over his grubby white vest and baggy pants. 'Sit down, please.' He waved a hand of dog-eared playing cards graciously at a vacant area of mat and spat a stream of red betel on to the ground beside him.

The loaded rickshaws looked more incongruous than ever as they sat unoccupied on the trail. We picked our way gingerly through the little blobs of red spit around the mat. Everyone was chewing betel.

Immigration held out a chubby hand for our passports and gave us a red grin.

'Where are you going?'

'Darjeeling.' Then I realised I should have said Calcutta.

'You have no Darjeeling permit. You must return to Kathmandu and get one.'

No way was I going to reverse that road journey, and a tense haggling ensued. It had been a long night and an even longer day, and my temper was beginning to wear thin at the edges.

'I am going to Sikkim and my permit is in Darjeeling. And if I can't get it, then one of your men must collect it. And I will sit *here* until it comes – then I will go to Sikkim!'

Immigration did not conceal his look of alarm before I noticed it. An obstinate memsahib sitting on his mat for an undetermined number of days evidently did not fit in with his idea of a peaceful life. Composure recovered, he solemnly handed over our exit cards. I had never filled one in so quickly. Then, with rubber stamp poised above passports, he asked for cigarettes. I had none, so gave him a lighter instead. A slow smile spread across his face, and the stamp descended. With agonising slowness, he began to fill out the details in the record book. A loud crash on the trail brought a welcome distraction from the tension as two rickshaws collided and their pedallers dismounted to argue and fight about it. Suddenly they decided to save their energy for pedalling, leaped aboard and clattered off furiously in opposite directions, the passengers clinging to their seats.

Meanwhile, Immigration had found out how to spell 'Sikkim', and was filling in the last column with a flourish.

We shook hands.

'Thank you. A pleasure to do business with you.'

He smiled broadly, redly.

We clambered aboard our transport and rattled off through the quiet afternoon paddy fields.

A huddle of thatched huts marked the start of another motor road and the first of a series of buses which would complete the route to Darjeeling. Ang found an empty seat and relapsed once more into unconsciousness. He gave the impression of being very young and inexperienced although the manager of the Sherpa Co-op in Kathmandu, Mike Cheney, had given his assurance that all his staff had many treks and expeditions behind them. With any luck, things would get easier once the buses and bureaucrats were left behind and the walking actually started.

We planned to travel east by road to Gantok in Sikkim and from there head west on foot along the Himalayan range to reach Srinagar in Kashmir seven months later. Peter Hillary and Arlene Blum had traversed the Himalaya in a similar way before, but with an elaborate system of support parties to keep them supplied at regular intervals along the route. I felt sure it could be done without a support crew. In the 1930s the English climber Bill Tilman had made long explorations with no more back-up than a local guide and a few spare bags of *tsampa*.

For the last few years I had been working as a freelance photo-journalist and had found that a lightweight, low-key, low-impact approach had worked well in getting to know the people I met without overwhelming them with an entourage of imported western culture. They were certainly uninhibited in talking to me and freely allowed themselves to be photographed. By meeting them on their terms rather than mine, I was seen as less strange and less of a threat. Although in the remote hills people lived very simple lives, they did so with dignity and I had no wish to introduce another culture which often makes people feel discontented with what they have. I was interested in learning about the way they perceived their world rather than superimposing my own perceptions on what I saw. It was lucky that I could speak both Nepali and Tibetan, as few inhabitants of either monasteries or remote villages spoke English.

I had never travelled lightweight for more than a month at a time but felt sure that it would be possible for any extended period so long as I was prepared to live on whatever happened to be available. There would always be *something* available. There were times during the months ahead when I looked back on such naiveté in disbelief, but then if everyone knew exactly what was going to happen to them when they set out on a journey, very few would ever set out at all.

I hoped that in the process of taking photographs and researching articles on this journey, I would be able to find out more about the Hidden Valleys of the Himalaya. Perhaps the people who lived on the periphery of these places knew the legends, history and possible location of these tiny Shangri-Las. Then I could learn how the great meditators are able to travel there. I did not want to admit to myself that this was the main reason for making the journey in case it turned out to be another disappointment. For years an inner restlessness had kept me travelling, from country to country, from one mountain adventure to another. I had reached enough summits to know that the answer lies within oneself, not on the summit of any mountain, yet the restlessness continued – a feeling that by exploring the outer world, I might catch a glimpse of the inner.

Pitting myself against higher summits and harder rock pitches had been recreationally refreshing and good fun but it had not revealed any lasting answers – except that if you have inner peace you can remain calm even in the so-called dreadful 'outside world' and if you haven't, you'll just drag all the hassles up the mountain with you. For a while it was easy to subscribe to the climbing theory that higher awareness is only available above the snowline or the 'E' grade, but the novelty wore off as quickly as the alluring sharpening of perceptions we had all been talking about. It was real enough, but it didn't last, and constantly risking one's neck to recapture it seemed like a bad recipe for longevity.

In addition to this, I had begun to see first-hand a change in Himalayan expeditions and to realise the price that professional climbers paid for success. The pressure of sponsors, media, and lecture tours often made the sport a focus of tension rather than enjoyment. The media wanted only one 'hero' per expedition, which naturally led to competitiveness rather than support and co-operation between members of a team. Becoming preoccupied with their public image, they missed the experience.

It was time to get away from all this and disappear into the remote mountains and valleys of the Himalaya for a while. My best climbing trips had been with just one partner on remote peaks in the Andes, and a team of two seemed a good number for the traverse. My climbing partner had recently married and settled down, so I telephoned a woman I had met briefly the previous year and, to my surprise, she agreed to go with me.

At first it seemed that our different personalities would complement one another. Fran was meticulous about organisation and methodical planning, while I had years of practical experience in the mountains. During the lengthy preparations, however, our interests began to diverge. She was looking forward to an opportunity to quit an unloved job and break into the world of the professional climber, with lecture tours and the resulting sponsorships. My lack of interest in her plans disappointed her, and led her to fear that I would leave her with ambitions which she lacked the experience to see through. I thought we could surely travel together and still pursue our own interests. While Fran was building a career I could explore obscure Himalayan myths for which she had a reciprocal lack of interest. I could not understand why she was becoming so tense and frustrated, but so long as we avoided each other, we got along passably well.

We arrived in Darjeeling on Christmas Eve. Morning sunlight washed away the cold fog and memories of the gruelling bus journeys. Darjeeling had become a fairytale city draped over a long ridgetop, houses and gardens spilling down the slopes into the tea plantations below. White Kangchenjunga floated above the cloud-filled valley.

It was no great surprise to find that the Sikkim permits still had not arrived. Learning that the youth hostel cost only eight rupees a night and even had hot water if you knew where to look, we hauled our luggage thither and settled down to wait for the ponderous Indian bureaucracy to regurgitate our papers.

For me, it was a welcome respite from the hectic business of getting this far; for the other half of the expedition, it was an agony of tension and frustration. She fretted constantly over the missing permits and the upset schedule, or else sank into a morose silence.

Ang seemed bored just hanging about the hotel, so I began to take him with me on forays into the surrounding area. He was too shy to venture more than a polite 'yes' or 'no' to any comment or question, and I felt as if I were making the journey alone, yet this had its own rewards. There were fewer distractions and more opportunity to notice what was going on around me.

Tenzing Norgay Road, like its namesake, climbs far up the ridge on which Darjeeling is built. I had a letter to deliver for a Tibetan friend, to her brother, Ngawang Norbu. The address given was simply, 'Tenzing Norgay Road, Darjeeling.' The standard Tibetan method of asking passers-by where I could find him was remarkably easy; Mr Norbu was a well-known character in these parts, being the editor of the *Tibetan Freedom News*. I found him sitting outside his office enjoying the sun, hands thrust deeply into the pockets of his down jacket. From the house next door came the cacophony of ritual instruments, while the sweet smoke of incense rose from a brazier outside.

Ngawang welcomed me in as if it was the hundredth, not the first, time we had met. Through a broken pane in the grimy glass of the downstairs window I could see the heavy printing press, old and solid, and spattered with ink. Narrow stone steps led up to the editorial offices – a grand title for two tiny rooms crammed with papers and files almost burying a couple of antique typewriters. Ngawang rummaged around for the latest edition, a small single sheet folded in half, printed in Tibetan script. He read through the current headlines: 'Guerrilla leaders from Amdo and Kham escape to India for treatment for Chinese bullet wounds, but after several operations die anyway.' Their pictures were not only in the newspaper, but on the wall of the office, draped in white silk scarves.

While the Khampas were fighting for freedom, the Tibetans who had fled to India were fighting for survival. I had spent the morning at the Tibetan Refugee Centre. Men, women, and children sat in rows spinning and weaving wool into carpets on makeshift equipment patched together from old bicycle rims and oddments from the local scrapheap. For people who had arrived destitute from a country which boasted nothing more mechanised than a prayer wheel, it had come as a shock to realise they would have to master technology – quickly – to earn a meagre living in someone else's country. The lucky few who learned quickly had already left the safe haven of the Centre and could be seen in smart business suits around the city, while a record book in the office told of the early days and the new arrivals in the tent camps:

'Land was allocated to each person of adult status. . . An adult was defined as a person over five years of age, and able to work.'

I followed Tenzing Norgay Road to the top of the ridge where the prayer flags around the little Buddhist temple flapped ghostlike in the damp air. The wind parted the mist and once again the snow-capped peak of Kanchenjunga appeared shimmering above the cloud-filled valleys like a mirage.

Many Tibetans believe that this corner of the Himalaya was once a Hidden Valley; a concealed sanctuary which was discovered at the beginning of the fifteenth century by a Tibetan lama called Rigdzin Godem. He found a pass leading across the snow mountains from Tibet to 'Bayul Demojong', the 'Hidden Valley of Rice'. He wrote a message describing his route and sent it back to his monastery tied to the neck of an eagle, but it was not until two hundred years later that another lama led a large group of Tibetans over the mountains to begin the settlement of Sikkim in earnest. Namkha Jigme was appointed the first Chogyal, or ruler of Sikkim, and the line continued up to the last Chogyal who lost

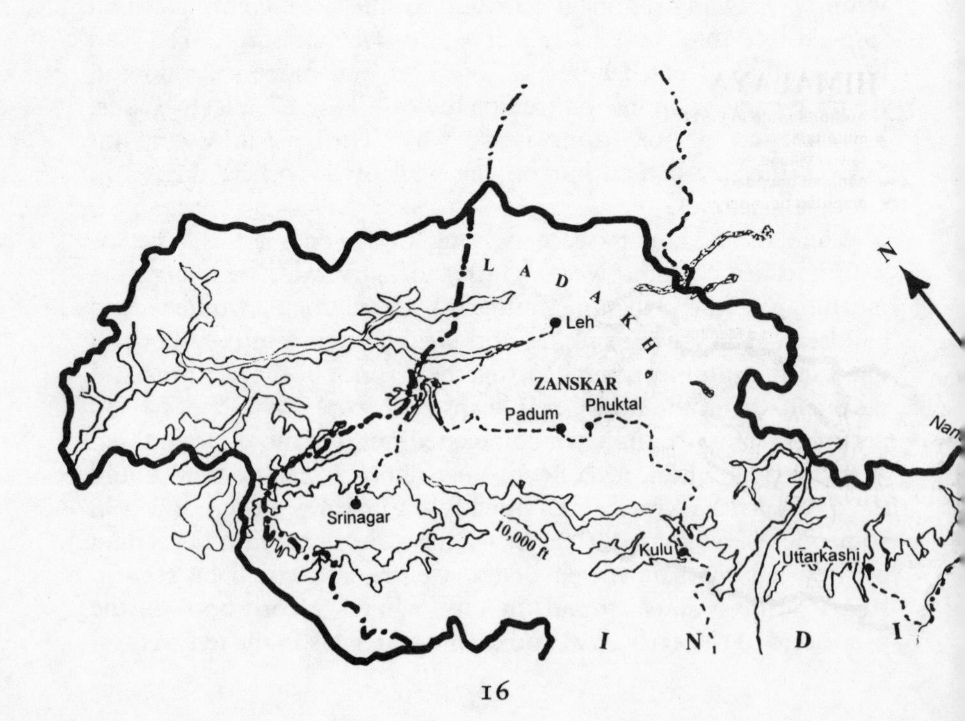

his throne when Sikkim was annexed as part of India in 1974.

Although the outer and inner Hidden Valleys have been opened, the secret part of Bayul Demojong still remains concealed in a remote valley beneath the snows of Kanchenjunga itself. While watching the shifting play of cloud and sunlight on the distant mountain, it was easy to believe there were still undiscovered valleys hidden beneath the cloud forest at its foot. The web of bureaucracy surrounding this Restricted Area is as much a barrier as the rugged terrain itself. Originally I had hoped that by calling the traverse an 'Expedition', the authorities would be persuaded to grant special permits for some of the western Restricted Areas. The Indian government had politely declined – and had then assigned a Liaison Officer for the journey through western India, at our expense!

The timing of the journey had to blend with the seasons. The high passes into Ladakh would not be cleared of dozens of feet of snow until the end of May. This meant crossing Nepal during the winter months, which I hoped would leave enough time to cross northern India and reach the rain-shadow of Ladakh

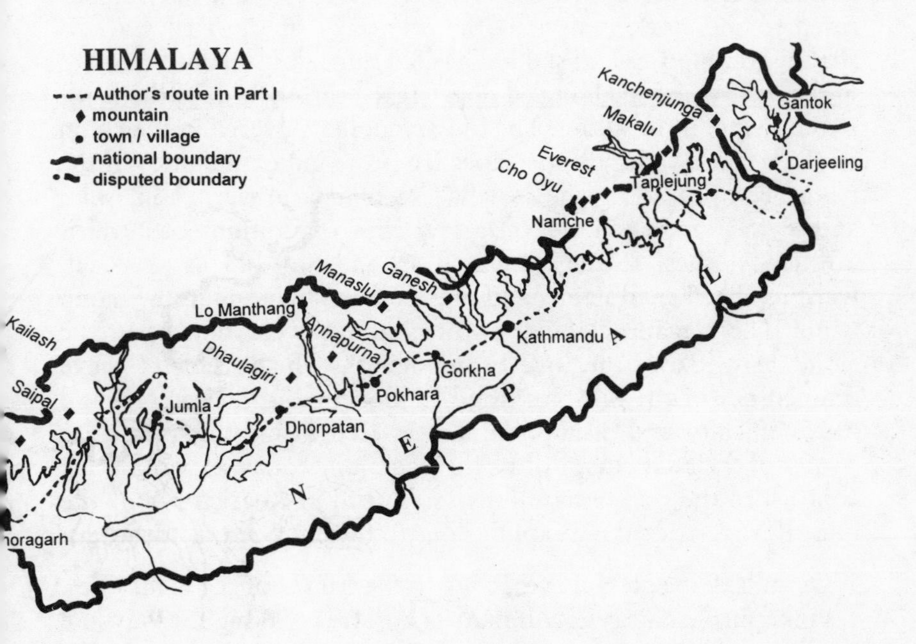

before the monsoon downpour transformed Garwhal into a leech-infested flood.

The bus arrived at the hilltop full to overflowing, but Ang and I persuaded the occupants nearest the door that there was room for two more. The road followed the same route as the railway track with frequent unmarked crossings. The bus driver was concentrating fiercely on racing the train down the grade, clearing crossings with barely seconds to spare. The hillside reared steeply in lush greenness above, falling away into near-vertical jungle below on the other side of the road. It would have been suicidal to try to get off, so I clung to the rail in the doorway, trying to think about something other than the squealing tyres inches from the precipice. After a particularly hair-raising slither around a perched hairpin bend, Ang looked across at me and said, 'Hm. Very close.' It was the first time he had been moved to venture any comment beyond polite assent.

The bus screeched to a halt in Darjeeling market, the driver looking delighted with the outcome of the race.

The market lay in the lower part of town; easy to forget for those living on the affluent upper hillsides. The coal-grimed streets revealed the stark reality of the workings of the city with its shabby warehouses and stalls. The cold rain left blackened puddles in the road where bedraggled dogs picked through the garbage for a thin living in the gutter. The Indian coolies shivered in their thin terylene clothes and plastic shoes from the industrial cities of the plains. Few people outside the villages would wear warm homespun and leather if they could get a few cheap imitations of coveted Western clothes, so they squatted around tiny braziers of coal, warming blackened hands and muddy feet, shivering in the damp wind. The elegant colonial gardens above were hidden in the cloud, leaving only the poverty and ugliness which seemed to have drained out of the hillsides. Rigdzin Godem and his eagle would have difficulty and disappointment in recognising this particular corner of their sanctuary of Bayul Demojong today. It was a stark contrast to the rich descriptions I had read in Roerich's book; he must have restricted his explorations to the more exotic locations:

> Orchids, like colorful eyes, cling to the trunks of the giant trees. Pink, purple and yellow bouquets are strewn along the way like

bright sparks. And these are not simply plants, many have their ancient powers of healing. . . Then, near Phalut, on the road to Kinchenjunga grows a precious plant, the black aconite. Its flower lights up at night, and by its glow one locates this rare plant. . .

I was as fascinated as Roerich by the ancient traditions of herbal knowledge that still remained in the Himalaya and hoped I would meet people on this journey who would teach me more about them.

I also tried, but failed, to find any reference to Csoma de Koros in Darjeeling. Roerich himself makes only a brief mention:

In the cemetery of Darjeeling is buried an enigmatic man, Hungarian by birth, who lived at the end of the eighteenth century. He came walking from Hungary to Tibet, remaining many years in unknown monasteries. In the thirties of the last century Csoma de Koros, as he was called, died. In his works he pointed out the teachings of Shambhala, designating the next hierarchy to succeed Buddha.

I was disappointed, but determined to follow up other clues along the route when there was more time. If I had known the terrifying situation into which I would get myself while tracking down the elusive Csoma de Koros, I might have felt rather less determined and more intimidated, but this lay in the unknown mountains of the months ahead.

To my surprise, the Sikkim permits appeared a few days before we were due to return to Nepal to meet up with Maila and Pasang, our trekking porters. Mike Cheney had arranged to send only Ang with us to India; the other two were to leave later, taking the same infamous night bus to the border, then transferring to another Nepalese bus northwards into the hills, to wait for us at the town of Ilam. They would bring with them the camping equipment for Nepal, as well as the clothes, walking boots, and rucksacks we had provided for them.

I confess that, until the promised permits appeared, I had been convinced that they were merely figments of the imagination. Within hours we were crammed into the back of a jeep heading for Gantok. I had felt disinclined to risk another bus for fear that kamikaze drivers were common in this area. It was a good choice until the jeep stopped at the second village and picked up an Indian family. As there were no vacant seats, they simply sat on top of us, dangling Grandma over the tailgate every time she was travel sick. Her obvious relief when they finally disembarked was echoed by my own.

The guards at the Tista Bridge checkpost gave scarcely a glance at the permits for which we had waited so long. The bridge itself seemed to lack confidence, with a policeman at either end signalling one vehicle across at a time. A heavy steamroller came trundling down the hill opposite, powered by a tractor perched and chained atop it. Surely the police would never allow such a leviathan on to their fragile bridge? After it had lumbered over, the jeep was waved across, and ground its way up the steep hill on the far side. At the top, scrub gave way to a forest of tall trees, long straight trunks reaching for the light and ending in a distant tuft of green. A jeepload of jolly Indian tourists sailed past, the occupants hanging out of the windows and waving.

2

Echoes of Tibet

།དོན་བདེན་རྫུན་གཞན་འབྱེད་བྱེད་པོ་ནི།

It was the slow patter of rain that awakened me next morning in Gantok. The night showers were easing, giving way to a soft mist which hung over the trees and gardens of the city and surrounding hillsides. Fran had already gone out, and I was eager to explore. A steep road led up the hill to the old palace complex of the Chogyals of Sikkim. At the top of the hill the mist grew thinner and watery sunlight shone on the Tsuk Lha Khang, the Royal Chapel. Inside, the wall paintings were mellowed with age and shadows, illumined only by a few butter lamps and the rays penetrating the dusty windows, with the faded smell of incense a haunting memory of a past already half-forgotten. There were no monks, only soldiers guarding the gateway and a group of tourists photographing each other by the door. I sat down in the arched entrance to put on my shoes, under the painted stare of the Guardians of the Four Directions. These are depicted at the door of all Himalayan Buddhist temples.

A busload of plump Bombay tourists erupted suddenly at the gate and poured into the temple in a flurry of gaudy saris and bangles, chattering above the blare of portable radios. Silence fell for a moment as Ang and I were left alone with the four Guardians.

'*Kukara*,' he said, disapprovingly.

I laughed. 'Squawking like chickens!'

A moment later they all came flapping back through the door like rumpled peacocks in retreat, and turned to face the old caretaker who had evicted them. He stood on the step, muttering under his breath and closed the door firmly behind him. The multi-coloured crowd backed slowly away from him, before scuttling off in confusion in the direction of their bus. Ang could hardly conceal his amusement.

'Shoes on – no good. Making noise – no good. All out!' He shook his head. 'Gompa* not understanding.'

Rumtek stands high on the hill opposite Gantok city, with a deep valley between and the Himalaya emerging from cloud behind it. The road twists and climbs through a forest of fluttering prayer flags that surround the monastery. I knew nothing about Rumtek except the historical background, and there is little enough of that. It was built by the sixteenth Gyalwa Karmapa, the head of the Kagyu sect of Tibetan Buddhism, after his flight from Chinese-occupied Tibet in 1959. It is styled as much like his original monastery as possible, and, apart from the Sikkimese greenness, it does feel very 'Tibetan' here, with the red-robed monks sitting about the sunny courtyard, or spreading barley grains to dry, robes flipped back out of the way.

A small room within the pagoda roof of the temple was almost filled by the new gold chorten which contained the ashes of the Karmapa. They were still waiting for his reincarnation to be recognised. Around the walls were the statues of Marpa, Milarepa, and the whole lineage of the Karmapas up to the sixteenth.

There was a clattering on the stairs, and an uncharacteristically fat young monk arrived breathless, remembered himself, and prostrated three times before the still-powerful earthly remains of his teacher. Then he hurried over, pulling a dog-eared photograph out of his robe.

'Are you the *inji* they've been talking about? You have been to Lhasa?'

How quickly gossip spreads in a monastery! That brief conversation with one of the monks had taken place barely ten minutes before.

'Do you know my uncle? I think he is in Lhasa. I want to know if he is still alive and maybe have his address.'

How often have I been asked this question? And every time with the same pain and hope in their eyes – and the same disap-

---

* Gompa (Tibetan) – a place of meditation; a temple or monastery

pointment when I shake my head, wishing they were not so naive as to imagine a meeting like that could chance in such a vast country, wishing that all families scattered by violence could be reunited. Then I glanced again at the photograph.

'Yes, I met him last year. He's working for the Chinese Tourist Association. Give me a pen and I'll write down the address.'

The fat young man beamed with enthusiasm and dragged me off to his room for writing materials. He plied me with cups of butter tea while a crowd of young hopefuls crammed themselves through the door, all clutching photographs of lost relatives – but the faces that stared up from the yellowing paper were all strangers to me.

On the hillside above the peacock aviary and the gardens around the Karmapa's house stands the little pink *ani-gompa*, the nunnery. The five grey-haired, gap-toothed nuns in their patched maroon and saffron are very much the poor relations of the elegant and well-organised establishment below, but the smiles of delight as they sat me down and rummaged around for a clean teacup made a welcome fit for a queen. They probably don't get many visitors up on that hill.

The little shrine in the corner of the room was covered with a battered sheet of plastic, upon which was set a motley assortment of Buddha statues and plastic flowers. A Nescafe tin stuffed with nasturtiums reminded me of a Zen Buddhist friend in America who had used a saki bottle for the flowers on his shrine because it was so decorative – until he was told by a Japanese visitor what it was, and that it was not appropriate.

Through the window I could see a lone white house set high on the hillside where the prayer flag forest was thickest. This was the place of retreat, and visitors are asked not to go near in case they disturb the meditation of those within. Some of these meditators would have renounced the world for a period of weeks, but for most it would be months or even years before they emerged. Such an intense pursuit of spiritual realisation is said to produce spectacular side-effects such as the 'inner fire' by which Milarepa warmed himself while meditating among the snows of the Himalaya. Or there is the art of *lung-gom* by which the ancient adepts travelled vast distances in a series of untiring leaps. Apparently, in order to begin the practice of learning to 'fly' in this way, one must first dig a hole the height of oneself and sit in the bottom of it in the lotus position. When, in this position, you are able to jump level with the top of the hole, you are ready to *begin* receiving instruction! But as one lama pointed out, 'If your only aim is to warm the body, you do not need to meditate; it would be easier to turn on the central heating.'

I spent the evening in the hotel, swapping jokes with Ang and the Nepalese waiter who was feeling homesick. Fran returned late, having been to a bar with some British tourists. Ang sensed her irritation at our jokes and laughter, made his excuses, and left. I hesitated, wondering if I should do the same. She lit a cigarette and inhaled tensely.

'I can't understand what you're saying in Nepali, and it makes me feel left out.'

She spoke as if on the edge of tears. I began to feel sorry for her.

'Why not tell me what the problems are, instead of picking fights? Maybe I can help.'

She let out a long sigh of exasperation before speaking slowly, as if to a child.

'You still don't understand, do you? I don't *want* to be patronised. What are you trying to do? Destroy the last little bit of pride I might have left?'

In the last weeks her rapid swings from aggression to pathos and back had left me confused. I was not proving as useful to her plans for a new career as she had hoped and she seemed convinced I was holding something back.

'All this supposed sympathy – it's just your underhand way of getting at me. You've got to *fight* for what you want in this world and I'm going to do *anything* that's necessary to get what I want out of this trip.'

I felt baffled. 'What more do you want? You're the official leader, handling the money, and I've given you information for your articles and slide shows. There isn't any more.'

'I'm afraid you'll just go off and do your own thing.'

The idea was becoming more attractive as days went by. The prospect of a seven-month running battle was less than appealing. Still, I felt sure that if I agreed to everything she wanted and then left her to get on with it, she would soon settle down. After all, it takes two to make a fight.

I went back to my room to write.

It took a day to retrace the journey from Gantok to the Nepalese border, and another to disentangle bureaucratic snarl-ups with re-entry visas and reach the market town of Ilam. This marked the end of the motor road in the Nepalese foothills, and from here we would travel on foot. The market filled the town's main square and overflowed into neighbouring streets. Stalls and racks of saris in crimson, purple and aquamarine were jostled by others heaped with terylene sweaters and shorts in scarlet or yellow, while wedged between were smaller blankets displaying plastic tea-strainers, combs, and bangles. The people from the surrounding villages bargained hard for precious items to carry home, raising a babble of voices as colourful as the merchandise.

Maila and Pasang had been anxiously watching every bus in anticipation of our arrival. They pushed a way for us through the crowd and the smell of sweat and mothballs to the rickety warren of a hotel where they had stashed the tents and trek equipment. Like Ang, neither spoke much English, and for a minute I struggled to comprehend the torrent of Nepali as Maila hauled out an alarmingly large array of bags and boxes.

'We need to hire three local porters tomorrow,' pronounced Maila.

'No we don't. The five of us are supposed to be carrying everything between us. That's what we agreed, and why you've all been given warm clothes. We won't get far with local porters – they'll freeze.'

I had hoped we could manage with only two porters but a recent climbing accident had left me with a crushed vertebra and stern warnings from the doctor about load-carrying. Reluctantly I had asked Mike Cheney to to find us three, but an additional three would destroy the whole low-impact ethos I had hoped for.

'Not possible carrying, memsahib.' He continued to heave boxes and baskets from the pile in the corner.

'What is all this stuff?' I began rummaging in the baskets.

'I gave him seven hundred rupees of the expedition money for food when we were in Kathmandu,' said Fran defensively.

'But we're supposed to be living off the land where there's food available in east Nepal. . .'

I detected another storm brewing, and abandoned the plan that had been forming to throw out the glass bottles of ketchup, jam and gourmet foods that were piled on top of the protein rations intended for west Nepal where, by all accounts, there was no food available for travellers. I tried to persuade Maila to carry a little more himself and manage with just two more local porters. Maila possessed a stubborn resilience to my bargaining, and I felt we were getting nowhere. Suddenly Ang said he would carry a double load, tied two bundles together, dumped the load in a corner, and went out to start cooking supper.

Next morning Maila hired the two extra porters and we set off, Ang lagging behind under his extra load. It was a far cry from the way I had anticipated this journey. I had envisaged travelling light and living simply, sleeping in local farmhouses, putting up with the fleas and the diet of rice with rice, and perhaps seeing a little deeper into this place. Now I felt like a tourist, surrounded by an entourage of servants whose job it was to feed us Western food and keep us in as much Western comfort as possible – in other words isolate us from the country we were in. In spite of this, it was impossible to feel discontented for more than a few minutes on a beautiful fresh morning in the hills, with the sun catching the snow on the distant mountains beyond.

Although it was January (winter in Nepal) the air was warm in these lush valleys and the women wore soft, brightly-patterned saris as they worked in the fields. The rivers flowed from north to south, and as we were travelling from east to west, the route constantly climbed ridges and then descended into river valleys.

A few days of leisurely walking brought us to Phidim, a cluster of thatched cottages and gardens full of laden orange and banana trees entwined with clusters of purple bougainvillaea. Women, like orchids in richly-coloured saris, leaned in their doorways and gossiped in the sunshine. A Rai woman sat weaving outside her house, the long warp threads stretching across the yard and her children climbing round her feet as she passed the weft from hand to hand and the delicate geometric pattern took shape.

'Ah. Good afternoon. I am village policeman. Please, show permit.'

He looked an unlikely constable in his neat Nepali hat, tunic, and white baggy pants, but he politely escorted us to the army barracks where two bronchial sergeants tried to figure out what to do with Kathmandu-issued trek permits. It seemed they had few tourists through Phidim. There was a dark little jail in the corner of the compound, with two pairs of handcuffs hanging empty from the bars. I wondered if they ever put anyone in there from this village of flowers.

Ang's expression of relief as we left was unmistakable. I did not treat the police with the same awe that he did, and he was convinced that eventually I would suffer for it. Yells from above made him jump visibly, but it was only the entire Phidim division of the Nepalese Army enthusiastically directing us further left. During the last two days in Gantok Ang had managed to overcome his shyness enough to talk a little about his village and family, but now that he was once more a porter under Maila's direction he had relapsed into his habitual 'yes' and 'no'. I had redistributed the loads more evenly, but I still wondered how he managed to keep up. He only stood the height of my shoulder, which together with a mop of unruly hair and a turned-up nose made it hard not to think of him as about fourteen years old.

Towards the end of the afternoon I noticed Ang helping Fran as she limped her way heavily down the last hill with the aid of a stick and a knee bandage. A cold had replaced her earlier stomach upset, and I decided to hurry ahead to try to ensure that just this once her tent would be up and a hot cup of tea ready when she arrived. I found Maila in his usual role of directing operations – except that there was nobody to direct as Pasang had gone to fetch the water.

'Come on, Maila, this is no time for role-playing. You light the fire and I'll put up the tent.'

Maila looked embarrassed, wandered round in a circle, and came back to base. Lighting the fire was not a Sirdar's job. Neither, apparently, was carrying any equipment; he had left the new large rucksack in Kathmandu and brought only a small daypack incapable of holding more than a few necessities. He had given me a martyred look when I had presented him with some of the excess from Ang's load a few days before. He was modelling his role on that of Sirdar of a big expedition with perhaps fifty staff and several hundred porters to co-ordinate. In our meagre circumstances he was a captain without troops, yet he still endeavoured to maintain an image which I found greatly entertaining in spite of having to put up the tents myself. Before long Ang arrived, lit the fire and made the tea.

We had been travelling very slowly and I began to feel uneasy about getting across Nepal with our 90–day visas. Next day, map in hand, I cornered Maila at the evening campfire.

'Look, this is Nepal. We have to be across it in ninety days. That means Ilam to Kathmandu in twenty-five days.'

Maila stared solemnly at the map. He was a handsome lad, with eyes that wouldn't meet mine and a bland smile that belied the sharp intelligence with which he reasoned things out. His real name was Munghal Tamang; Maila simply means 'second son', a label used frequently in a land where people often have several names, none of which are for common usage. Mike Cheney employed mainly Tamangs; he said they were 'sharp'. I was beginning to see what he meant.

Maila finally made his pronouncement.

'Not possible.'

'But it's got to be possible. We must start at seven o'clock and walk faster, and spend less time over lunch.'

'Nepal, one hundred and fifty days.'

'Look we don't need all this fancy sahib food. Just cook one *dal-bhat* (rice and lentils) for all of us and lunch will take half the time.'

'*Yess*, memsahib.' But I could tell by the way his eyes shifted and moved away, things would go on exactly as before. Providing every comfort was his job; the problem of the visas was not.

I wandered to the edge of the trees and watched Kanchenjunga shimmering in blue evening mist. We had been climbing all day and there was frost on the dry grass of this ridgetop. Smoke was rising from houses in the village, seeping out between the wooden roof shingles. The villagers were inside cooking supper. Only crazy Westerners stand outside in the frost and cold to watch Kanchenjunga fade into the night sky.

I awakened to now-familiar sounds of Pasang crashing around in the pots and pans. Although small and nimble even for a Sherpa, he had a great affinity for things that crash and clank. I could always hear him coming up behind me on the trail, scampering feet in rhythm with the rattle of aluminium cooking pots in the basket on his back. He enjoyed any opportunity for a chat and a smoke with the local girls, and was often poking his head over people's hedges to see what their gardens or storerooms had to offer, on the excuse of keeping us stocked with fresh produce.

Somewhere along the way Maila bought a chicken and it later appeared chopped and boiled on a bed of rice. Boiled chicken Nepali-style means chopped complete with bones, and, on examining my plate more closely, I discovered one of its (boiled) feet, complete with claws. This I returned to the camp kitchen without comment. Later, Fran told me that she got the (boiled) head, complete with beak, but in the dark she did not figure this out until she was chewing through it.

I suggested to Maila that if in future he felt the urge to buy a chicken he and the Sherpas could eat it themselves.

'*Yess*, memsahib.'

A long descent through the village of Chainpur led past pots of geraniums at the windows and brass water pots at the village tap. The river was not difficult to ford in the dry season, and from there it is only a short distance to the airstrip at Tumlingtar. Two large grey water buffalo were wallowing in a muddy pond, languidly blowing bubbles and flaring their nostrils at intruders. A siren sounded from the small white airport building, and within seconds half a dozen skinny youngsters hastily appeared as if from nowhere and dragged away the goats and cows which had been grazing on the grass runway. The Twin-Otter from Kathmandu bumped to a halt, then took off again in the direction of Biratnagar, while the village relapsed into a sleepy silence.

An aged Chettri woman gave me a wrinkled smile of welcome. Lal Kumari remembered my previous visit when she had teased me for my impatience as I waited three days for a delayed flight out to Kathmandu. Her job then had been to pluck and cook chickens in the little shack of a restaurant by the airstrip. Now, two years later, she was living in a farmhouse three fields away. From the large quantities of chicken feathers blowing about the yard it seemed that her job, at least, had not changed.

That evening I heard a hideous clucking and squawking and looked out of my tent thinking another one had gone to its doom, to see her putting all her chickens in an enclosed basket hung high on the wall of the house. At intervals one would get tired of lying at the bottom of a large pile of flapping birds and fight its way to the top, amid a basketful of squawked protests.

After dark I was awakened by a terrible howling and wailing which had every dog in the village barking and snarling in pursuit. The noise increased, as if all the banshees of hell were being let loose in the village, until at last the sounds began to fade in the distance and the dogs fell quiet. Next morning I asked what it was about, and Ang said they were *shell*, a bit like a dog. . .

'But how big are they?'

He caught the note of awe and mischievously held his hands wide above his head. Lal Kumari was laughing, bright eyes taking in the impatient foreigner who had never heard jackals before.

'They come and eat my chickens! That is why I hang them up on the wall, in a basket. . .'

The Sherpas were dividing the equipment, for we had joined the main trekkers' route over the Salpa La to Kathmandu and here our ways were to diverge. It was an issue that had been tacitly avoided since leaving England. Fran felt that the traverse would not be prestigious enough without some winter climbing, and so she had planned to cross the 18,000-foot Tashi Lapcha pass, which would be a serious climb in the January blizzards. Although we had high-altitude boots and clothing adequate for winter snow and ice, our staff porters had only leather walking boots. In my view, it was not safe to attempt a winter crossing unless everyone was properly equipped. Diplomacy not being my strong point, I had said so, dumping my high-altitude kit in England and telling Fran to do the same. Instead she had discussed her route at length with an experienced Himalayan mountaineer and considered that my opinion counted for little by comparison. Neither of us would agree to the other's route. I had found an alternative way to the south of the main trail which could be done safely with trek equipment, and I still felt uneasy about Fran and those porters on the Tashi Lapcha.

'Are you sure you can get a rope in Namche – for the two abseils down the Rolwaling side of the icefall?'

'Oh, I'm not doing it if there are abseils. I've never fixed an abseil by myself before. It's just a case of us taking different routes to Kathmandu.'

I stared at her. Was she being deliberately perverse? After all her consultations she must have known about the abseils. With a look of disappointment, she turned her back on me. I had spoilt her plans for a prestigious climb and had been paying for it with her moods over the past two weeks. She was now in no mood to discuss things further with me. We both knew that if she couldn't cross the high pass and didn't want to come with me she would have to take the ordinary Everest trekkers' route. I wanted to say something to console her and clear the air, but she kept her distance.

The loads were packed and Sherpas were shaking hands. I gave her a hug but she twitched away from me and walked off very quickly. Maila, Pasang and the larger of the two local porters followed. Ang heaved the other porter to his feet and we turned west, toward the towering hulk of the Mayam Danda.

3

The Shaman's Song

།ངས་སྒྲུ་མའི་དཔུང་ཚོགས་ཉིད་ལ་རེ།

Ang had not been in this part of the country before and was constantly having to ask the way – not an easy task as only a few newly-established farms intruded on this part of the hillside. A maze of tiny, indistinct trails ran in every direction as if following the exploratory route of the first intrepid Nepali explorer to bush-whack his way through this hot, sweaty, cricket-chirping jungle. We thrashed our way into a clearing where a young couple were chopping diligently away at some charred tree roots.

'*E! Dai! Dingla jaane bato ye ho?*' ('Hey, brother, is this the way to Dingla?')

'*Ho!*' The farmer waved a sooty hand at the skyline above us, where clumps of giant bamboo were silhouetted against the sunset.

We left the couple to complete their new farm and add another patch to the growing swathe of Nepal's deforestation. In the twilight it was easy to lose the trail and crash through chirping undergrowth. It seemed hours before we stumbled on to the cobbled streets of Jaupokhari, shadowed by towering bamboos. The door of the village shop was open wide and the yellow light of a kerosene taper shone out and flickered on the faces of people sitting and gossiping in the square outside.

'*Bas painchha?*' ('Anywhere to stay?')

This prompted enthusiastic but conflicting information from the villagers until a small child was despatched to lead the way to a thatched cottage on the edge of the jungle. I squeezed through a narrow doorway and groped in utter darkness to a wooden balcony at the back of the house. The eaves of the roof overhung to pots of geraniums which served as railings. It was considerably less smoky than the chimney-less inner rooms, and was dimly lit by the stars beyond the geraniums and bamboos.

There was clunking on the stairs as Manbahadur the porter struggled to negotiate the doorways with his laden doko.

'Aah! Very difficult in dark!' He sat down, gnome-like in his pastel-blue Nepali smock and baggy-pants, and mopped his face with his sleeve. His thin spindly legs and big round belly betrayed his lack of practice at carrying heavy loads, but he was a pleasant fellow with whom to travel; his face bore the same beatific grin whether he was struggling uphill through the jungle or relaxing on this balcony with a cup of lemon tea from the kitchen.

Ang and Manbahadur were exchanging news with the lady of the house – a necessary politeness in a part of the country where newspapers were non-existent. I was drowsing in the corner when Ang nudged me awake.

'She wants to know how old you are.'

'Thirty-three.'

She seemed surprised, and said something to the others.

'Did she just say she thought I was eighty?'

Ang looked embarrassed. He admitted that since we had entered this remote corner of the country, where there were no trekkers, people often asked him this question because the only time they had seen 'white' hair was on very old people. There was also confusion because I was wearing baggy cotton trousers instead of a sari. I told them about punk rockers in England, with black plastic bags for clothes, and pink and green hair. They smiled politely, but clearly didn't believe a word of it. The moon rose slowly above the giant bamboos as sleep blurred sound and vision and the tropical night swallowed up the soft voices.

We left at first light, before the sun made the uphill slog unbearable. Three girls were walking down the hill from the spring, copper water pots gracefully balanced on one shoulder. After the ritual exchange of 'Where from?' and 'Where going?' their curiosity began to show.

'Boy or girl?'

'Old person?'

This time the joke was on them, because this time I was in earshot and recognised the Nepali phrases. I burst out laughing. Realising they had been overheard, the girls retreated in confusion, giggling, towards the village. I felt reassured by the ambiguity of my status. The prejudice against Western women travelling in remote parts of Asia was clearly a Western one if the locals were not even sure whether I was male or female, let alone eighty years old!

By the time we stopped for lunch I was living up to my 'white' hair. My feet and back ached from the weight of the backpack and the distance we had travelled. Not only were we walking faster, but also starting earlier and walking until dusk, stopping only briefly for a simple meal of rice and vegetables at mid-day. We were covering twice as much ground in a day as we had before reaching Tumlingtar. One of the village grannies surveyed my lethargy and sore feet with a gap-toothed cackle. Presumably this was meant to indicate sympathy because she reached inside the complex cummerbund of cloth that the hill women wear round their waists, and drew out a small cloth pouch of seeds.

'Get you up the hill quicker!' she cackled, dropping some into my hand.

I crunched a few, and they did. They tasted like strong cough drops whose vapours penetrate right into your head and wake you up. Ang found a small bottle of volatile oil extract in a dusty corner of a village shop.

'*Alanchi*. Good medicine. Same as this.' He pointed to the remaining aromatic seeds in my hand. 'Good for colds and headaches, but this,' – he drew out a small package from his pocket – 'this is better. I buy in Gantok.' Carefully he unwrapped the crumpled package to reveal a small lump of black gum. It smelt of liquorice but tasted bitter.

'*Pongmar Nagpo*,' explained Ang.

I was looking at the concentrated extract of Roerich's 'rare and precious' Black Aconite.

'Where did you learn about medicine?'

'My father. Big Lama in our village. He know all this.' ('Lama' is Tibetan for 'Guru' or spiritual teacher, but Sherpas tend to use it for anyone who can read a scripture text. In context, they will distinguish between a High Lama, an ordinary monk, or a married farmer like Ang's father who officiates at village ceremonies.)

Ang had persuaded me some time before to make a detour to his village. He had probably not seen his family for months, and his father sounded an interesting character. Meeting him was something I looked forward to in the days ahead.

The trail climbed steeply and the air grew cold with the gain in altitude. The villages and terraces gave way to gnarled cloud-forest smelling of damp leaf-mould underfoot and with trailing lichens wafting in damp mist between the trees. Soon the ridges and landmarks by which we might have navigated were engulfed in cloud and the trail ran out into a swamp. We lost an hour backtracking to the windswept stone chorten where we first went wrong. Ang and Manbahadur left me guarding the loads – from what, I did not like to ask – and set off in opposite directions in search of a shepherd to give us the way.

It seemed a long time before they returned, and we bore left and upwards towards some herders' huts where the shepherd had said we could spend the night. After three hours the trail was clear of the clinging forest and out on open pastures of winter grass with scattered clumps of leafless thorn bushes. Poor Manbahadur was trailing further and further behind as the air grew thinner.

Ang yelled encouragement. 'Come on *bai*! You can make it.'

An indistinct reply came from below.

Ang sighed and swung off the trail to a lone thatched shelter where a couple of ragged children were blowing on the embers of a fire. A quick exchange in Sherpa, and Ang threw the tent on to a flat area of ground.

'You here. Me and porter in cow-house.'

I looked at the roof-only 'cow-house'. It seemed a chilly spot to spend the night at 12,000 feet in January. Ang had a new 'expedition' sleeping bag, but Manbahadur boasted only a thread-bare blanket. At first Ang was too embarrassed to accept the loan of my mattress and down jacket on Manbahadur's behalf, but concluded it was better than trying to thaw out a frozen porter the next morning.

The cold gripped the hillside as evening drew in. I sat for a while, muffled in sweaters, listening to the low bong, bong, bong of heavy bells as the cattle returned to their shelter for the night. Clouds sank into the valley with the cold air and suddenly the whole mountain range of Makalu and Chamlang emerged like a mirage, closer and higher than I could have believed possible, glowing a fiery pink and orange in the last rays of sun. The peaks hovered above the shadowed cloudbank until snow and light faded to purple, then a deeper blue that melted into the night sky.

Sherpa legend has it that the sacred valley of Khembalung, the

'Valley of Incense Plants', lies hidden somewhere to the north of the great massif of Chamlang. At the time when Guru Rinpoche (Padmasambhava) brought the teachings of Buddhism from India to Tibet, he lured away the evil king of Khembalung, sealed the borders of the country, and set the gods to watch over it and keep it hidden from the world. Among the many sacred texts hidden by Guru Rinpoche there are guidebooks to Khembalung, but only the true followers of Guru Rinpoche, true practitioners of the teachings, can discover the texts, or follow the directions to the Valley. If intruders try to reach Khembalung, snow leopards will attack them on the mountain passes, or mist will come down and conceal the way. According to the legend these are manifestations of the guardian deities.

The texts describe Khembalung as a kind of paradise of plenty; rivers flowing with milk, caves full of jewels, and springs of youth-giving water. Yet even these are not the real treasure; this is less tangible – a kind of subtle radiance or power which can lift the mind beyond dark, heavy thoughts and emotions:

> Just by being in Khembalung, compassion and kindness will naturally increase, and greater wisdom and knowledge will come. To meditate for one year in Khembalung is better than for a thousand years elsewhere. . .

It was the deeper symbolism of the myth that fascinated me. The legends made it clear that there was more to finding Khembalung than stomping through the mountains with a map and compass. There was still so much to learn about the way in which these valleys were concealed. The guidebooks implied that to understand this dimension one had to learn to transcend one's ordinary perceptions and concepts of reality. This is the way of the yogis and great meditators.

The wound was badly infected, the wrist red and swollen. The filthy bandage peeled away stickily, greenish pus clinging to it and more oozing from the ugly festering gash beneath. Suddenly the thumb flopped down in a sickeningly unnatural movement and I realised the tendon must be severed. The woman was shivering with cold and fever. She would only get the tendon repaired in hospital now it had pulled back into her arm. There were antibiotic tablets in the medical kit, but without supervision she might take the whole course at once. I cleaned the wound with boiling water – only hand-hot at this altitude – and covered it with lint and antibiotic powder. Thus protected, it seemed safe to let her replace the cleanest of the original grubby bandages. I gave her more dressings to change each day, Ang translated from Nepali to Sherpa, and she tucked them into the front of her dress. She seemed gloomily resigned to the entire weirdness of being scrubbed and bandaged by a white-haired stranger who had suddenly appeared in a yellow space dome behind her cowshed.

Having announced an early start the next morning, I lost all credibility by being found fast asleep when my patient arrived with a bowl of hot boiled curds for breakfast. She looked much better already – people who have never used an antibiotic in their lives often respond almost magically to their first encounter. She gave knowledgeable directions for crossing the Mayam Danda, waving her bandaged hand towards the misty hillside above.

The Mayam Danda is not a pass but a long ridge which rises well above the tree line. It is barren, rocky country where the earth's bones protrude through thin soil and scraggly withered grass hisses in the wind. First scramble at altitude always leaves lungs burning in the thin air, especially when the trail is a barely perceptible line of wear up steep rock and slippery turf.

I was anxious to get off the ridge before more cloud came in. It would be easy to descend the wrong side of something very big in this barren wasteland. The ridge fell away steeply in a series of ravines. There was snow underfoot now, no more than a frosting on the spiny rocks but thigh-deep where it had drifted, and I stopped several times to wait for Manbahadur. With his awkward load he could easily have slipped and fallen a long way, but he kept appearing out of the fog, smiling placidly as ever as his bandy legs ploughed through the wet snow. Ang paused, scanning the ground for footprints which would indicate the direction we should go now that the trail was under three feet of snow and mist obscured all the landmarks. . .

'No people,' he announced gloomily. 'Just *jangu*.' He pointed to the wolf tracks which led away down a ravine and fell silent again as the tension grew and the mist rolled in more thickly across the hilltop. It seemed endless, this smudgy whiteness and the crunch of our footsteps in the crystalline snow. We were descending now, but whether we were right or wrong it was impossible to tell.

There were voices in the mist, and a couple of young Sherpas were looking as surprised to see us as we were relieved to see them. They directed us down to the left of the ridge, where their *dzos* (yak/cow crossbreeds) were grazing the foggy grass. The tension was broken, we were on the right road, and Ang was whooping and shouting and leaping down the hill, calling that he would go ahead to cook a long overdue meal.

It would have been a good idea, but we missed him in the fog and it took an hour before he caught up with us. We were very hungry. Manbahadur grabbed a cookpot and disappeared to fetch water, while Ang teased a flame out of a pile of twigs. I decided that, in the circumstances, we could dispense with Raj-style protocol for a while. Ang turned round from lighting the fire and his face assumed an expression of horror as he perceived a memsahib sitting in his kitchen – peeling potatoes! Temporarily at a loss over what to do, he pretended not to notice, and hurriedly brewed some tea. Then he spread his foam mattress a suitable distance from the cooking area and carried my tea over to it.

'Tea, memsahib.'

He hovered, tea in hand, waiting for me to comply. It was much more interesting to watch how quickly and efficiently they put a meal together over a twig fire, but obviously Ang had been mortally offended. He could only interpret my offers of help as a reproach that he was not doing his job adequately. I moved out and drank my tea. It is sometimes easy to forget how aware the Nepalese are of their place within the caste system, and the place of others. Everyone knows and understands their rights and obligations within this social framework. *Sahib* is the caste of a foreigner and there was no point trying to impose Western ideas and confusing the way people here were used to doing things. Ang had already dispensed with the elaborate meals and unnecessary trimmings which had been slowing us down, and the system we now had was a reasonable compromise. I knew that within a few hours he would be back on familiar territory and was hoping that our schedule would become more tidy.

The ochre and white houses of the Rai village were tinted red in the setting sun. Smoke rose through the heavy grass thatch of the roofs as the villagers began cooking their evening meal. A few stragglers were on their way home from the fields, and a girl carried a heavy brass water pot back from the spring. The sound of flutes and drums drifted down from a wedding party at a house on the hillside above.

Steep stone steps in the terrace wall led down to the house of a Rai couple whom Ang knew. Nanda Maya was standing in her doorway, enticing a brood of half-grown chicks into the house with a handful of dried corn. She was tiny and fragile, stooped and old, yet beautiful in her faded sari and ropes of jewels. She beckoned us in to sit by her fire while she settled the chicks for the night under an upturned doko in a corner of the room, safe from the appetites of the *shell* whose eerie voices already echoed in the forest beyond the village.

Nanda Maya set a battered cookpot on the three stones set in the hearth.

'All we have is *diro*. . .'

I nodded assent. I detested the stuff, but did not want to embarrass Nanda Maya. She scooped out handfuls of the toasted millet flour and stirred it energetically into boiling water as it thickened instantly. There is nothing exactly wrong with diro except that it has no taste, and has the consistency of the coarse, solid mud it so closely resembles. And it sits like mud in your insides while your digestive system tries to figure out what to do with it – usually with no great success.

I intercepted Nanda's questions as the firelight shone red-gold on her heavy jewellery.

'No, not eighty, only thirty-three! Where I come from many people have white hair as children.'

'Ah! My hair is white because I'm old – and look! So much falling out as well.' She held up a wisp of thin grey hair and laughed ruefully. She pointed to the heavy gold and turquoise hanging from her left nostril. 'Why don't you have one?'

'We don't use them in the nose, just the ears – and smaller than yours.'

She fingered the heavy gold discs that covered her ears, suspended by chains looped over the top.

'They seem not heavy now. So many years I've had them.' Then she saw my socks. 'What's this?'

'Keeps your feet warm in the snow.'

'Maybe I should try.' Although her feet were tiny, the dried calluses on the sole were so cracked and wrinkled that the woolly sock would not slide over them.

'How do you put them on your feet?' Then she saw my soft pink feet and laughed out loud. '*E!* They're just like hands! And you really couldn't walk without shoes. . .'

For some years I had assumed that the Nepalese words for 'leg' and 'foot' corresponded with the English, but this is not so. In a land where so many walk barefoot, the vital part of the limb is the sole of the foot, which must be tough enough to withstand stony tracks and even stretches of seasonal snow. All the rest is 'leg'.

Not only the words, but also the regional accents, were beginning to emerge for me as I listened to people from different areas and altitudes and began to perceive how Nepalese can distinguish the *jat*, or caste, of people they meet by their accent as well as their clothing, jewellery and features. Different altitudes in these mountains are inhabited by different castes. The Brahmins and Chettris, the high-caste Hindus, farm the lush, low-lying rice paddies, while Rais, Mangars and Limbus inhabit the hillsides a little higher up. As one climbs, one may pass Gurung or Tamang villages, and the Buddhist Sherpas and Tibetans eke out a living in the highest and most inhospitable mountainsides that can possibly be farmed. Each different ethnic group has its own language, so people use Nepalese for conversing at the local markets which they visit regularly to exchange their produce for that of a different altitude and climate, farmed by a different *jat*.

Nanda's husband returned from the wedding feast and sat down by the fire. He paused, hand outstretched, to take the offered cup of tea.

'Did you use the pot you cooked the spinach in?'

'Yes, but I washed it after I cooked the spinach in it.'

'Well washed?'

'Three times.'

'That should be all right.' He turned to Ang. 'I must not eat green vegetables for one month.'

I was curious. 'Why not? Are you sick?'

He looked at me, as if for the first time.

'Because I am *Dami*,' he said enigmatically.

I asked Ang why a shaman should abstain from vegetables but he just shrugged.

'I don't know why. I am not *Dami*. Maybe his god told him not to.'

There was nothing in the old shaman's outward appearance

to mark him as different from others apart from the quiet dignity with which he held himself in spite of his bare feet and patched clothes. His special clothes and implements would be carefully wrapped and put away. Before the old man had finished eating, a woman from a nearby village came in to ask if he could find the whereabouts of her brother who had disappeared two weeks ago. Evidently this did not require the full paraphernalia of a trance because the Dami simply took out a worn wooden rosary and began dividing the beads in a complex pattern. Then he consulted a dog-eared book of astrological charts before telling the woman that her brother would return of his own accord within a week. I had already heard enough stories of the accuracy of these mountain seers to suspend disbelief. I had only once before seen a Dami in action, and it had led me to wonder from what source their skill came.

I had been working as a guide for a trekking group on the route that circled the Annapurnas. The weather was cold and there had been over a foot of snow on the 17,500-foot Thorung La pass. With two clients recovering from altitude sickness in Kagbeni, I scarcely noticed the cookboys' apology that came with the tea.

'Sorry no biscuit. Biscuit porter late.'

An hour later a white-faced Sirdar burst in announcing, 'One porter dying.'

I pushed through the crowd of gawpers and hangers-on who were blocking the doorway of the ramshackle shed which was serving as the camp kitchen. Several of the porters were crying and wailing around the inert form of a young woman while someone in the shadows was chanting the last rites. I elbowed through the crowd, arriving at the girl's side at the same time as the trek doctor. The Sirdar was explaining hurriedly that the porter had collapsed, vomiting from food poisoning after eating lunch in one of the grubby teashops below the pass. Her husband had carried her for four hours to the camp, by which time she was in a coma.

The trek doctor was from Florida and had probably not seen many cases of hypothermia but took only two minutes to make the diagnosis after feeling the temperature of the girl's body and limbs. We wrapped her in sleeping bags and packed water bottles filled with hot water around her torso, trying at the same time to explain to her family why they should not keep moving the bottles to her limbs as this would draw blood away from the vital organs.

After an hour there was little improvement. The young woman's eyes were still rolled upwards in their sockets with only the whites showing.

Suddenly the crowd at the door fell silent and drew aside to let in an extraordinary character. He was small and wizened, wearing threadbare Nepali clothes and a pair of red moon-boots gleaned from a passing expedition. He carried a leather pouch and a large hand-drum adorned with clusters of coloured quills and feathers. He sat down by the girl's head and gave orders to the cookboys. The family were whispering among themselves.

'He's the local shaman,' I translated. The doctor's eyes widened in disbelief. They obviously didn't have many shamans in Florida.

The Dami began to chant and sway as he took grains of rice from his pouch and threw them violently on to the girl's face. One of the cookboys returned with a pair of metal tongs heated red and glowing in the fire. The Dami took them, and pressed them, hissing, on to his protruding tongue. He circled them slowly over the girl's face as if he was going to brand her with them. To my relief, all she got was another handful of the rice while the Dami sizzled the glowing tongs on his tongue again, without any apparent ill-effect. He handed them back to the cookboy to be re-heated, and the performance was repeated. I was becoming mesmerised by the chanting and the glowing light of the tongs in the dark shelter, wondering if the doctor's patients in Florida would ever hear about this. Suddenly the girl began to babble, incoherently at first, as if she were talking in her sleep.

'I can't find my load! Oh, I will lose my job! . . . Ohh, I'm so cold, so cold, I don't have any legs. . .'

She gasped a couple of times and opened her eyes. Slowly they focused on her family, the American doctor, and the Dami. Then, with a sigh, she turned over and slept. The Dami stood up, accepted his fee from her husband, and left.

We were on the road again at dawn and reached Ang's village an hour after dark, tripping and stumbling up the last hill by torch-light. The dogs set up a chorus of baying and snarling as we approached, and even Ang hung back and yelled for someone to hold them so that we could enter with our legs intact. The single-storey stone farmhouse had small shuttered wooden windows and a low doorway. Ang's family were sitting round the open fire while a fat pot of potatoes bubbled on the three stones of the *chullo*.

Ang sat down by the fire and began to exchange news as if he had been away only a few days instead of months. His mother bustled round making sure everyone had enough potatoes, all plump smiles and striped apron. It was her that Ang resembled more than his father, who was tall and thin with a long nose – unusual for a Sherpa. Ang's younger sister Kamali came in from tying up the dog which was still growling sulkily outside.

'It will have got used to you by tomorrow,' she said reassuringly. I hoped she was right.

Ang's wife sat at the edge of the group, waiting attentively on her parents-in-law. Ang had told me it would take another year before he had saved enough money for them to build a house of their own on a portion of his father's land.

A minor contretemps seemed to be erupting between Ang and his wife. I thought she was demanding more housekeeping money but apparently the discussion was of longer standing.

'She no like farm. She want teashop in Kathmandu.'

'What do you think?'

He wrinkled his flat nose. 'Kathmandu difficult place. Expensive. Maybe I try.'

I said nothing. He had seemed so out of his depth in Kathmandu that I doubted he would really enjoy the teashop business. At the same time, once they had started to feel restless it would be difficult to remain content on an isolated hill farm.

We rested for a day at the stone farmhouse. I was glad to ease aching feet and watch the family move about their chores. Toasted barley was ground in a stone hand mill and mixed with hot tea to make *tsampa*, the staple of Tibetans and Sherpas who eke out a subsistence living on the highest cultivable part of the Himalayan hillsides. Ang's father was philosophical about the harsh life and uncertain harvests.

'Yes, some years, it is difficult. We plough and plant, as our fathers did, but if the gods are not happy, the hail comes or the rain does not come. Then the crop is less and we search in the jungle for plants to eat. But most times, it is good. We do the pujas, and the gods are happy.'

He spent more than two hours that day chanting from a heavy Tibetan text, amid all the traditional paraphernalia of bells and hand-drums. The cacophony of sound mingled with the rumbling of the tsampa mill and the clucking of chickens in the yard outside the open door.

Ang was searching through the dusty shelves, muttering 'Khatak, khatak. . .' under his breath. I watched his progress, idly wondering what part of the religious ritual required a ceremonial white scarf. Finally Ang found what he was looking for. He carefully folded the scarf (which had the appearance of having been recycled several times already), placed it over the top of the teakettle, and poured a potful of boiling tea through it.

'Why did you do that?' I asked curiously.

Ang looked up, a little startled at the question. 'I can't find the tea-strainer,' he said.

I reminded myself not to read too much ritual into events in future.

Manbahadur the porter had decided that leaping up and down snowbound hills at all hours of the day and night was not quite what he'd had in mind when he left Ilam on a warm, sunny morning. I paid him off, and next morning he headed for home (via a seven-day walk through the southern valleys to the nearest bus route) with a smile of undisguised relief. Ten minutes later Ang arrived with his brother-in-law – our replacement porter.

'Much stronger than Manbahadur.'

Phurba was no bigger than Ang, but he was wiry and strong-looking, swinging the heavy doko on to his back and taking it to his house to pack his own kit on top. His luggage comprised a spare T-shirt, a blanket, and a religious text.

'Phurba very good lama,' Ang assured me.

We were on the road early the next morning. Ang's father draped our necks in white khataks and delivered a homily on taking care and not running unnecessary risks.

Because we walked until it was too late to put up the tent, I spent the first night in a herder's hut in the company of his children, goats, chickens, and considerable numbers of other smaller livestock which invaded my sleeping bag and spent the night biting large areas of my anatomy.

The following night promised better things. A Sherpa farm-house on the outskirts of Salleri Bazaar had running water piped through a rubber hose to a tap in the yard and a spare upstairs room used for storing barley straw. There was a stone hearth in the corner of this room-sized tinderbox which, to my surprise and horror, the Sherpas intended to use. This was confirmed when

Phurba casually poured kerosene from the borrowed pressure lamp over a handful of straw to start the fire.

'Don't you think this is taking unnecessary risks?' I asked.

'Very useful,' said Phurba cheerfully, brandishing the frying pan. 'Too much snow on Lamjura. Need plenty pancakes.' So I gave up worrying about being incinerated in my sleep and joined in the pancake session. Ang would still not let me near his cooking utensils, so all I could do was spread jam and eat. In the circumstances I was not complaining.

The sky was a heavy grey as we began the climb to the Lamjura, and a cold wind whipped down from the mountains to the north. Phurba's worn-out sneakers had no grip on the old frozen snow underfoot, so I lent him my boots as my running shoes were still gripping well. He winced as he jammed his broad feet into the narrow boots.

'Maybe cut,' suggested Ang mischievously, brandishing the kitchen knife.

'My boots or Phurba's toes?'

Phurba looked alarmed. 'No problem,' he announced hastily, and set off.

By the time we neared the summit of the Lamjura it was snowing hard and drifting across the trail, blotting out everything beyond a radius of ten yards. The last time I had crossed this pass it had been a pleasant grassy hill in summer rather than a wasteland of drifting snow.

The grey light was deceptive, shifting between the snow and cloud, and making it difficult to judge distances. Suddenly I stopped and looked back, my eyes straining to catch the movement of a deeper shadow within the shifting cloud. I felt uneasy, apprehensive, yet didn't know why. Conditions were bad but we were coping easily, so why was I imagining what this storm would be like higher on the mountain? The ridge which we were crossing ran northwards to a series of peaks then dropped again to form another pass – the Tashi Lapcha. I pushed the thought aside. The others could not possibly be on the Tashi Lapcha in this blizzard. They would never attempt to cross the pass when there was no one in the party capable of fixing the abseils for the descent on the far side. They would have cut across to the Lamjura and were probably a day ahead of us, squelching along the valley in the pouring rain.

Ang and Phurba were yelling at me to keep moving. We were

descending now, feet skidding and sliding in the new snow that turned to mush as we lost altitude. The mush was still ankle-deep when we reached the first Sherpa 'hotel', whose proprietor looked surprised to see three bedraggled figures crawl in out of the storm. We joined several other travellers round the fire. They had intended to cross the pass that morning but had seen the weather and stayed put. A pot of noodles was already steaming on the *chullo* – a welcome hot lunch after a long morning sustained by cold pancakes, although they had proved surprisingly good fodder for plodding through blizzards.

We reached the valley by nightfall. Next morning the rain had stopped, although the sky was still grey and rags of cloud clung to the pass like giant prayer flags. Two more days brought us to the roadhead at Mandu, above the Tamba Kosi. From here, we would take the local bus into Kathmandu to resupply – and to find out what had happened to the other half of the expedition.

The road was little more than a dirt track awaiting completion that had cut the village in half. Either side of the slash of rutted red mud a line of wood and corrugated iron shanties had sprung up as city entrepreneurs moved in to take advantage of the road-head trade. The ochre and white farmhouses lay beyond, while the local people still seemed to be wondering what to do about this tentacle from Kathmandu that had suddenly appeared on their doorstep. Some of them were labouring on the road construction, pounding the rocks with small hammers to make gravel.

4

The Rinpoche

།སྔོན་ཡོད་ཡོད་འདྲ་བའི་བན་ཆན་དེ།

Back in Kathmandu, it was interesting to watch the accumulated grime of weeks disappear into the shower in a matter of minutes. The cheap flea-pit of a hotel boasted the excellence of plentiful hot water, if you didn't mind picking the cockroaches out of the shower first.

I went round to the Sherpa Co-op to see if there were any messages from the others. While most tourist offices in Kathmandu were smartening up their premises to attract up-market customers, the Sherpa Co-op seemed to consider such things unnecessary. I picked my way along damp-smelling corridors and past storerooms piled with old tents and kerosene stoves to Mike Cheney's office. His stooping figure and quizzical smile seemed as unchanged as his quarters which had the colonial atmosphere of the tea plantation he had left behind.

'You're not the only traverse team in the field you know. There's a chap out here from England now. He's soloing it with his girlfriend.'

He had waited weeks to tell me this. I fixed him with a look reserved for occasions like these.

'He's soloing it with his girlfriend,' I repeated slowly and carefully. 'I suppose that makes this the first non-existent traverse of the Himalaya then?'

Mike's smile became positively animated. A chauvinist maybe, but with style and a sense of humour. The others had not arrived back, but Mike was unconcerned.

'They probably decided to fly from Lukla rather than walk –

and there have been no flights for a week because of the weather. They're probably stuck up there in the snow waiting for a plane. Come back in a few days and ask again.'

There was nothing to do but wait, although it seemed pointless to continue the partnership. Our ideas and objectives were too different. All the same, I could hardly disappear without letting her know, and I was still uneasy about why they were all so late. I took the bus to Boudhnath to deliver Ngawang Norbu's reply to my friend Samten.

I climbed over a new consignment of Tibetan wool for her carpet weaving business and found her in the kitchen priming the kerosene stove to fry sugar bread for the Losar festival. I had forgotten that Tibetan New Year was only a week away. Samten read the letter without slowing down bread production, my supply of butter tea, or her opinions on rent increases and the rising price of food. The baskets and bags of rice, fruit, and meat on the kitchen table had obviously cost her some hard bargaining that morning.

I laughed. 'How's the carpet business?'

'*E!* Getting worse. The Chinese keep raising the price of wool – now buying from Australia is cheaper! And how to compete with these big factories?'

She waved a floury hand at the stock of goodies on the table. 'This – all Tenzing's money. Expedition just finished.'

'I thought he was going trekking this year.'

Her face clouded. 'Always he say, "Just one more. Expedition is best money." He's going again soon. If he does not come back, what will we do?'

Tenzing was one of the few Tibetans to break into Sherpa-dominated expedition work. His strength and ability to carry the climbers' oxygen at high altitude had brought him a steady stream of jobs. Now, with three major expeditions a year and a friend recently killed while climbing, the strain was beginning to show. I knew Samten was hoping he would 'retire' to the safer option of trekking.

Samten's children smelled the frying sugar bread and came piling in from a rowdy game outside. I extricated myself from the melée and walked up to Kopan.

The muddy jeep-track meandered through the fallow rice paddies on the outskirts of Boudhnath before climbing the tree-covered hill on which the monastery stood. Looking down from the hilltop I could see the whole of Kathmandu spread across the flat valley like a map. A brown pall of fumes hung over the city centre but up here the air was clean and the surrounding hills were etched clear in the sunlight. A gnarled pipal tree cast dappled shade on the courtyard and the red-painted temple. A fountain played beneath a shrine to the Buddha Tara, the female embodiment of compassion. Young Sherpa and Tibetan monks were walking to their classes while a group of small boys were teasing and chasing each other in the courtyard – a game guaranteed to get them a ticking off from the disciplinarian for being late.

A path led through the vegetable garden to the visitors' quarters perched on a sunny ledge above the rows of spinach and carrots. A blonde girl was sitting outside polishing a set of brass offering bowls. She smiled, and spread a sweater for me to sit on. There seemed to be no other visitors.

'It's very quiet at the moment,' I said.

She nodded. 'There was a course for Westerners a few weeks ago and some of us stayed on to go into what we had learned in more depth. Now there are only about five of us here. It's a peaceful place to meditate.'

There was no need to make conversation. I sat and listened to the rustle of the trees and the squeak of the girl's polishing rag. When her polishing was finished, Marian offered tea and the loan of her notes from the course.

She went off to meditate while I sat in the sun and read.

> According to the buddhist teachings, no matter how confused or deluded we may be at the moment, the underlying and essential nature of our being is clear and pure. In the same way that clouds can temporarily obscure but cannot damage the light-giving power of the sun, so too the temporary afflictions of body and mind – our confusion, anxiety, and the suffering they cause – can temporarily obscure but cannot destroy or even touch the fundamentally clear nature of our consciousness. The ultimate purpose of all spiritual practices, whether they are called buddhist or not, is to uncover and make contact with this essentially pure nature – the inexhaustible source of love and wisdom within the hearts of all beings without exception.

It seemed less exotic but more immediately practical than jumping cross-legged out of holes in the ground. Perhaps I would stay here for a few days.

The first pale rays of sun crept through the dawn mist that shrouded the trees. My mind was supposed to be meditating, but it wasn't. It was drifting into the rose-tinted mist beyond the window and becoming busy with what was to come, and what had already gone.

Kopan was just as Marian had said, a peaceful place in which to meditate. There was also time to spend in the library, and evenings to enjoy with Marian. She was a quiet, self-effacing woman with a dry sense of humour and none of the new convert's pious self-righteousness. Not that 'convert' was a real description for someone who had spent years in search of a philosophy which would stand up to questioning, to being challenged. She had read every metaphysical work she could find, and thought deeply about what she studied. Since coming to Kopan, she said, she felt settled. The Rinpoche's writings and teachings had answered her question; now she needed time to assimilate them. When she asked me if I would like to join the three-day Nyungne retreat, I was prepared to trust her judgement.

'It's mainly fasting and meditation – a method for mental purification. There's also ritual and actual washing to emphasise the point.' She laughed. 'Mind you, at three in the morning in the middle of winter you can bet it'll be more ritual than actual!'

One of the students who had previously participated in Nyungne warned that some people found the physical discipline of the long hours exhausting. In the event I had few problems as my time in the mountains had left me lean and fit, but after three days of attempting single-pointed concentration without food it was my mind that was exhausted.

According to tradition, the Nyungne practice was introduced by an eleventh-century Kashmiri princess who became known as Bikshuni Lakshmi. A sympathetic and compassionate person, she was so shocked when she discovered that animals were slaughtered for food she decided to renounce life and become a nun. She was an accomplished scholar, skilled at logical debate, and received meditation instruction from a Tantric guru. Eventually she became the abbess of a monastery and held this position for many years until she fell ill with leprosy.

The monks of the monastery then threw her out and left her to die in the forest. This is not the sort of behaviour that Buddhism advocates, but perhaps one cannot expect all monks to be perfect. Lakshmi crawled to a cave and collapsed, calling on Chenresig, the Buddha of Compassion, for help. The Compassionate Buddha appeared to her in a radiant vision of a white figure with a thousand arms, each with an eye in the palm of the hand to see all the suffering in the world. The spiritual medicine he gave to the dying woman completely cured her illness. She then flew with the Buddha to the realm of enlightenment and danced in the sky with the Dakinis. . .

It is difficult to express in words the actual experience of meditation, even at the basic level at which I was practising. It is small wonder that the writers of the ancient texts lapse into poetry and allegory to describe the transcendent experiences of their saints and heroes. I was as intrigued by Dakinis as I was by Shambhala. Both seemed to be enigmatic symbols of something on the periphery of perception, even language itself. Dakinis, whether they appear as beautiful goddesses or ugly hags, are symbols of enlightened feminine energy, yet they are often more than just symbols. Lakshmi herself is often referred to as a Dakini. The Compassionate Buddha taught her the Nyungne fasting practice and instructed her to teach it to as many people as possible, especially lay people.

Lakshmi's personal attendant had come into the forest looking for her dead body. When she found the abbess fully restored to health, she suggested they return to the monastery to teach the fasting meditations to the monks there. Lakshmi is reported to have responded, 'That monastery? I wouldn't go there to pee!' I felt quite encouraged to hear that even great saints who have danced in the sky with Dakinis can be moderately grumpy at the thought of their erstwhile persecutors. However, compassion prevailed and the monks were the first people to receive the instruction before Lakshmi taught the fasting practice to many lay people. Today the Nyungne practice is widespread among lay people in the villages of the Himalayan region, and is regarded as a powerful means of spiritual purification.

At the end of the retreat I walked down to Boudhnath to take the bus into the city. After the long hours of silence and stillness the noise and fumes of the traffic seemed overpowering. The colours of the wares in the little shops had an intensity and brightness I had not noticed before. All my senses were heightened, reeling at the overload of colour, sound and movement.

An Indian beggar sat on the stone paving by the chorten. A few coins lay on a scrap of sacking on the ground and a pair of crutches leaned against the white wall behind him. His legs were metal and plastic below the knees. I stopped and stared at him, my mind racing back to my time in Tibet, to the dark room in a Chinese hospital stinking of cheap disinfectant and rotting amputated toes, to the dark eyes of the Indian pilgrim who had crossed the Himalaya barefoot. He still had the same wild, staring look . . . but there were so many crippled Indians in Nepal. How could this be the same man? Suddenly his eyes focused on me and he sat bolt upright, staring and pointing.

'You. Ladakh, Dharamsala.' He spoke slowly and clearly, then his eyes glazed over again and he leaned back against the wall of the chorten. Shaken, I dropped some rupees on to the sacking and walked on.

The changing images of Kathmandu appeared in quick succession, each one etched sharp against the teeming background of the city. A group of German tourists, crispy-clean in their drip-dry and sunglasses, stepped their clean shoes carefully through the market where vegetable sellers tried to protect their produce from the attentions of passing sacred cows. A chicken picked unseen grubs out of the dirt at my feet, one leg anchored to a brick with a piece of blue wool. A gilded serpent rose above the rubbish dump that had once been Nagpokhari, the Serpent's Lake. Even now, the old Naga retained some shred of his dignity in spite of the string of somebody's kite that had tangled in his whiskers.

Ang and Phurba were sitting outside Mike Cheney's office, talking to two strangers. I could not understand why the newcomers greeted me as if they knew me. Suddenly, with an almost physical shock, I recognised Maila and Pasang. Not the Maila and Pasang I had last seen in east Nepal. There were shadows of exhaustion under their eyes, their faces tight and expressionless. They moved clumsily, hands swathed in heavy white bandages with dark stains oozing through from inside.

Maila answered the unspoken question. 'Frostbite. Pasang, five fingers. Me and memsahib, one finger.' He hesitated. There wasn't much more anyone could say about frostbite. It was a case of wait and see how much finger you had left at the end of the waiting.

'What happened?'

'We get to Thame. Bad weather. Try Tashi Lapcha but not possible – too much snow. Two days coming down. . .'

Pasang tried to joke about his own clumsiness with bandaged hands, but the humour was brittle and there was fear mixed with the pain. What did the future hold for a boy without fingers?

'Other memsahib want to see you.' Maila led the way and I followed, trying to force rational thought into a mind numbed with shock.

She was eating egg and chips at a table on the lawns of her hotel. One finger was heavily bandaged. The five of us found chairs and sat down. There was an awkward silence.

She said, 'I'm not giving up this trip.'

I stared at her blankly. What trip? That belonged to another world. She began outlining her plans to recover in Kathmandu, then fly out with Maila and rejoin the traverse further on. Pasang's fingers would probably not heal in time. . .

I said, 'What do you feel about it all?'

She hesitated at the non-sequitur. 'Well, I'm disappointed I didn't succeed at the Tashi Lapcha, but I'm still determined to complete the traverse. If you keep going – '

'I think we should give the money that's left to Maila and Pasang and go home.'

Her voice became soft and persuasive, almost tearful. 'We can't give up now. My family gave up so much for me to be here. I have to get something out of it, for their sake.'

I felt trapped. I could hardly ditch her just after she had been injured.

I stumbled back to Kopan in the dark, wondering what I should do next – wondering what I should have done to prevent all this from happening. Marian took one look, pushed me into a chair and fed me cups of tea. She listened thoughtfully and it was a while before she spoke.

'Compassion isn't about blaming yourself for everything that happens – or giving in to whatever someone demands, or expecting everything to work out, or even the recipient being grateful. When you feel you've done what you can – leave it, or you become part of the problem. I'm getting out of my depth – you should talk to the Rinpoche.'

I stood outside the temple by the Tara shrine, waiting to be called.

Zopa Rinpoche. Until now it had just been the author's name on some of the books in the library, and the intangible presence behind the tranquillity of Kopan itself. It would not have occurred to me to seek an interview with a High Lama. They seemed too venerated, remote, absorbed in contemplations of Eternity or whatever it was they contemplated. I couldn't see how someone like that could possibly be interested in the kind of mundane problems I was dragging around. I shifted the silk khatak awkwardly from one hand to the other, still unfamiliar with the refinements of Eastern protocol. I was sure to drop the khatak or do the prostrations wrong or commit some other breach of etiquette. A young monk beckoned me over, helpfully rearranging the folds of the khatak as he showed the way to the Rinpoche's room above the temple.

I paused outside the open door to take off my sandals, catching the faint scent of incense and saffron from within. The room was filled with dappled sunlight and the rustling of the pipal tree outside the open window. Zopa Rinpoche was sitting on a cushioned bench at the end of the room. He seemed to radiate a calmness that was pervasive, a stillness within that dancing green sunlight. He motioned me to sit, then replaced his hands within the folds of his deep red robes. He was neither young nor old, almost timeless, as if belonging to another world. Everyday problems suddenly seemed incongruous and self-perpetuating and I wished I had come to learn about his world instead of bringing mine in with me.

'So what was it that you came to ask?' He spoke clear, educated English, quietly, unhurriedly. I told him what had happened, that I felt responsible for other people's safety, and worried about what might happen next.

Suddenly he laughed, a hearty fresh-air laugh that sent the creeping doubts scuttering back into the shadows. 'So you feel responsible for everything that happens around you?' There was a pause, then his expression became serious. 'If you are to continue, there are things that you must understand. There are powers that live in the Himal; guardians. . . You cannot see them but you would be wise not to ignore them. There are mantras which can protect . . . but first tell me the name of the pass you must cross.'

'Thorung La.' There were probably other passes further west, but the only available map was so sketchy it was impossible to name them.

The Rinpoche took out a small box inlaid with turquoise. He was making the kind of divination the Tibetans called *mo*. I wondered what he saw as he searched the future. Finally he emerged from his concentration.

'Don't go. This way is full of danger for you. You must find another way.'

We sat and talked for over an hour. Afterwards, I could not remember a word that was said, or even if we spoke at all. I was aware simply of a growing understanding of the tangible and intangible forces which affect our lives, and the link between the powers outside and within ourselves. Apart from the safety factor, the Rinpoche clearly did not consider the physical aspects of the coming journey to be important, yet he seemed to understand the nature of my inner search better than I did myself. When I left, although I could not put it into words, I knew that a bond had formed – or in Tibetan terms re-established itself from previous lives – and that slowly, over the years, this would lead into dimensions less tangible yet far more powerful than those I was pursuing in the mountains.

I went over to say goodbye to Marian, but it was a tawny bundle of fluff that leaped out to greet me, tripped over its own paws and rolled down the steps. Marian scooped up the puppy in one hand.

'One of the boys brought it in this morning because some children were stoning it down in the village. Can you take it with you? I'll be flying home soon, and there will be no one to look after it.'

The puppy was already pulling strands of silk out of the khatak which the Rinpoche had blessed and draped round my neck. I tucked the wriggling fluff-ball under my arm out of harm's way, and succeeded in getting it back to my hotel without mishap. The advantage of patronising an establishment where one cohabits with cockroaches and geckos – apart from the economy – is that the management turn a blind eye to the odd puppy being smuggled in and out. After a few futile attempts at eviction, I resigned myself to the fact that nothing was going to keep it out of my bed. At least dog fleas don't bite humans. Or so I hoped.

In true Cinderella style, it was perhaps fitting that the first social engagement for the former unwanted stray was a formal lunch at the Indian Ambassador's residence. I had first met Mr Sarin in Delhi, where he was the head of the Indian Mountaineering Foundation. He had since been appointed Ambassador to Nepal.

I left the puppy outside the front entrance to the Residence, happily chewing the trouser leg of an immaculately uniformed doorman. Lunch was served on the terrace above the front garden. The other guests arrived in a swirl of silk saris and heavy make-up, or in crisp business suits with careers in mind, and the conversation was careful and appropriate. I laboured through the meaningless pleasantries, regretting the wasted opportunity as Mr Sarin is an intelligent and interesting man and a provoking conversationalist.

It must have been the smell of tandoori chicken and spiced kebabs wafting down to the flower borders that suddenly brought an embarrassingly familiar howling and wailing from below. The polite exchanges trickled to a halt while the Ambassador and his wife craned their necks over the stone parapet to see what all the bedlam was about. Mrs Sarin brushed my apologies aside with a gracious wave of the hand.

'Oh, it's so *sweet!* Poor little thing, it must be *so* hungry. Here, you must take it something.'

She swooped on the dishes of gourmet Indian cuisine, picking out dainty morsels by the dozen and piling them on a spare plate while her husband filled another. I hoped the dog's coarse breeding showed in its stomach as well as its manners. It was barely weaned and had been living for the last few days on yoghurt and rice pudding. I need not have worried. It ate the lot, then rolled over on the sunny grass with a contented burp to sleep it off.

Before I left, Mrs Sarin took me into the kitchen and filled a bag with leftovers for the spoiled brat, while the cooks watched in amazed silence.

Ang and Phurba had been stocking up on provisions for the next stage of the trek. Due to the delay, there would be no time to walk the section from Mandu to Gorkha which would have crossed the area directly north of Kathmandu. These valleys were easily accessible from the city if I ever wanted to explore them in the future – unlike the far west of Nepal. One 30kg load of high protein and calorie rations was set aside to be air freighted to Jumla (the regional capital) where food was in short supply.

Pasang was at the hospital on a course of treatment that was due to be completed before his half of the team left Kathmandu.

He was hoping his insurance compensation would have arrived by then so that he could return home. Fran had decided to wait for the insurance money before flying out to rejoin the traverse in Jumla; she and Maila would bring the food with them. We arranged to use the airline office in Jumla as a contact point for letters. Expedition funds were now a tenth of their original glory, probably because of the others' rescue expenses, and £300 seemed a fragile amount with which to be setting out. If only I had realised the futility of worrying when so many factors were unknown. If only there had been something to spend it on.

After the debacle at the Indian border with missing permits I decided not to entrust my passport to the Sherpa Co-op again and went down to the Immigration Office myself. The officer in charge shook his head sympathetically when he saw my proposed trek route, then issued the permit with a look that said he didn't expect to see me again.

Samten had heard disquieting rumours that an American volunteer had been murdered near Dhorpatan and she urged me to go to see her friend Tsering Choedrak who had a weaving business in Dhorpatan. He and his family spent the winters in Kathmandu to sell their carpets.

Tsering was clearly embarrassed about the murder so close to his own village. His battered face wrinkled into a frown as he spoke.

'It was not Dhorpatan people of course. It was those Kami people in the jungle beyond our area. It's bad in those parts – not safe, like the rest of Nepal. You must walk together and only camp beside good quality houses.' He clasped my hand earnestly. 'You must stay at my house in Dhorpatan. It's locked up for the winter, but my friend has the key . . . you will find good people in Dhorpatan!'

Departure plans were curtailed the next morning by a raging fever and sore throat. I crawled off to the Tibetan doctor in Boudhnath. He was alone in his small dispensary, the walls of which were lined with shelves of herbal remedies. I had not expected him to be a shaven-headed monk and wondered who would translate the medical terminology. He smiled a greeting and took my hand, feeling for several pulses in my wrist and fingers. I was still waiting for him to ask what my symptoms were and peer at my tonsils when he offered his diagnosis.

'You have a fever and a sore throat,' he said, in English. He smiled again and took down a heavy glass jar containing large brown hand-rolled pills.

'Crunch or swallow,' he said cheerfully, as he wrapped them in a piece of brown paper. The very size of them made the latter option a formidable undertaking, even without a sore throat.

Months of plain rations ahead made a good excuse to stuff oneself with goodies beforehand. The Green Dragon Cake and Pie Shop stood on the corner of Jochhen Tole, alias Freak Street, a veritable zoo of trinket sellers, hash traders, money changers and ageing hippies left over from the sixties. Heavily scented Indian incense failed to conceal the sweet smoke of marijuana wafting into the street through the open door. Inside, a sheet of paper pinned to the basketwork which covered the walls read, 'Smoking Of Ganja Is Not Allowed On Premises.'

I squeezed into the only vacant seat at a small table near the window. Behind me a group of overland travellers draped in scarves and gaudy jackets from the bazaar were discussing the advantages of an ascetic life while working their way through double helpings of chocolate gateau. The table opposite was half hidden by billowing clouds of smoke as two long-haired young men passed an overstuffed joint back and forth. Their conversation was slow, with lapses of several minutes between responses, demonstrating how literally the term 'spaced out' could be taken.

'D'ya get that letter from ya folks?' Pause.

'Yeah. No money though. . . They were talkin' about gettin' a *job*. . . career. . . Man – I came t' Kathmandu to find the *meanin' of life*. . .' Longer pause.

'Yeah, man. . . they're in a diff'rent spatial orientation. . .'

Outside, the street lamps cast auras in the dusty air and the street hustlers clustered moth-like in the pools of light.

'Buy hashish, opium?'

'Change money?'

'Buy carpet?'

It was time to leave the city.

5

A Hunter from Dolpo

།བརྟགས་ཚ་ན་ནམ་མཁའི་བྱ་རྗེས་འདྲ།

The driver turned the volume on full, distorting the cheap recording of Hindi pop songs, until the whole bus reverberated to a wailing reminiscent of a thousand cats being slowly and simultaneously fried. The bus itself was painted with gaudy pictures of Hindu gods and tassled like the Tata truck it was trying, suicidally, to overtake. The rear of the truck read '*HORN PLEASE*' in large decorative letters and the driver was doing his best to oblige, competing with the overloaded stereo for final destruction of the passengers' eardrums. It was a relief when one of the rear tyres burst and we had a half hour break while the crew replaced it.

I took the puppy for a short walk and it promptly threw itself down an embankment. I spent a few alarming moments clinging to trees and near-vertical shrubbery a few hundred feet above the foaming waters of the Trisuli river before my dog and I were on level ground again. It waddled over to the bus completely unabashed. Back on board the dog announced loudly and continuously that it took a dim view of bus travel and was relegated to the floor. Ten minutes later it had disappeared from between Phurba's feet. I began a frantic search through the baskets of vegetables under the seats. The other passengers were a sporting lot and soon most of them had joined in the grovelling. I had just become convinced that the dog had decamped in disgust at the last tea stop in Mugling when there was a yell of triumph from the back and a grinning Mangar lad hoisted the plump wriggling bundle above his head. It was passed from hand to hand amid the jokes and laughter of one of the most cheerful busloads of people I had met.

'Where are you taking it?'

'Looks nice with that red ribbon on!'

'Very small dog for trekking. . .'

It was rather a small dog to take trekking. Fifteen minutes on the trail out of Gorkha the front end collapsed, so I packed it into the top of my rucksack. It seemed content enough to ride in style, chin and front paws hanging over the edge of the canvas.

A large haystack overtook us on the way up the trail, only a sinewy pair of legs and bare feet visible below the huge load. A little further up, both haystack and owner were propped against a stone wall.

'Good afternoon,' said the haystack owner, sounding terribly British. 'Bit warm, what?'

He looked like any other hill farmer, dressed in nothing but a cotton *lungi* wound round like a skirt. He could interpret baffled British expressions as well as the language.

'Gurkhas,' he explained. 'Home on leave. Thought I needed a bit of exercise – been down the pub with the chaps a bit too often.' He patted his stomach ruefully. He was rather fatter than most hill farmers I noticed, now that he had mentioned it.

The Gurkha regiment took its name from the Gorkha region. The Gorkha kings probably originated from Rajasthan; Rajput princes fleeing to the hills from the Muslim invasion. In 1768 King Prithvi Naryan Shah – now Nepal's national hero – ousted the Malla dynasty from the Kathmandu Valley and 'unified Nepal'. By 1814 the Shah dynasty had expanded the borders of Nepal to twice its present size, which became a threat to the British administration in India. The Gorkha kings lost the ensuing war and a great deal of their empire, but the British generals were so impressed by the tenacity of the 'Gurkha' soldiers that they began recruiting them for their own army. The name remains, although today the recruits come from all areas of Nepal. Many are Buddhists, for whom killing is a sure ticket to hell, but it did not seem quite polite to ask the farmer how they resolved the contradiction.

We walked on together for a while, until the size of the haystack and the legacy of too many British pints began to make themselves felt. The haystack fell further and further behind and I caught up with the Sherpas making camp on a fallow rice terrace below the old fortified palace of Prithvi Naryan Shah, which now stood empty on the hill behind the town.

The dog made a beeline for the kitchen as soon as it was out of the rucksack. I curled up with my diary, listening to the conversation round the fire. There were three Sherpas now; I had felt the need for safety in numbers after hearing so many stories of bandits in West Nepal. Gyatso was a head taller than Ang or Phurba and walked with a lumbering, rolling gait which had already earned him the name Balu, the Bear. He came from a remote area east of the Arun and spoke Sherpa in a different dialect to the others. I found I could understand much of the conversation as they had to revert to Nepali to make themselves understood.

'Balu, how old are you?'

'Nineteen, I think.'

'Can you read?'

'No.'

Balu was a dreamy character and was soon getting cheerfully blamed for everything; 'Oh, Balu put too much sugar in the tea', or, 'Where's Balu?' 'Don't know, I sent him for water ten minutes ago and he disappeared!'

Neither Phurba nor Balu had any experience of working for tourist treks, but what would be more relevant in the region for which we were heading was their experience of surviving on isolated hill farms where storms and crop failures could sometimes mean the difference between life and death. Even in the lowlands their help was invaluable in finding food supplies and hospitable houses where we could cook. We had already met two hungry and disgruntled trekkers who, although delighted to be off the tourist trails, complained that they were not allowed into any houses. They had no way of knowing that the area was inhabited by high-caste Hindus for whom an outcaste in the house brings caste pollution, and must be avoided at all costs. If an outcaste were even to enter a Brahmin house during the preparation of the meal, the food would have to be thrown away uneaten. We now had lightweight tents to use in Hindu areas and unpopulated mountains, but they gave no shelter to the cooking fire. In non-Brahmin areas we squashed into a villager's one-room cottage with the family, dogs and chickens, in spite of the fleas.

From the camp, the snow peaks of the Ganesh range were visible further north up the valley of the great Buri Gandaki river.

I had heard about a Hidden Valley which is said to lie north of Ganesh and Manaslu Himal, somewhere in the Restricted Area up near the Tibetan border. It is called Kyimolung, the 'Valley of Happiness'. In this magical place a three-tiered pagoda temple stands on a ridge below a snow mountain. Maybe one day I would find a way through the net of bureaucracy and explore up there as well, but for the moment there was no permit for a detour.

In accordance with the Rinpoche's warnings, I had found a route skirting south of the Annapurna massif instead of crossing the Thorung La. Ang looked disappointed; he had wanted to show his brother-in-law an area he knew from his work with trekking groups. Disappointment soon turned to relief as each day brought violent rain storms and gusting winds. Sometimes the clouds would break up for long enough to reveal the spreading whiteness on the mountain to the north. There would be metres of snow on the Thorung La. It was not until later that I learned how many people had become frostbitten or died on the pass in the exceptional storms of that early spring.

Phurba had heard about Phewa Tal but had never seen it. When we reached Pokhara, he went to see for himself that such a great expanse of water really existed.

'Rara Tal near Jumla is even bigger,' I promised him. It still seemed distant and unreal, a hypothesis based on a smudgy blob on my map.

The lake shimmered in the dawn light, ripples spreading from the heavy dugouts slipping across the surface. Some were already on the beach, with barefoot farmers unloading churns of milk to sell in Pokhara.

The trail to Beni was thronged with porters and mules travelling in each direction. Farm produce was heading for the markets of Pokhara, while kerosene, biscuits, plastic *chappal* (sandals) and packets of cigarettes were being lugged back up into the hills. We rested with a group of porters carrying bleached white flour marked 'American Foreign Aid'. I added the weights printed on the bound-together sacks. Ninety kilos. I looked at the calf muscles of the porters. Cautiously, I braced the namlo on my head and heaved. Nothing happened. It felt as if it were nailed to the seat. When the onlookers had finished laughing, Phurba hefted the load with a grunt, and then replaced it on the chautara.

'Hm. Difficult but possible.'

We left, and the porters went on resting.

'They not live long if they carry so much weight. They are too greedy – they told me they are paid for each kilo.'

A piteous wailing and squealing from the puppy heralded the approach of another mule train. Ever since an unfortunate encounter with a justifiably irritable cow, it had developed a pathological fear of anything that was large and had hoofs. I scooped the fleeing creature into my arms, from which safe perch it yapped cheekily at the passing mules. No sooner was it back on the ground than it discovered a clutch of chicks and a broody hen eating left-over rice and dal under an upturned doko. A few good yaps and snuffles, and the basket was leaping round the farmyard propelled by a squawking panic-stricken hen, leaving a self-satisfied puppy to finish off the rice. Feeling hot and extremely embarrassed, I removed my dog from under the curious stares of the farmer and his family and hurried off after the Sherpas who had had the good sense to make themselves scarce. When, at lunchtime, a rather larger and more aggressive chicken helped itself to the brat's lunch and sent it packing with a few well-aimed pecks on the nose, I felt it had got no more than it deserved. It was a peeved, hungry, but sadly unwiser dog that set out on the afternoon trail.

We stocked up with provisions in Beni. It took an hour of shopping to fill every rucksack and doko to capacity. After that, it would be a case of buying food where we could find it – *if* we could find it.

'Don't we have enough? It's getting too heavy.'

Ang was buying more rice and Phurba peered out from beneath his overloaded doko.

'Big load – small problem. No food – big problem!' he said cryptically. He spoke as if from experience.

The route left the valley of the Kali Gandaki at Beni and headed west. The Dhorpatan road was a sudden contrast to the domesticated farming country around Gorkha and Pokhara. The sides of the valley rose steeply above the trail with outcrops of brown rock breaking through the dry grass and scrub. Where the valley fell back a little, terraced fields perched on the slopes, some brilliant yellow with oilseed *tori*, while others grew a deep green, speckled with the white pea flowers of next year's dal. A spiny grey cactus grew over the stone walls around the fields, its small red flowers a bright warning to anyone foolish enough to try to climb over.

We camped near a small farm set on the north bank of the river, isolated from other settlements by a stumpy *sal* forest. Ang had bought some meat at the market in Beni. As soon as the first whiff reached the puppy's nostrils the creature lost all restraint and it had to be forcibly prevented from following the stew into the pressure-cooker. These invasions of the kitchen caused chaos as it was alternately tripped over or trampled on. I resigned myself to guard duty.

A girl wandered over from the farm to see what we were doing. She might have been ten or twelve and, like most children, was more interested in the puppy than camp chores.

'*Raamro kukur ho.*'

I found it rather difficult to agree that it was a nice dog in the present circumstances. Ang was quicker off the mark.

'Really good dog. Special memsahib dog. Look, special red ribbon round its neck...' He spruced up the battered piece of nylon rag round the dog's neck as he kept up his sales pitch. 'And you have to feed it yoghurt every day and meat once a week.'

The child was entranced, arms full of fat puppy. 'So nice. No dog at our house...'

And so, in the midst of the opportunity presenting itself, I gave the puppy away.

The campsite seemed empty and gloomily quiet after it had gone. It was much better off on a farm. Trekking across country was no life for a small dog which hated being on a lead. It had already come close to being eaten by farm dogs whose territory it had trespassed, not to mention the trouble it had caused to people's chickens and cookpots. But it still seemed very quiet and empty without it.

There was no baying and howling coming from the farm the next morning, so the dog must have been adequately fed. The trail climbed, then contoured the north side of the gorge. At Tatopani there were rough bamboo shelters and a smell of sulphurous water wafted up from hot pools on a rocky bank of the Mayagdi Khola. A crowd of Nepalese, all men, were wallowing naked in the hot water. The women hovered, fully clothed, looking for a quiet spot for washing the family laundry. Had the place been deserted I would have risked a breach of Nepalese protocol and gone for a bath, but I could hardly do so with the place already fully occupied. I decided rather resentfully that Nepalese protocol had been invented by Nepalese men in order to have the hot pools to themselves.

Further upriver at Dharbang the Mayagdi Khola foamed out of a gorge on the right, flowing straight from the Dhaulagiri massif to the north. The trail twisted and climbed, clinging precariously to the rock walls of the gorge. Steps had been cut into the cliff and a cavelike roof arched overhead. Below, dark green pools of cold ice-melt from Dhaulagiri swirled round smooth grey rocks before plunging on towards the hot springs of Tatopani. The place had a dark, shadowy beauty that was at the same time oppressive as clouds drifted across the sun and a chill wind rattled the dry leaves on the thorn bushes. I shivered, and found myself repeating the Rinpoche's protection mantra as I walked.

A stream flowed into the Mayagdi Khola from the right, leaving a small triangle of gravel at the confluence. A huddle of untidy huts stood at the base of a cliff, smoke rising through the rumpled thatch on the roofs. The occupants were as unkempt and sooty as their dwellings, but they were friendly enough and volunteered the valuable information that the route now cut straight up the hill and that there was no water available before Dharapani on the ridge three hours away. Balu was sent to look for dry twigs while Phurba carefully removed insects from a small patch of ground before setting up the *chullo* of three rocks to support the cooking pot. He always took great care to avoid killing any tiny creatures which happened to get in his way. After the water had been put on to boil for tea, Ang bargained for some pieces of smoked fish he had seen above the hearth. I noticed Phurba's expression of distaste at the mention of fish. He said something in a low voice, whereupon Ang bought some pieces of smoked buffalo meat instead. The shrivelled, blackened lumps were added to the lunchtime stew where they did little to enhance it. I was doubtful whether the fish would have been any better, but surprised that Phurba should offer any opinion on food. He always wolfed down whatever was put in front of him and then looked round hopefully for more.

'Don't you like fish?'

He looked up, hands clasped round a chipped enamel mug of tea. 'Yes, I like it, but I am the same as the fish. This life killing, next life very bad.'

'But you didn't kill it.'

'It is different for lama. This time, no fish. Maybe later, no other meat.'

'Why are fish and buffalo different?'

'They are same. We are all same, all linked.'

Phurba's rudimentary English and my grasp of Nepali were insufficient to pursue the question further into the realms of metaphysics, but I admired Phurba's determination to stick to his beliefs in the face of our limited supplies of food. I did not usually eat fish or meat, but had decided that during this journey I would accept anything edible that became available.

At first I had wondered why a 'very good lama' had accepted a porter job for weeks of strenuous walking across inhospitable country. His wife had told me he made enough money selling butter in the markets near their farm, but she too seemed to think it was a good idea for him to travel. Curiosity led Phurba to explore his own country – and, he hoped, India as well – but he also nursed an ambition to learn English. Within hours of setting out on the trail he had pulled a small black notebook from his pocket and read out the English phrases so that I could check the pronunciation. Already literate in both Tibetan and Nepali script, he would write the words phonetically in Nepali. I soon found that helping Phurba in his struggles with English was rapidly increasing my knowledge of Nepali. Even so, real conversations were few and uncomplicated. The Sherpas were busy with their chores and, after a day walking from dawn to dusk, all the while on the lookout for good photographs, I was too exhausted for much conversation. I would spend an hour or so in my tent with my diary and then collapse into a deep sleep that lasted at least ten hours.

It was a long haul to Dharapani. We rested with a group of Chantel carrying supplies of salt from Beni to their home in Gurjakhani on the slopes of Dhaulagiri. Many of the village names in the area end in 'khani', meaning mine, but the copper has long since been exhausted and the Chantel have returned to work on the surface as farmers or porters. They spoke Nepali with a strange accent, and even Phurba had difficulty understanding them. Squares of nettlecloth were drawn over their shoulders and knotted in front to form a kind of jacket. When they lit up heavy smelling pipes Phurba set off up the hill. He avoided tobacco smoke as meticulously as he avoided fish.

Dharapani was little more than a scattering of farms on the crest of the ridge where the pine forest gave way to terraced fields, a bright patchwork falling away below to the dusky shadows of the river valley. The brown and purple mountains rose to the north, their summits swallowed up in layers of brooding dark cloud. A distant rumble of thunder shook the valley and a sharp wind from the hidden snowfield stung my face. Instinctively I quickened my pace. If the storm would hold off we might make Lumsum by nightfall.

The cultivated terraces ended as suddenly as they had appeared, leaving a barren hillside of dry winter grass flattened by the keening wind. A flash of lightning behind the stormclouds lit the valley with an eerie light for an instant before the thunder rumbled again. I broke into a run to catch up with the others. The powers that lived in the Himal were breaking loose, and whether one gave them embodied form or not, there was an almost tangible energy roaming that vast place, which made me feel uneasy. It was harder to be sceptical of demons when not walled in by the noise and concrete of a city; when not in a country that foolishly prides itself in keeping such powers at bay.

With the next great clap of thunder came the rain – stinging, driving sheets that within minutes had the trail ankle deep in muddy water. The rain became hail, slashing lumps of ice the size of marbles. Above the noise I heard Phurba yelling from the shelter of a small stone hut beside the trail. I squeezed through the low doorway, thankful to be out of the wind and drenching rain.

'Lumsum maybe tomorrow,' said Phurba unnecessarily.

We were lucky. The previous group of porters to use this shelter had not used all the dry firewood they had collected and the Sherpas already had a small blaze going. There was even a pile of dry bracken at the end of the hut which promised a comfortable sleep. Ang phlegmatically resisted my offers of help, so I strung wet jackets near the fire, then settled in a corner with my diary, breathing the tang of bracken and woodsmoke, and listening to the wind outside.

It rained all night but morning dawned cold and clear. Only the devastation remained – flattened crops and piles of mud and debris strewn across the trail. Visible for the first time in the clear morning air, the snow peaks of Dhaulagiri, Churen Himal, Gurja Himal, and Putha Hiunchuli towered above us, rising up from the brown hills on the other side of the valley.

We spent the following night partway up the Jaljali Danda in an abandoned hut perched above the valley with only the snow peaks for company. The inhabitants of Lumsum had advised us to make use of it as crossing the pass would be a long day without water while the winter streams were frozen. Unfortunately information was all that the villagers in Lumsum had to spare, and Ang gloomily rooted among the dwindling supplies for the evening meal. After seven days on the trail from Beni, we were running low on fuel again. Ang left Balu to oversee the stew while he cooked a pile of chapatis to fuel us through the following day in the snow.

A yell from the kitchen jolted me away from the sunset and inside to see who had been scalded. Balu had been daydreaming and the stew had boiled over into the fire. The stew had been saved, but not the last shreds of Balu's reputation.

Ang was shaking his head. 'All no possible,' he sighed.

It was true. Balu was pleasant, but he was lazy and seemed to have little idea of how to go about camp chores. I knew Phurba had been covering for him, fetching water, making tea, and peeling vegetables.

'You should have a strong talk with him,' I advised Ang.

He looked perturbed. 'I no like. . .' And so it would go on. Balu would only function if a strong leader insisted that he did so, while Ang's reluctance to lay down the law explained why he had not made it up the ladder to be Sirdar of a big group, and why he often resorted to taking porter work.

The winter snow lay packed and deep above the hut and soon the trail was buried altogether. We plodded through the smudgy whiteness between the trees. All the streams were frozen and the forest creaked in the cold air. For all his hopelessness at camp chores, Balu proved his worth time and again with his uncanny sense of direction. We soon learned that to follow him was to save ourselves endless backtracking.

We were almost clear of the forest when Phurba began a litany of demands for refuelling in a chant of broken English.

'Tea necessory, chapati also necessory . . . upside going no possible. . .' Phurba seemed to burn food faster than anyone; the only way someone with such a slight build could carry such a heavy load all day. Already I had noticed in myself an increased dependence on regular meals for the energy to keep moving.

As we ate the clouds thinned and a watery sun broke through. The snow peaks glistened on the far side of the valley, elusive as a dream with clouds drifting in and hiding them once more. Another Hidden Valley is said to lie concealed in the icy wilderness behind Dhaulagiri, guarded by passes almost 20,000 feet high – not a side trip even to consider in this season, with this weather. One story tells of a hunter from Dolpo to the north of these mountains, who, in a rocky valley near Dhaulagiri, heard the sound of temple drums and lamas chanting. The sound led him to a cleft in the cliffs beyond which was a fertile country with a gompa set among the farms. The people welcomed him and invited him to stay, but he wanted to go home to fetch his wife and children. Although he was warned that he would not find the country again, he left his gun to mark the entrance to the Hidden Valley. When he returned with his family, his gun was hanging on a blank wall of rock.

The sky was darkening and we moved on before another storm broke. The top of the pass was a desert of bare rocks and frozen soil swept clean by the wind which hit us as we came over the crest. Ang and Phurba were both chanting protection mantras now as the wind brought the first flurries of snow. The summit was almost a plateau, frustrating our haste for tamer ground. Jagged rocky towers loomed above in the cloud, catching the wind and making it whine in its passage.

As the descent became steeper we slithered through the mush underfoot, weaving between the stunted trees. The snow turned to rain, whipping and hissing between the bare twigs, while the pass behind us glimmered white under the heavy clouds. The trail would be blocked for several days; we had crossed just in time.

The empty shepherds' hut was too good to pass by, even though it was only mid-afternoon. There was dry wood for cooking and drying out – and for all Ang's predictions of starvation, I knew there was an emergency stash of food in the bottom of Phurba's doko. A large potful of noodles disappeared into four people with uncanny speed, after which there was little to do but sleep.

I awoke before dawn. It was cold, and one bright star shone through a gap in the roof shingles.

Dhorpatan was unmistakably Tibetan, despite the style of the houses designed by a Swiss Foreign Aid team for the refugee Tibetans in the area. Even the gompa looked like a Swiss chalet surrounded by prayer flags. The place seemed deserted. Perhaps everyone had followed Tsering Choedrak's example and headed for the warmer climate of Kathmandu.

A movement behind one of the houses caught my eye. An old man was plodding up a side street with a shapeless bundle hefted on his back. Clearly, Phurba shared my anxiety that the last remaining inhabitant of Dhorpatan might slip away before we could do any shopping. He hailed the fellow across the distance.

'*Oi!* Do you have any tsampa or potatoes?'

'Huh?' The old man squinted at us curiously and shuffled closer. He was sunburned and wrinkled, dressed in an oily black home-spun coat that reached the top of his felt and leather boots. It was a few minutes before he and Phurba managed to establish communication in a kind of pidgin Tibetan. At last he broke into a gap-toothed smile. Yes, there were still a few people in Dhorpatan and a little food was for sale. At the mention of Tsering Choedrak's name, the old Tibetan's hospitality became galvanised into action. Of course we must stay at Tsering's house. He was the caretaker, and he would bring the key as soon as he had finished his business at one of the farms. Meanwhile, we could buy food and take it over to the house. He set off up the trail at a pace that would have been impressive even if he had not looked a hundred years old.

We approached the nearest house cautiously.

'*Oi! Ama!* Is there a dog here?' Ang yelled at the closed door. Obviously I was not the only one to have been chewed by a Tibetan mastiff. Right on cue, a ferocious barking and snarling came from within the enclosed yard, becoming suddenly muffled and protesting as one of the family controlled the animal by the standard method of sitting on its head.

The wooden door creaked open and a woman poked her head out. Despite the soot, she was fiercely, wildly beautiful with her high cheekbones and dark slanting eyes. Her hair was plaited in dozens of tiny braids laced with turquoise and coral. Three heavy amber beads were braided into the hair on her crown. The twee Swiss chalets had not prepared me for anyone like this, and I stood staring. Phurba was more collected – or perhaps he was hungrier.

'*E, Ama*, have you got any tsampa, potatoes, eggs, butter?'

She smiled, flashing perfect white teeth. 'Not much. Come in.'

For a moment I could see nothing but velvety blackness, until slowly the shapes of people detached themselves from their surroundings. There were two women in the house – and presumably one more person in the yard, judging by the muffled and indignant canine shrieks still coming from that direction.

'*Cha?*'

The question came from the shadows, and without waiting for an answer the woman began to blow on the embers, illuminating her face with a red glow. The tea was true Tibetan style, thick with tsampa, salt and globs of butter. We made small talk about the weather and the price of food, as well as the condition of the route to Pokhara. Ritual politeness having been observed, we then bought all the tsampa, eggs and potatoes the family could spare and made our way to Tukden's 'hotel' for sugar.

The 'hotel' was scarcely bigger than an ordinary house, but it was here that the summer mule-trains from the south offloaded goods such as sugar, rice, and tea. It was very much off-season – with snow on the passes and the village almost deserted – and there was just one lad in charge of the place. Dusty corners revealed a residue of commodities, and we reached Tsering's house with stores replenished. An enormous mastiff hurled itself into the attack and almost choked when it reached the end of its chain. Suddenly the old caretaker appeared from behind the house and grunted something at it, whereupon it immediately changed character, whimpering and snuffling at his ankles and shrugging its bristling shoulders at us as if we had lost all importance.

The house was by far the largest in Dhorpatan, serving also as a small weaving factory. The front room was well-lit by large, south-facing windows and contained a row of tall, heavy looms for weaving rugs. None of the looms was strung, as most of the weavers were, like Tsering, in Kathmandu for the winter. At the back of the house a series of smaller rooms comprised the living quarters.

Ang wanted to make a cake now that we had the ingredients and were in civilised surroundings. He had made several during the first part of the trek, although he had showed little interest in eating any of them himself. It was the recently-acquired ability to make such a specialised Western dish that was important to him. The old caretaker was invited for tea and cake. He watched the proceedings with a bemused expression: they obviously didn't make many cakes in Dhorpatan.

At last there were sufficient supplies of food available to justify some rest days. I found it a delight to be able to spread out my few belongings and know I would not have to cram them all into a rucksack in the half-light of the following morning. Since leaving Beni we had been covering as much ground each day as possible so as to reach Dhorpatan before the food ran out. There had been almost nothing in the villages along the way. The winter drought had affected supplies even in east Nepal, but it was more acute out here, where food was generally less plentiful. Now the drought was breaking in a series of violent storms, but the hail was probably destroying more than it was watering.

Dhorpatan was a friendly oasis in a vast hinterland of barren hills, parched farms, and frozen mountains. The quiet warmth and hospitality of its people blended subtly with the frosty air and the cold snow peaks surrounding the village. Everyone was busy, but no one seemed to hurry, and there was always time to stop and chat. It was uncertain what lay ahead, except for the rumours that said it would be harder than what had gone before; but here the sun was shining and the 'good people' of Tsering's Dhorpatan exuded a tranquillity that was infectious. For the moment, I was utterly content.

I spent much of my time in the sunny courtyard of Tsering's house, catching up on details in my diary. Phurba spread out his notebooks and set himself lists of words to memorise. Ang baked another cake. Balu slept.

The caretaker returned with more eggs. He was as curious about Phurba's homeland as he was about mine.

'Is Solu Khumbu like Dhorpatan?'

'Same crops, bigger mountains, more people.'

'Do you have lamas and gompas too?'

'Plenty of those. Not Swiss like yours.'

'Only the gompa is Swiss. Our lama is Tibetan. He's away in Kathmandu now.'

The conversation became more involved with religion, and I could not follow it. Villagers usually asked the same questions about my home as they did the Sherpas, with the exception that I had never been asked about my religion. Perhaps they assumed that sahibs had no religion.

Phurba had taken out his carefully wrapped *peja*, the Tibetan text he had brought from home. On the rare occasions when he had time to himself after the camp chores he had read from it in the lilting chant of the Buddhist tradition. Usually he had to make do with chanting mantras while he scrubbed pots or tended the fire.

I leaned across to see if I could decipher the script. On the open page was a line drawing of a lotus with the compassion mantra OM MANI PADME HUM arranged in a circle on its petals. The syllable HRI was set in the centre of the lotus.

Phurba looked up and smiled. 'Reading peja – very difficult. But *understanding* is more important. Dharma comes from here.' He pointed to the centre of the lotus, then his own heart. 'It is here in your heart and mind – and when we practise Dharma it shines out from us, like the sun.' He smiled again and continued his conversation with the old Tibetan, happy with his books and philosophical discussion. I wondered again why he had decided to work as a porter. Then I realised it did not matter to him what he did. He was content simply to be what he was; to experience whatever he happened to be doing and make it part of that practice. It was this acceptance of himself that gave him a lama's dignity, whether he was clowning with Balu or scrubbing pots.

'*Oi!* Get up! Get up! Tea!'

Phurba's English was improving, but I knew that Ang had been lecturing him on the lack of standard phrases he considered suitable for use with Western clients. As it happened, I was already up and packed. I had woken early, thinking of the caretaker's concern for our safety and his warnings about the solo Westerner murdered by the Kamis the previous year. I followed Phurba back to the kitchen. Balu was emerging from his sleeping bag, snuffling and rubbing his eyes in a good imitation of his namesake.

'*Oi! Rambahadur!* Get up!'

Phurba prodded the lazy bear-cub mercilessly with his toe. He deserved worse; making the tea was the cookboy's job and Balu hadn't managed it once since we had left Kathmandu. Phurba poured his own tea, then held it up as an offering to the unseen Buddhas before he drank. Five minutes later he was scrubbing the soot off the teakettle and yelling at Balu to get the baskets packed.

We left the silent village with the dawn light pale behind a mackerel sky. The boggy flatland of the valley floor was frozen crisp and shaggy mountain ponies grazed the sour grass, tails to the wind. The flat Alpine meadows dropped into the steep gorge of the Uttar Ganga, and the path descended to the bridge that was the gateway to Dhorpatan. Protective wooden figures were carved on the sides of the bridge, guarding the village from the fierce powers that lived in the wild hills beyond.

At the bridge I stopped and looked back. The village was hidden behind the shoulder of the hill, already part of the pattern of what had passed. The future lay in the brown hills beyond the narrow valley of the Uttar Ganga, with the ephemeral present at this fragile bridge which linked the two. The contentment I had felt in Dhorpatan had taken its place in that pattern while the hopes and fears of the journey took their turn in the cycle. I knew it would be foolish to come back in the hope of recapturing the spontaneity of that experience, like the Dolpo hunter who tried to engineer a return to the Hidden Valley – and found the passage between the worlds closed.

6

The Land Where the Jumlies Live

།བྱའི་སྐྱང་པ་ཡིད་ལ་འཁོར་ཙམ་ལས།

The trail climbed until it contoured precariously along the steep south side of the gorge. A line of porters passed, eight tiny figures in rags and jewels, bent under their loads. They were the only people we saw all day. The valley was home only for birds and animals; the brown marmot perched on a rock, jays screeching in the bushes, and wild ducks below in the river. I watched them swimming against the swift current of the Uttar Ganga to snatch out small silver fish. An eagle wheeled overhead, its shadow darkening the dry grass and sending small birds twittering into the cover of the thorn bushes. A dark forest swallowed us up, firs and evergreens casting pools of shadow across the path.

The forest gave way to dry grass and rocks once more before the first village appeared, dun-coloured mud walls and flat roofs blending with beige grass on the opposite side of the valley. The village was terraced with tree-trunk ladders linking the roofs which doubled as village streets.

A tiny trickle of water and a small terraced field marked a lonely night's camp. It was hard to follow Tsering's advice and camp only by respectable houses when there were hardly any houses at all. I was not even quite sure what the correlation was between non-respectable houses and the apparently murderous *Kamis* – the perpetrators of crimes generally prefer the scene to be someone else's doorstep.

I had never quite understood why Hindus and Buddhists alike seemed to regard this caste of metalworkers with such a strange mixture of fear and contempt. Perhaps it is the almost Faustian power they are perceived to gain by forging and controlling the metals of the earth. Even in my own culture, there are enough old songs and stories about blacksmiths with magical powers to suggest that this association of ideas is universal and deeply embedded in the human psyche. Out here, where the gods, spirits and protectors of earth and mountain are still treated with great respect, those who take and forge their metal are bound to be regarded as powerful enough to get away with it, and yet are seen as disturbing a profound and sacred balance that might be better left alone. And perhaps there is also an underlying awareness that while in peacetime the Kamis make and mend essential farm implements and cooking pots, on demand they could also make weapons of war.

Not that this prevents anyone eagerly seeking the benefits of the Kamis' trade, and they often become quite wealthy. I had seen an itinerant Kami at work in a Sherpa village the previous year. He would spend a few days at each farmhouse while he completed his contract. Before he could start work at each house he visited, he had to build himself a small bamboo shelter in the yard. In this he would work, eat and sleep. Regarded as an outcaste, he was not permitted to enter any of the houses. I could not tell whether the rumours about the Kamis and the murder were founded solely on caste prejudice, or whether, being pushed to the periphery of society, they had become as dangerous as their reputation. So little was known about this western area of Nepal and the diverse groups of people living here.

In spite of my apprehension I felt an exhilaration to be in such a wild and remote place, surrounded by jagged peaks turning red and gold as the sun dropped behind the purple clouds in the west. Even the Sherpas were exclaiming on the size and beauty of the mountains.

'Like ours at home. . .'

'Do you often think of home?'

Ang nodded. 'Many time. Night time, body sleeping, mind going everywhere, going home. . .'

Perhaps we are all doomed to spend some time wishing we were elsewhere. I knew how restless Sherpas become after months tied to the farm.

Everything was frozen in the morning. So, apparently, was Balu who spent the whole of breakfast time shuffling and blowing on his fingers. Phurba was cheerfully unsympathetic.

'I showed you how to wear your down jacket inside your sleeping bag. You'll learn.'

Balu made a wry face and hefted his load with a grunt.

The snow mountains shone cold in the dawn light, and the rocks of the trail had a hollow ring under our feet. Dolpo lay to the north of the valley in a wilderness of snow-covered mountains. It was still a Restricted Area; while intruding Sahibs earned little more than a ticking-off and a future visa problem, any Nepalese found with them could face several years in jail. It seemed irresponsible to break the rules if to do so would get one's employees into serious trouble.

The shortage of available firewood drew us to make lunch near one of the villages where we could buy a bundle from the locals. Before long we had the undivided attention of everyone who could walk the intervening hundred yards. In the absence of newspapers and telephones it is hardly surprising that passing travellers warrant thorough investigation, and by now I was used to the ritual questions of 'where from, where going, what business?' What did make me uncomfortable were the rare occasions when nobody asked anything, and this was one of them. The whole crowd just sat and stared at point-blank range, pointing and making comments among themselves – and coughing noisily over us and our food. I knew one of the rudest breaches of Nepalese etiquette is to stare at people who are eating. Usually one has only to turn one's back on the offender to make him acutely aware and embarrassed about his manners – and he will quickly disappear. Not so this lot. Even when I moved to the other side of a stone wall I was pursued by half a dozen gawping bronchial children. I resigned myself to it. After all, it was their village.

As we were leaving I asked for directions and was told we were on the wrong road. We would have to backtrack two hours to the bridge we should not have crossed. No wonder they were surprised to see us.

It was a despondent party that set off back up the road by which we had come. Suddenly we were hailed by a loud voice from behind.

'NAMASKAAR, SAHIB!'

The young man and his smile were as large as his voice. He greeted us expansively, palms pressed together at his breast. He wore the knotted-blanket jacket of the hill people and carried an empty bamboo doko slung loosely across his broad shoulders.

He fell into step with us, eager for news, and was soon being plied with questions himself about the road and the availability of water and supplies. No need to backtrack so far, he assured us. There was a ford just five minutes up the trail. He was going that way and would guide us.

'Ford' was a bit of an understatement. Perhaps there was an unusual amount of melting snow coming down from the mountains, but it was probably considered quite normal by the inhabitants of these wild hills. Even the Sherpas were having to steady each other as they balanced their loads in the waist-deep, swift green current. I hesitated. It looked horrendous. Well, they were nearly across, so it had to be possible. I plunged in. The rocks underfoot were slimy with weed, and after two steps I went under. I felt the current tearing my balance loose, flinging me down stream. I hit a boulder, grabbed it and stood up. It was not until later I remembered passing the time waiting for a delayed flight by taking turns with the Sherpa staff to stand on the baggage scales in the airport – and discovering that Sherpas are far heavier and more solid than Westerners. Maybe this gives them a built-in advantage when crossing rivers in flood.

I tried again to step out into the torrent – and the Uttar Ganga threw me against another boulder. I pulled myself out of the water, spluttering. I had now reached the last boulder and ahead lay fifty yards of open river, green and deadly fast. I tried to brace myself by gripping the slimy rocks with my bare toes, but they were as slippery as oil. Suddenly there was a shout and a shrill whistle from the far bank as our new acquaintance plunged back into the water. He grabbed my arm just as I was going under for the third time, and kept an iron grip on my wrist as he dragged me across to the far bank. I noticed he avoided touching my hand.

We sat in the sun as our clothes steamed on us. I checked the cameras which I had crammed tightly in the middle of the things in my pack before trying to cross. They had remained dry, but my sleeping bag had not. Phurba spread it over the broad top of his doko to dry as we walked.

'Why wouldn't he touch my hand?'

'He is *Kami*.'

I watched the retreating figure as he strode ahead up the trail. After all the fear and rumour, the only Kami I meet pulls me out of the river.

That evening a beautiful pyramidal mountain hovered in the

rose-tinted clouds of Dolpo. Sisne Himal was to haunt us for the next few days, a mirage of mist and light that sometimes seemed nearer, sometimes further. Jumla lay at the foot of its western flank, still many days distant. The formidable rock wall of the east side of Dhaulagiri stood stark and black at the head of the valley behind us.

A lone hut wafted smoke across the empty hillside. Outside, an old man smoked a pipe and watched Sisne Himal fade into purple.

'*Oi, Babu!* Anywhere to camp?'

Slowly, the old man removed his pipe. 'This field be empty.'

The 'field' was a tiny terrace barely the size of the hut, but it looked adequate and there was a pile of dry leaves in one corner. Ang and Phurba began spreading them under the tents to smooth over the large clods of dry earth.

'You mind you put 'em back in the morning,' said the old farmer. I regret to say we didn't.

The villages in this arid valley had nothing to spare except for the two manna of walnuts we bought in the village of Kankari. I sub-titled it 'Village of Flies', and it certainly had more flies than walnuts. Several days later found us camping on the gravel beach of the river with the last of the food staring inadequately from the bottom of Phurba's doko; an emergency can of tuna, together with a few spoonfuls of sugar and honey, and enough flour for a few chapatis. I was sure Ang had not come across canned tuna before, but as I didn't want to offend him by invading the kitchen, it was a case of wait and see. My suspicions were confirmed when I saw Phurba scraping the last of the honey on to his tuna sandwich.

'Oh, don't! It will taste horrible.'

'Ex-cellent!' Munch, munch.

I tried my own sandwich. Sure enough, Ang had mixed the last of the sugar with the tuna. It was not as awful as I would have imagined, but then I was ravenously hungry.

It was a long, thin day to the market gardens of Musikot, where the evening sun reddened the ochre walls of a small farmhouse standing in a rich field of cauliflowers and spinach. A young man weighed out the vegetables by the *darni*, (about 2.5kg) using a hand-held balance, while I took artistic photographs. Never had vegetables seemed so beautiful. The lush greens of the riverside paddy fields seemed exaggerated in their brightness after so many days of faded grey and brown in the highlands. Flowers bloomed everywhere, and the chirp of crickets vibrated on the warm evening air. We should have walked at night, for the days were now unbearably hot. The Thuli Bheri river flowed past, cool and green and mocking. We crossed it on an impressive Foreign Aid suspension bridge to reach Jajrakot.

There were a few shops in Jajrakot selling rice and dal that had been portered up from Nepalganj in the Terai, on the East-West highway. The rice was Foreign Aid, too, if the words JAPAN NOT TO BE SOLD printed on the sacks were anything to go by.

It rained in the night, but the sky had cleared by morning and Phurba broke into his tea-making and his morning mantras to call me outside to see the *Kharzhang*, the morning star, bright in the storm-cleared air. There was no sign of the others, so I walked to the top of a nearby hillock to watch the dawn fade the sky to rose. A mist hung over the river below, and the tents were dripping with dew.

The route had turned northwards from Jajrakot, heading for the 13,000-foot Chakhuri Lekh which separated the valleys of the Thuli Bheri and the Karnali. The weather did not promise well for high pass crossings with sudden storms of rain or hail moving in, bringing lower temperatures and high winds. The trail meandered along the tropical valley, following the natural contours but always climbing steadily towards the pass which I estimated must be five or six days away. We passed a line of porters with laden dokos. Incongruously, there were bamboo tables and chairs lashed on top of two of the dokos.

'What are the tables and chairs for?'

'Sahib,' grunted the table porter, sweat dripping off the end of his nose.

The 'Sahib' was resting at the next chautara. A pale-skinned paunch overhung the top of his ankle-length cotton *lungi*, sporting curly ginger hairs which matched his beard. He looked us up and down, then ignored me and addressed Ang in fluent Nepali.

'Where are you going?'

'Er, Jumla.' Ang looked across at me, embarrassed at the breach of protocol.

'Why are you going to Jumla? Don't you know there's no food available?'

'Yes, very difficult,' agreed Ang diplomatically. He shuffled apologetically, then set off up the trail. The stranger turned to me, still aggressive and still speaking Nepali.

'You have no business going to Jumla. There are serious food shortages in this area.'

'It doesn't appear to have affected you,' I said in English. Two people conversing in a second language seemed ridiculous. To my relief, he followed suit.

'Oh, I always get fed; I'm considered kind of important. I live here – I'm an anthropologist.'

No wonder he resents another white face, I thought. Some of them get very territorial.

'What are you anthropologising?'

He ignored the intended jibe and launched into his pet subject. 'Poetry and literature, trance songs, shamanism.' He imbued the words with a mystique designed to invite more questions which he obviously wouldn't answer, so I didn't ask.

After an hour of walking, the only water we could find for lunch was a rather murky pond surrounded by mud churned up by water buffalo hoofs.

'Boil it well,' I advised Ang, who was trying to scoop the cleanest layer from the surface. The anthropologist and his entourage caught up. He licked dry lips at the sight of the steaming tea-kettle, so I invited him over. He sat on a shady rock and wiped the sweat off his face.

'Do you always drink out of *bisi* ponds? There's a good spring twenty minutes further on.'

'Usually the locals are very helpful in advising us where there's good water.'

The implied reproach hit home, and he immediately became more helpful.

'Show me your map and I'll mark in some of the main springs and villages.'

The combination of local knowledge and the ability to read a map was indeed a boon as few villages were marked – usually in the wrong place. Ang brought the tea on an improvised tray with a separate bowl of sugar to impress the visitor. I smiled as I thought how long it was since such 'sahib' trimmings had succumbed to the harshness of the terrain.

The anthropologist was writing the village names on the map in flowing devangari script. Phurba would have to read them out to me as I could only decipher the equivalent of block capitals. By the time the anthropologist set off in pursuit of his own lunch he was being almost friendly, and wished us luck crossing the pass.

My next cup of tea was Sherpa readymix straight into the enamel mug and the 'tray' was back in its rightful role as the lid of the rice pot. The original bamboo tray had fallen apart long since and the blackened remnants of the cloth that had covered it were wrapped around the flour because the bag had split. Other trimmings had gone the same way; hot wash water was impossible when firewood was scarce (which it usually was) and a separate 'sahib' meal would have been a joke as all we had left to cook was rice, flour and dal. I wondered, as the anthropologist had suggested, whether we were taking food from the hungry mouths of the local people, but came to the conclusion we were not. Supplies were being portered in and the villagers would simply use our rupees to restock at local prices. Poorer people without enough to tide them over until they could restock were, sensibly, refusing to sell. We were paying slightly enhanced prices and no doubt great numbers of large trekking groups would unbalance the local economy, but the overall shortages and the remoteness from Kathmandu made the event unlikely.

Over tea, the anthropologist had launched once more into the subject of his research, candidly enough for me to realise that the people of the mysterious far west did not give up their secrets easily. Very little is known about the reasons why the great Malla Kingdoms of Jumla and Hadsinja had fallen into decline, having once stretched beyond the present borders of Tibet and occupied parts of the region of Kumaon in India. By painstakingly researching the songs and poetry of these remote hills, the anthropologist hoped to discover more about the indigenous shamans and the power they still held in this strange culture which was all that remained of the ancient kingdoms.

The link between caste and occupation seemed stronger out here in the west. We came to a village of shoemenders and stopped for some quick repairs to badly-worn footwear. In the next village the women sat in pairs along the single village street, turning out clay chilums by the dozen. While one woman turned a spindle supporting the pipe by means of a leather thong, the other put the finishing touches to the unfired clay with a sharp stick. We were just entering the area of the far west where every male over the age of ten – and most of the women – spent much of their time puffing at clay chilums like these.

The village of Barakot looked as if it had been moulded from clay then painted in bright primary colours. No sooner had we left its double row of crooked houses behind than a downpour of rain sent us running for shelter under a huge overhanging rock. We scattered in search of twigs but there was no time to collect dry wood before everything was soaked. An old man wearing thin homespun was crouching by his doko of firewood under the rock when I returned.

Phurba bounded over, like a waterlogged elf shaking droplets from his hair.

'*E, Dai*, have you got any firewood to sell?'

'*Paundaina*. All gone from round here. These days we have to go up to the jungle for it. Takes all day.' He indicated the smudge of trees on the ridge high above. Phurba's cajoling finally persuaded him to sell a few sticks to supplement what we had already scavenged.

'*Ke ho?*' The yellow and blue closed-cell mattress looked incongruously bright in the knobbly hand.

'For sleeping on,' I said. 'More warm, more comfortable.'

The old boy roared with laughter. 'That's no good! You spend all your time sleeping, you never get anywhere!'

I asked about the pass above.

'Not possible. Too much snow. Six people tried and they died in the snow.'

I resolved to ask for a second opinion the following day. The old man noticed our dinner was ready and politely drifted back to his village.

'I make extra rice this time,' said Phurba. 'This Japanese white rice – like plastic! *Looks* very nice, but half an hour after eating, I am hungry again!'

I laughed. Phurba's appetite was becoming legendary, but he was right about the polished rice. It boiled up to fluffy piles worthy of cookbook photography, but there was no body to it, and as fuel for steep hills it was sadly lacking. I found my own attitude to food had changed over the last few weeks. The strenuous walking and scarcity of supplies had made the relationship between food and the energy to survive more vivid than anything I had experienced in the affluent, overfed West. Surprisingly, I did not find myself fantasising about gourmet meals when times were lean. Perhaps this was because all my attention was focused on the stark reality of investigating every possible source of supply as we went along. There was no time or energy to spare for luxurious fantasies. I noticed that as I became increasingly absorbed in the daily issues of finding enough food and energy to keep going, I had much less mental energy to think about Shambhala and the Hidden Valleys. It was as if the very process of the journey was beginning to take the place of my thoughts and projections about it.

I did not read through my diary until I had been back in England for almost a year and was surprised to see my apparent preoccupation with food. It took an effort of will to shift my perception back to the way it had been in those lonely hills where gourmet considerations such as 'flavour' and 'appetite' no longer exist; where you concentrate simply on finding enough fuel to keep going for another day. It was only then that I recognised the habitual filtering of communication through one's own personal and social condition. If I was able – even for a few minutes – to misinterpret myself, how then was I perceiving others?

> *Wednesday 16th March.* A month since we left Kathmandu. A month of not hearing an internal combustion engine, the squeal of brakes, a crowded market-place, the blare of a radio. But the Himal is not silent. My perceptions have become attuned to the subtle sounds of the hills; the passage of the wind through the heavy leaves and gnarled limbs of the rhododendron trees, the bark of a dog in a distant village. Then, from the terraced fields below us, still shrouded in the damp dawn mist, rises the haunting song of a woman, already at work in the dew-heavy winter wheat. The melody rises and falls, thin and fluttering on the still air, until the song is taken up by other women's voices, lifting the music beyond the farms to the hilltop where we stand listening. This is the sound of Asia.
>
> The sun comes over the edge of the eastern mountains and warms our faces. I could go on for ever the way it is now... But nothing goes on for ever the way it is now. It is all moving and changing like the noisy river that flows beside the trail; Nepal is flowing past as our legs move, and the country and the people are changing even as I am changing...

There was pink cherry-blossom in the last village before the pass. We put down our loads and searched among the low stone houses for someone who had some cornmeal to sell. A child beckoned us through a low doorway and up narrow twisting wooden stairs. In the room above, the farmer sat crosslegged on the wooden floor puffing at his chilum, surrounded by his wife and seven children.

There was a pause. The farmer handed the chilum to his wife, and looked at us.

'Where are you going?'

'Chakhuri Lekh.'

He took the chilum back, and drew on it slowly.

'You go up there, you die.'

There was another pause, then Ang showed him our 'good shoes' and asked if it might be possible with enough equipment.

'I don't know. Not been up there this year. Maybe you can do it and not die. Better have some food to take with you!'

He moved aside so that his wife could pull out a basket of cornmeal from the pile of baskets and cloth bags set against the wall. Our battered old tea-towel was laid on the floor while she carefully scooped the cornmeal into the manna measure. Everyone chanted the counting softly in unison as the measure was emptied into the tea-towel. We bought eight manna (one pathi in these parts) at twenty rupees a pathi – a reasonable price considering they had a complete monopoly – but money has not yet become a god here. The woman leaned back and smiled, then hefted the heavy basket back to its place in the pile at the side of the room. The farmer sent one of his children to fetch a glowing ember to relight the chilum, and once again the heavy sweet smoke filled the room. It did not have the acrid sting of tobacco smoke – perhaps it was marijuana; there was enough of it growing in the fields around here.

We left them smoking contentedly, and stumbled back outside into the sunlight.

Now surely we must be beyond the last house – but around the next corner was a tiny shop. I confess I thought it was a half-ruined cowshed until I looked inside and saw the little shelves of dusty cigarettes and biscuits. The wizened Nepali shopkeeper said it was expensive because it took twenty days to porter it all from Nepalganj. My reckoning said thirteen to fourteen days, but maybe the loads were huge and heavy. Such were the tales of the desolate pass above that I bought a few packets of stale biscuits for dire emergencies.

It was all uphill from here, as it had been since we left tropical Jajrakot. As the trail continued to climb steeply, rhododendron and pine forest gave way to rocky alpine meadows by the end of the afternoon. Nobody wanted to do any chores while the sun was still above the mountains, so we sat around the campfire drinking tea and watching the sun slip imperceptibly towards the red-tinged snow of the horizon. A lone figure walked across the empty meadow towards us. He was barefoot and dressed in patched and ragged creamy wool homespun with a piece of dark red cloth tied like a cloak around his shoulders. As he turned I saw the ends were not flowing loose but gathered round in a bundle on his back. I wondered what he was carrying. And what was he doing up here alone, so far from the last village?

He walked directly over to us, and sat down by the fire. He paused a moment, watching us quizzically, and I felt as if my very thoughts were being scrutinised. Then he greeted us, and his smile lit up the whole meadow! He had an ageless face, with strong features, and those penetrating eyes were deep-set, and dark like his long hair which flowed out from under the strip of white cloth wound turban-like around his head.

Soon the conversation was roaming from Pokhara to Kathmandu to India. This man had travelled far indeed, and was thoughtful about what he had seen. Unlike the other villagers in this area, his Nepali was clear and easy to understand, but I felt no need to join in; I was too absorbed in listening and watching him. His expressions and hand movements seemed perfectly aware, as if he were the most immaculate actor in the world. He knew he had my whole attention and was enjoying it.

'Is she American?'

'No, I'm not,' was all I could manage as I emerged from my trance.

Phurba said, 'She's a Nepali from Kathmandu but her hair changed colour from too much walking!' Everyone enjoyed that one.

I offered him a cup of tea, but he refused with the same broad, enigmatic smile.

'No, thank you, I never drink at this time and I've just had one.'

Where in these lonely hills, I wonder, has he just been drinking tea? I wanted to take his photograph, but was afraid to break the spell, afraid of offending him. I brought the camera out cautiously, as if I was perhaps only going to clean it.

'Hah! Photographs!' He laughed and struck a pose. 'Are you going to give it to me now?'

'No, it has to go to England first.' I took out the dull black cassette that contained his picture. I could see his quick mind taking in the details of the camera's innards in the few seconds it was open.

'So you will bring it next year! My house is down there' – an encompassing sweep of the arm in the direction of downhill – 'and my name is Kali Bahadur Bowra Chettri Dami. So when you return, you can easily find me. . .'

It occurred to me that it was his poise and detachment from worldly things which allowed him this wholehearted, childlike delight in me and my gadgets without a trace of awe or envy.

Phurba asked, 'Why is your hair long?'

'Because I am *Dami*.' Everything was falling into place; of course he could not drink with us outcastes if he was a Chettri, a high-caste Hindu, but it was nice of him to be polite about it. But Hinduism is only a recent veneer over the ancient Shamanism of these remote hills; Kali Bahadur Bowra Chettri Dami is a shaman. I wondered why he was up here in the mountains. Again, Phurba was ahead of me.

'Where are you going?'

'Up there.' He waved his hand in the direction of the ice and snow above.

Just the emptiness and the solitude and the sky. Or did he have a special ritual to perform; a meeting with one of the 'powers that live in the Himal'? I wondered again what he had in that bundle on his back.

He stood up to leave.

'You have another day's walking before you reach the pass. You must find the place they call Tamtu. There is a great cliff by a river, and a cave in the cliff where you can sleep safely. Then you must leave in the early morning and cross the snow quickly before the sun makes it dangerous. Good luck!' He waved, and flashed his radiating smile, then turned and walked briskly towards the snowy heights above, leaving the meadow quiet, and tamer in the aftermath of his presence.

In the last glow of sunset a sliver of crescent moon hung over the silhouetted peaks of the Himal. In the clear cold air the full circle of the moon glowed faintly. Above it was one bright star.

Phurba followed my gaze.

'That is the *Karzhang*,' he said softly.

So the Karzhang is the morning star, and the evening star too.

In the cold darkness, I listened for the Dami's drum calling up the spirits of the Himal, but he was gone, deep into the jagged ice and rock above, while frost crept across the meadow, glimmering faintly in the light of the Karzhang.

The Lekh rose above a maze of grassy ridges intersected by forested valleys. In places the forest had been blasted by lightning, charred trunks pointing blackened fingers at the rocks above. The trail ran out into a landslide, a sweep of rock and loose earth down to the river. From above, Balu yelled and pointed at two lithe tawny shapes disappearing into the dappled sunlight between the trees. Too fast for a bear, too big for a wolf –

'Tiger,' said Ang. We didn't see them again.

Three men and a boy were waiting where the trail rose above the treeline. They were heading back to their homes in Jumla after being away for the winter and had decided to cross the pass when they heard there would be other travellers on the road. The men wore leather sandals bound with woollen rags but the boy's feet were bare, blackened with the dust of the route. Already there were patches of snow even though the trail artfully snaked along dry ridges and sunny rock slopes. At a bend in the river was a south-facing cliff with the dark smudge of a cave at its base. Ang and Phurba headed for the cave while the Jumla men sat and smoked their pipes.

'We camp further up, by the big rock. Quickest over the snow tomorrow morning is better.'

I walked down to the cave, thinking about the boy's bare feet and how Pasang's fingers had looked and the fear in his eyes. I rooted out Ang's sneakers from the pile of dokos.

'You don't need these now you've got the expedition boots. I'll buy some more in Jumla.'

He looked at the sneakers. They were well-worn, but he would clearly not have given them away until they were falling to pieces if he were back home. He looked at the snowy lekh above, then walked back towards the trail, waving the sneakers.

'*Oi!* Small *Bai*! Shoes!'

A diminutive figure broke away from the group and scampered across the frosty grass. Ang returned, grinning.

'Using shoes very quick. Big happy now.'

Evening was closing in and the meagre warmth of the twig fire was barely enough to boil up the last of the cornmeal. I hoped there would be supplies available in Jumla.

Footsteps crunched across the gravel by the river and a lone figure dumped his basket on the grass and stepped into the circle of light around the fire.

'Where going?' Ang's voice had an edge to it. Nepalese rarely travel alone.

'Jumla. Looking for work. No travelling friend with me, and they said in the village you would cross Chakhuri Lekh. Can I cross with you?'

Phurba's laugh broke the tension. 'No problem! Sit down – here, have some tea.'

The stranger edged into the offered space by the fire and wrapped his hands round the mug of tea. He might have been almost thirty, but he sat hunched over the fire, patched clothes pulled tight around skinny shoulders. He had probably always lived by casual labouring and his conversation revealed little hint that he ever hoped for anything better.

The cave was lined with dry grass from previous travellers but there was a gnawing chill flowing out of the snowbanks surrounding it. Phurba looked critically at the traveller's thin blanket and spread one of the unused tents over him. Stars were still shining in a dark sky when I awoke to the sound of Phurba's mantras as he brewed the morning tea. We left before dawn touched the snow, with yesterday's ice-melt solid and slippery underfoot. The stranger had wrapped strips of wool and leather round his ankles for warmth but there was no grip in his worn-out sneakers and he walked behind in our footprints.

It was hard to believe this was only a *lekh*, a hill bare of snow in the summer months. The expanse of whiteness stretched in all directions and we sank thigh deep in the snow as soon as the sun softened it. From the top of the pass the Jumla valley spread out below, and beyond the white peaks of the Western Himalaya with Sisne and Kanjiroba standing out from the line of the range.

The snow had drifted on the north side and the deep cold powder made slow going. Already clouds were boiling up from the forested valleys to the south and an icy wind whipped up flurries of spindrift. In his hurry to get out of the coming storm Balu forgot his laziness and ploughed ahead, only to stumble and fall in the deep snow. The plastic tarpaulin slithered off the top of his basket and down into the snowy bowl below. He set off to retrieve it.

'Balu – don't! That's an avalanche slope!'

Phurba read the snow as I did and began to yell at the boy in Sherpa. Balu stopped at the edge of the unstable snow looking puzzled, then shrugged and returned to his load.

The sky darkened as cloud engulfed the mountain. Rumbles of thunder growled overhead and a vicious wind whipped up blinding spindrift. Once again, we had crossed just before the storm blocked the pass behind us. We seemed to be having uncanny luck – either avoiding a pass altogether that was completely blocked by snow, or getting across each subsequent pass with no time to spare before storms closed in behind. Or was it just lucky coincidence? There was no question in the minds of the Sherpas that Zopa Rinpoche's knowledge extended far beyond our comprehension and that following his advice and using his protection mantra was the sole reason that we were succeeding, despite the appalling conditions. Even though I felt great respect for Rinpoche as a profoundly wise and compassionate person, my western-conditioned mind still resisted the thought that his clairvoyance might extend beyond the ability to clearly understand the minds of his students, and encompass a knowledge of what was happening – or would happen – in the distant mountains as well. But now the coincidence theory was being stretched beyond probability.

The descent steepened and the snow became wet and mushy as we lost altitude. It became difficult to stay upright. Ang was ahead, stomping the snow into submission with a solid Sherpa plod, while I tried shoe-skiing which was less tiring, except on the occasions I missed a turn and wrapped myself round an unyielding tree trunk. Phurba began imitating the technique, shussing through the slush with remarkable agility, basket and all. No one saw what technique Balu was experimenting with at the back, but its failure was heralded by a yelp of alarm and I turned to see his basket bouncing down the slope just before it hit me and knocked me into a snowdrift. The others were sprayed with assorted kitchenware which they then had to retrieve from the forest. Balu was ordered to walk ahead.

Camp that night was a damp and dismal affair in a muddy grove of spindly trees. It was still drizzling next morning, and after a few hours the valley ran into a steep-sided gorge, with the trail clinging to a ledge halfway up the northern cliff. In places the cliff overhung the trail far enough to catch at our loaded packs. It would have been easy to slip, and that meant a fall of several hundred feet to the rocks in the river below.

The storm caught us in the centre of a huge amphitheatre, and the hail and wind combined to bring rocks down from the cliffs above. We cowered in the inadequate shelter of a small overhang at the base of the cliff while rocks continued to crash round us on all sides.

The others looked singularly unconvinced about the safety of the place and moved to leave. I struggled to overcome my own feelings of vulnerability as another missile embedded itself in a patch of muddy grass a couple of feet away.

'No, it's better we stay here. I've done it before, rock-climbing – '

A crash of thunder right overhead seemed to shake the whole cliff and a sideways gust threw stinging hailstones into the scant shelter. I tried not to look at the dizzying drop below but it was a poor choice between that and an eyeful of hail.

Suddenly it was over. As abruptly as it had started, the storm blew on up the gorge, leaving behind a patchy blue sky and piles of hailstones melting in the thin sunshine.

7

Lost Cities in the Desert

།རྗེས་བརྩལ་ན་བརྗོད་བྲལ་སྟོང་བའི་གཞིས།

I had expected Jumla, the regional capital, to be a fairly large town, but as it came into view at the centre of a broad valley it appeared small and compact. Indeed the old town was little more than a single flagged street bordered by flat-roofed houses and shops, with a few muddy twisting side alleys running out into fields. A tangle of electricity wires, kerosene street lights, and an open drain enhanced the prestige of the main street with spaces between filled with the colourful displays of a street market. The twin cupolas of the mosque-like temple stood at the end of a street, surrounded by tall prayer flags. The modern administrative buildings lay scattered across the far bank of the river.

The woman in the Royal Nepal Airlines office looked suitably baffled by my questions. She directed me to the control room where a group of smartly-dressed Nepalis were gathered round the wheezing radio. The flight from Nepalganj had just been cancelled, and with thunder rolling round the hills and snow almost down to Jumla, it looked as if the Kathmandu flight would have to be cancelled as well. Then the radio went dead.

'Agh! I *knew* we were running out of gasoline!' The controller shrugged resignedly. 'Can I help you?' He ruffled through his passenger lists, but there were no Western names listed on flights past, present, or future. More significantly, there were no boxes of food supplies waiting for us. The others were clearly not coming.

I walked across to the telegraph office to find out why. It was the most excitement the telegraph operator had seen all year.

Helpfully he went through every entry in his log for the past three months, confirming that very few telegrams are ever sent to Jumla, and certainly not one for us.

The Post Office stood next to the Telegraph Office; a similar two-storey white-painted building with a corrugated iron roof. Ten minutes of conversation with the bespectacled clerk convinced me I had just wasted the efforts of the past few days in writing letters for the last postbox before the Indian border.

'Sorry, mudum, only airmail if flight departs same day as posting. These will go porter to Nepalganj.'

'But Nepalganj is twenty days away in good weather – and right now the Chakhuri Lekh is under ten feet of new snow.'

'Sorry mudum, Post Office regulation.' Finally he agreed to fetch the Big Man.

The Big Man seemed puzzled that I was so concerned that my letters might take over a month to arrive. He was far too polite to point this out, and was doing his best to be helpful. Eventually he agreed to hold the letters until the next flight if I would put them all in one large envelope. He weighed the package carefully and announced that it was now heavier; I would have to pay an extra 25 *paise*. Even by Nepalese standards, this indicated a precise and careful approach to Post Office regulations. I handed over the coin.

At that precise moment, a megaton wind gust hit Jumla and with a rending and tearing worthy of the Last Judgement the Post Office roof blew off. Everyone moved cautiously to the door and peered out. The roof lay in a heap of crumpled timbers and twisted metal in the dusty compound outside. A shaken bystander confirmed that there was no one underneath it, so we all drifted back inside again just as the occupants of the now roofless first floor offices came clattering down the stairs clutching antique typewriters and sheaves of yellowed, dog-eared papers. Then everyone shrugged and went back to what they were doing or not doing before the roof blew off.

It was a dry, if crowded, night at the home of a friendly Jumli shopkeeper and his wife and eleven children: incentive enough to be on the road again the following day. Several hours of diligent hunting had replenished supplies of flour, oil, sugar, dal and rice. It would run out sooner than the concentrated supplies we had been expecting, but we would just have to hope there would be a chance to restock later. The Jumla rice, at least, was a pleasant change from the Japanese plastic variety. The reddish-coloured grains have a pleasant nutty flavour and it was easy to see why precious sacks of it had been portered to Kathmandu for Maharajas' banquets in the days of the ancient Malla kingdoms of which Jumla had been the capital. The skill and strict following of the lunar calendar for growing rice at 7,000 feet were brought to Jumla originally from Kashmir, and careful planting out is done to escape the frosts. To grow rice in these snowy valleys seemed impossible.

Several helpful Jumlies had tried to decipher my map without much success. They had never heard of the villages on the map, and those they knew weren't marked. I pencilled in their villages on the spots I thought they were likely to be, hoping to correct mistakes as we went along and not get too hopelessly lost in the meantime. It would probably mean that even if we arrived at the other end, we would never be quite sure where we'd been, but it was the best map available, so there were few alternatives.

The Sherpas were habitually anxious about our meagre supplies and in spite of the drizzle made the effort to investigate every village we passed, finally being offered eggs and chickens in Padmara. A tree-trunk ladder led up to the village street – the flat roofs of the lower tier of houses. There were three tiers in all, built against the steep hillside. Within minutes I was marooned in a sea of curious children. The women in these villages looked almost Muslim, wearing layers of dark sacklike homespun swathed over their heads, shoulders, and everything else. They were friendly, but cautious with strangers and pulled their shawls closer around themselves when they spoke to us. Only the children were uninhibited enough to show off their jewellery, which they wore in great swathes of turquoise, coral, and old Indian rupee coins inscribed VICTORIA, QUEEN AND EMPRESS. Ang appeared from one of the houses, swinging a scrawny chicken by its legs and with a clutch of eggs wrapped in the grubby remains of the tea-towel. The villagers had never seen the newly-issued twenty rupee notes and refused to accept them, so I had to collect all our spare change and offer them coins instead.

Ang handed the chicken to Balu. 'Don't put it in the basket, it will shit on the cookpots.'

Balu swung the chicken by its feet as he walked.

'Look out, you're beating its head on the ground,' I said.

With a shrug that said 'So what?' Balu hoisted the unhappy bird a few inches higher as it swung.

By mid-afternoon the drizzle had turned to sleet and the heavy clouds brought an early twilight to the valley. The snowbound lekh loomed ahead, glimmering white in the gloom, while another storm moved up the valley behind us. We needed a place to camp, but the steep terrain made that an impossibility. A shepherd stood watching us from the flat roof of his hut, shoulders swathed in thick homespun against the bitter wind.

'*E, Dai!* Anywhere to camp up here?' Phurba looked anxious.

'Not here. Any further and you're on the lekh. Deep snow up there.'

I wasn't sure if it was polite to ask, but times were hard. 'Could we camp on your roof?'

He looked at the mud roof under his feet. 'Hm. No stomping around and breaking it now.'

The tents were up minutes before the storm hit and buried them under inches of snow. Having satisfied himself that the pegs were not protruding through his ceiling, the shepherd offered to let us cook in his woodshed.

The chicken sat gloomily on the mud floor of the shed while the Sherpas discussed who should kill it.

'Hey – Balu – you want to eat chicken?'

Clearly Balu did, but wasn't going to let them pass the buck so easily.

'These lama people – all same. They sit there going OM MANI PADME HUM and saying, "Oh, we should not kill anything," but when it's cooked they like it well enough.'

The others roared with laughter at the joke on themselves but offered no defence. Balu and the chicken disappeared into the blizzard and Phurba fled in the opposite direction. The chicken reappeared with a quill feather stuck right through its head by the eyes – very dead. Balu had done this kind of work before. An hour later the chicken had become the Nepalese version of chicken stew – a mixture of stringy meat and splintered bone for which it seemed hardly worth breaking one's Buddhist precepts. When the last spoonful of stew was finished, Phurba retreated to a dry corner with his rosary, muttering mantras.

'How many for one chicken?' I was curious about such cheerful hypocrisy.

'Maybe one thousand.'

I could still hear Phurba chanting, muffled by the deep snow, as I crawled into my damp sleeping bag and fell asleep. By morning the tent was sagging under the weight of snow outside and ice that had formed inside. It was an effort of will to force cold limbs out of the soggy sleeping bag and feet into frozen boots. Outside, sunlight hung golden on frozen waterfalls on the crags. Nearly nine inches of cold powder covered the tents, and Ang and Phurba were digging a snowdrift out of the woodshed. Balu was shuffling around in a pair of wet tennis shoes.

'Where are your boots?'

Balu shuffled off to fetch water. Ang answered for him. 'They need fixing so he throw away in Jumla and buy canvas shoes instead.'

I could see from Ang's expression that he had already failed to reason with Balu on this subject. If only the boy were more experienced. If only Ang were more forceful... I rummaged around for a pair of dry socks.

'If you lend him your gaiters as well, he should be all right.'

Ang took the socks and stomped off, muttering recriminations in Sherpa against Balu and all his ancestors. Still, harsh words were better than frostbitten feet and we still had two days of these frozen lekhs ahead of us. Before I had the tents packed, Balu was re-equipped, and the others were lecturing him on the dangers of frostbite.

'Why has he got Phurba's sunglasses?'

'His broken.'

'So what do we do when Phurba goes snowblind?' Trying to control my impatience at the late start, I sat down to repair the broken glasses with dental floss and sticking plaster.

For the next two days we saw few travellers. Only Tibetans from the remote villages near the border were well-equipped and hardy enough to tackle the deep snow and bitter wind. They walked in groups of four or five, felt and leather boots creaking in the frozen snow, backs bowed under loads of sheepswool destined for southern markets.

From the crest of the last pass, the whole of the Kanjiroba range spread across the horizon, with Saipal distant in the haze to the northwest. Beyond, in Tibet, stood the holy mountain of Kailash, the centre of the world for Buddhists and Hindus alike; the jewelled palace of a god is said to stand on the summit. From

Lake Manasrowar at its base flow the great rivers of southern Asia; the Indus and the Sutlej to the west, and the Tsangpo, later the Brahmaputra, to the east. Pilgrims from all the Buddhist and Hindu countries of Asia make their way across the mountains and deserts to make the traditional three circuits of the holy mountain. Each circuit involves not only four days of hard walking, but also the crossing of a rocky pass almost 19,000 feet high.

Some people associate Mount Kailash with Mount Meru, the centre of the world in Tibetan mystical geography. Mount Meru is thousands of miles high and is surrounded by seven concentric rings of golden mountains, and four continents, one at each of the cardinal points. Shambhala is said to be situated on the southern continent. However, there the similarity between the mystical and the geographical sacred mountains ceases, because most of the ancient texts describe Shambhala as being further north than the Himalaya. If Shambhala lay south of Kailash that would place it somewhere in the dusty hills further west, where our route was heading. Although this location did not correspond with any of the texts, I found the thought intriguing nonetheless.

The trail led down through a forest carpeted with ever-softening snow, sun sparkling on white-laden branches that dripped and dumped their loads on unsuspecting heads. We had descended into spring. There was a warmth and richness in the smell of resinous pine needles underfoot, and the damp decay of walnuts lying where they had fallen. Pink cherry blossom and green leaves filtered dappled sunlight, soothing eyes strained by the searing brightness of the wastes of snow. The valley exuded a warm sleepiness after the bleak dampness of Jumla and the wolfish cold of the lekh. I wanted to rest, to catch up on food and sleep and change into dry clothes.

The circled letter H of an emergency helipad was scored in the meadow grass, probably for use in the summer. There would be no helicopters while everything was snowed in and as it was the only piece of flat land, we pitched camp on it.

The afternoon passed pleasantly, dedicated to mundane domestic chores, and the camp soon sported several lines of washing. It seemed incongruous that a party of uniformed soldiers should suddenly appear on such a homely scene.

They stood and watched for a while, until one stepped forward and coughed politely. His uniform was crisper and more heavily decorated than those of his companions, but his dialect took some translating. I eventually gathered that he was explaining why I really shouldn't camp on their helipad, because you never knew when a passing helicopter might want to use it. It seemed unlikely that any helicopters would come this far when even winged aircraft could not reach Jumla, but perhaps he knew something I didn't. We moved the camp further up the hill.

The few villages in the area were filthy and dilapidated, and the people in rags. Everyone had the same answer: 'No food, nothing to sell. Even our own is not enough.' These low-lying Brahmin villages contrasted sharply with the prosperous little Buddha-Chettri settlements on the hills. The Buddha-Chettris were shepherds, with flocks large enough to keep them from the poverty of the valley dwellers. We had seen them at dusk at one of the higher camps, silently bringing their animals down from hillsides that had been officially declared a nature reserve, and from which sheep had been banned. I never found out whether these silent shepherds considered themselves to be Buddhists or Chettris, or a strange mixture of both.

The Brahmin villages were dirty and unkempt, swarming with flies that buzzed constantly around the huts. Usually high-caste Brahmins were the elite of Hindu society. What had happened to them since the decline of the great Malla kingdoms of Jumla and Hadsinja? All that remained of an empire which had reached into parts of India and Tibet were the overgrown remains of strange stone carvings on the empty hillsides. The more recent carvings were much cruder, mainly wooden effigies on the bridges and beside the springs to scare away the malevolent *bhuts*, the harmful ghosts that haunt these desolate hills.

Back in Jumla I had become involved in a conversation with David, a British foreign-aid worker who had been stationed there for the past two years. Although still dedicated to his job and determined to help, he had become increasingly disillusioned and pessimistic about any real chances of improving the lives of the impoverished farmers of the far west.

'Poverty seems to be ingrained in the culture now. It's no good us coming along with new stock, new grains, new production methods – if the people here don't really accept these ideas as useful to themselves then the project will never become self-sustaining.'

'Why can't they see that what you're offering is useful?'

'For many of them, it's too much *dukkha* – too much trouble. I went to see an old farmer the other day in one of the outlying villages. There's a swamp all round his house; his *bisi* has foot-rot from standing in it and he has to walk through it himself every time he goes outside his door to take a leak. All he has to do is to dig a trench to drain the water off and he can have a vegetable plot instead of a swamp. But it's too much *dukkha*. He can't be bothered. It's not his fault – his family have been so poor for generations they seem to have lost any aspirations to be anything else. Where do you start?'

I had heard of other aid projects running into similar difficulties. In other parts of Nepal the problem was often that peasant farmers were so deeply in debt to local money lenders, usually Brahmin landlords. Because the rates of interest are so high, and because the peasants are so used to being in debt, much of the benefit brought by foreign aid often simply goes to pay off the loans.

David said, 'It's going to need more than foreign technology and ideas. Somehow the ideas have to be blended into the existing social system – and frankly, some of the dogmas and inequalities in this social system could do with throwing out. I'm not saying our system's perfect either – no system is – but at least we eat.'

The outlet from Rara Lake breaks through the rock barrier to the west and plunges through a deep gorge to join the great Karnali which flows from Humla and Mugu in the north. There were no trails marked on this section of the map, so it seemed a reasonable guess to follow the river. It was a wet and difficult descent over slimy rocks and sticky clay, with only sulky wet firewood on which to cook. Before we reached the Karnali Ang had a fever and was trailing behind.

Balu, Phurba and I collected wood and brewed tea. I was thinking of going back up the trail to look for Ang when he stumbled into camp and threw off his rucksack. Then he collapsed. It took the three of us to get him into a tent and covered with a sleeping bag. He was burning with fever. I had no thermometer in the medical kit, which was just as well for to know his temperature would probably have worried me even more. It was impossible to tell what was wrong with him. In any case there was no hospital for hundreds of miles, and no chance of getting him to one. I should have abandoned the whole thing in Kathmandu after the others got into trouble.

Phurba was concerned about food.

'We go tomorrow, or nothing to eat.'

With Ang unable to stand it seemed a limited choice. It rained all night and the tents sagged and began to leak.

Neither Ang nor the weather had improved much by morning. Phurba coaxed a sullen fire out of damp wood, and we managed to get Ang to drink half a cup of tea which he obviously didn't want. Phurba boiled the last of the flour and rice into a glutinous porridge. He emerged from Ang's tent with the food untouched.

'He says walking possible but carrying not possible.'

There was no food left to carry. Phurba kept a careful watch on him in case he toppled into the river below.

The country ahead was a dramatic contrast to the snowy pine forests of Rara. Dry cactus country stretched brown and barren with little cultivation. The rain shadow of the lekhs had compounded the droughts of the last two years, and little of the recent rain seemed to have penetrated here. Below, the Karnali was a brilliant turquoise slash of ice-melt flowing from Humla and Dolpo through the dry ochre and gold of the desert.

Water buffalo were wallowing in a green pool beneath the bridge. A boy lazed under a pipal tree, waiting to drive them home. Yes, he said, the Karnali came out of Dolpo, but he had never been there. If we turned south we would be on the way to Nepalganj, but he'd never been there either. He had never heard of Chainpur or Baitadi to the west.

'Find some Tibetans to ask,' Phurba suggested.

The trail degenerated into several pitches of rock-climbing several hundred feet sheer above the Karnali. It was not particularly difficult unless you happened to be carrying a doko or running a high fever. The desert heat was more exhausting than the wet cold of the highlands. We had to stop soon, food or no food.

A group of porters rested in the shade of the cliff. They were bringing rice and flour from Nepalganj to their villages, but they needed all they carried and wouldn't sell. As we were about to leave, a straggler limped in, nursing a swollen ankle. He finally agreed to part with a kilo of flour to lighten his load. While the bargaining was going on, some of his companions grew curious about the Sherpas' strange accents.

'Where are you from?'

'East side – Solu Khumbu.'

'*E?* Never heard of it. Are you sure you're Nepali?'

We camped in thornscrub beside the Karnali where Phurba gathered nettles to stew with the flour. It was so long since there had been any vegetables available along this route. The nettles boiled down to a hideous luminous green – like stewed pondweed – that was better eaten in the dark.

A herd of goats clattered through the scrub, nibbling at the trees, apparently impervious to the thorns. The herder sat and watched them.

'Are you going to Mugu?'

'Not Mugu. Humla. Everyone going north this time; Mugu, Humla. We are camped down there.' He waved his arm towards the southern trail. 'Two days' rest now, so the animals can eat. Then three more days on the road.'

Darkness fell, and I had to stop work on the map. The red line had caught up with the Karnali. The night was heavy with the rasping of crickets and the sound of the river. The full moon rose, its light haloed by the mosquito netting that hung in the tent doorway.

We passed the nomads' encampment early next morning. On the road, each goat carried homespun panniers stuffed with rice from India, and these had been unloaded and stacked into protective walls around the camp and covered with tarpaulins. Two children were stationed on rock-throwing duty near a cluster of goats and kids which were being hungrily watched by two huge vultures perched nearby. Further down, another group of nomads were laboriously catching their animals and strapping them back into their panniers ready for another route march on their journey north.

It was dusty, stony country. The Karnali slipped through like a heavy green snake without stopping to water the parched hills on either side. Only spiny cactus relieved the thornscrub and even the poorest locals wore leather sandals. Villages huddled wherever a stream could be diverted to water fields that splashed a brilliant green against the dun-coloured desert. A fisherman hauled in his net from the turquoise water. His catch, four tiny fish, lay in a basket beside him.

'Only two rupees each,' he offered.

There was some discussion and hesitation, but the fish did at least have the advantage over the chicken of being dead already. Ang handed over the money, but Phurba lunched on dry chapatis. I was beginning to understand a little more about Phurba's attitude to fish, although most of this was from observation and guesswork as Phurba made no further attempt to give explanations.

Buddhism does not clothe itself in fixed rules of behaviour; there are guidelines, but these are regarded as good advice rather than divine decrees. The ideal is to avoid harming any other living being – but even without the use of microscopes it is easy to see that this is not possible. Even to walk across the ground is to squash countless tiny creatures underfoot. In Tibet, if the population had been prohibited from eating meat, many of them would have died, because this was a staple for the nomads in the desert. So people compromised as best they could, accepting that just by being alive they must automatically bring harm to some other creatures, but always striving to do their best to limit that harm as much as possible. The most likely reason for Phurba's attitude towards eating fish was that they were so tiny that it took several lives to feed one person, whereas a large animal such as a buffalo would feed many people, and even a chicken would feed several more than a fish.

Ang was recovering from the fever, but he was still weak. In any case, our progress was slowed by the flowing woolly tide of sheep and goats moving northwards along all the trails. The nomads transported their sparse possessions slung in bundles on their backs or loaded on to their dzos – usually with a couple of gawky chickens perched on top. Even the children carried bundles of cookpots or their small brothers and sisters. A woman walked with a calf slung across her shoulders, while behind her a man staggered under the weight of a dead sheep dangling a tell-tale bloody leg. One goat had been late in kid and two small white heads poked out of her homespun panniers.

The nomads were a rowdy, lively contrast to the local farmers who seemed to spend most of their time smoking their clay chilums and watching the marijuana growing in the fields. They would trek once a month to the district headquarters in Maitadi to collect their dole of foreign aid rice 'from the King'. Only the rowdy nomads had any spare food to sell, and there was little enough of that. There were not even any nettles left; the nomads had been through and eaten them all.

Balu was sick with stomach cramps, so we took a rest day despite the grilling heat and the ever-present swarms of sandflies. The little beasts seemed to be an integral part of the cactus desert, feasting on any areas of exposed flesh and leaving a hole the size of a large pinhead streaming blood. In two days the pinheads would swell to angry red itchy lumps which easily became infected. Sandflies were not the only denizens of this spiny, prickly country. My diary records:

> I don't know what it is but it's five inches long and black and hairy, and it flies. Phurba says 4 stings kill you.

A few lean days later, near the village of Patharkot, the trail was almost blocked by a family of Tamangs cutting up a dead cow. Severed bloody limbs were strewn across the trail and quivering slabs of red meat were being tossed into a doko.

'What happened to it?'

'It fell.'

Fell, or was pushed? The bank above it was hardly precipitous. Better not ask such a question in a country that holds the killing of the holy cow a greater sin than homicide. One way or another, it fell – and hungry Sherpa eyes were already fixed on its earthly remains.

Ang shuffled awkwardly. 'Do English eat cow?'

To a Buddhist minority living in a Hindu country it must seem as if the whole of the rest of the world abstains from cow. Officially, beef does not exist in Nepal, where even imports are banned. The meat would soon spoil in the tropical heat, so there was no point in buying much.

I was saved any delicate philosophical dilemmas about the relative de-merits of eating beef by the persistence of the dizziness and queasiness that had haunted me for the last few days. The others were suffering from it too, and our pace was slowing as the mysterious sickness took hold. I could not tell whether it was some strange virus picked up in one of the squalid villages, or an allergy caused by so many sandfly bites, or simply the effects of weeks of living on starvation rations – mainly nettles. I found it increasingly difficult to remain objective about my own condition and so found it more alarming to watch the symptoms manifest themselves in the others. They would lose concentration on packing or camp chores, either meandering off or lapsing into inertia and staring into space.

I spent the next few days wandering an alien land that bore only superficial resemblance to the country through which we were travelling. I constantly stumbled off the trail, and several times Phurba had to grab my sleeve and haul me back on to the route again. Lightning flashed from behind the darkening hills and storms brought a heavy oppression to the air. Sometimes the thornscrub and dry grass would fade, leaving only a parched and barren desert seared by electric storms. As I drifted further and further into my own reality I could not tell which landscape I shared with the others and which was an hallucination.

My body no longer seemed to belong to me, moving slowly and automatically in a private world of laboured breathing rasping against a dry, parched throat. Thoughts seemed to drift in and out of this limited field of perception without meaning or focus until I felt they were no longer a part of my own mind. Separate from these scattered images was a force or will, as if another entity was following me, pushing me to keep going. Once before, in Tibet, some power such as this had forced me to keep moving and get out of a blizzard, but this time I knew my body had become much weaker, thinner, more drained of energy than anything I had experienced before. However hard I was pushed, or pushed myself, I knew it would not be long before my body would just stop of its own accord, wrung dry of the last drop of energy.

At night I would collapse into my tent, exhausted, yet sleep for only a few hours. The feeling of vertigo and dizziness pervaded my dreams and I would wake, sweating, dreaming of falling. To move on again in the clammy morning was an ordeal against which my body rebelled, yet from somewhere came the will to plod on. I no longer cared where I was going or whether I arrived; there was simply no choice, no hope or despair. To remain in this barren wasteland would be to starve to death.

At the crest of a low pass I sat down to rest in a patch of welcome shade. I was aware that I was resting more and more frequently and that the others were constantly having to wait for me. I knew it would not be long before the rest stops took over and I simply would not get up and start walking again. In this wilderness of dust and thornscrub and oppressive, thundery heat there were no hospitals, roads, or radio link with Kathmandu. To give up and stop moving would be to die here. I felt vaguely surprised that this realisation did not bring the expected response of fear or panic. Dying seemed now to be simply a natural and inevitable consequence of having been alive, and I accepted it with the same detachment I felt for my own body and its surroundings.

I stared at my hands and arms for a while, trying to remember how I had once felt so closely identified with my body; so attached to it. What I was looking at seemed strange and unfamiliar, black and broken fingernails, skin stretched tight over bone, fleshless and dry, burned dark and ingrained with dirt. It was almost as if I were already dead, a dried-up husk of skin and bone moving like a ghost through a dead landscape. What did it matter whether I stayed here or walked on a few hundred yards further?

8

Bears and Snowdrifts

།ཆོས་ཅན་གྱི་ཡིན་རྒྱལ་བསམ་གྱིས་ན།

I did not really notice when the country changed, but gradually I became aware that there were more people on the trail, porters carrying supplies up from the market towns of the Terai. The food was destined for the villages further up in the hills, yet some flour and sugar had found its way into the roadside bhatties and we could begin to eat again. At first I did not feel hungry and had to force myself to eat, but over the next few days I began to feel stronger, although the others still had to wait for me. To my relief the route climbed a little into the hills and the mornings, at least, were cool and damp.

The trail squeezed between a huge rock overhang and a small stone hut. A carefully ochre-smoothed terrace had been built under the sooty rock roof three feet above the trail, fringed gracefully by drooping fronds of wet ivy. Inside the customised cave an old man sat cross-legged on a bamboo seat, tending an array of kettles bubbling on a twig fire. His wrinkled face peered out from the folds of a woollen blanket swathed around his head and shoulders.

'Any food to sell?' I asked.

'Well . . . not sure. I am only watching teapots for the owner. He's gone to fetch the *bisi* – I go and find him. You watch those teapots now.' He creaked to his feet and hobbled off up the road. Ang moved on to his vacated stool and blew on the embers of the fire. A minute later the ground began to vibrate with the thudding of hooves as five full grown water buffalo came pounding down the road at full gallop, heading straight for the three-foot-wide bottleneck where we sat. Everyone hastily tucked dangling feet out of the way. Suddenly a little girl of about seven stepped calmly out in front of the stampede and swatted the lead bisi smartly on the nose with a twig. The lumbering creatures executed a swivel turn that would have been the envy of a well-trained polo pony, and shot off in the direction from which they had come. The child smoothed her ragged dress, flashed us an enchanting smile and sauntered off in pursuit of the animals.

The owner of both bisi and shop appeared, looking equally unruffled, and grappled with the enormous padlock securing the flimsy wooden door. He had a few kilos of sugar and rice to sell; hardly a feast, but all I was counting was calories. Enough fuel to reach the border, if we were lucky.

Although I had been walking quite slowly, my head had cleared and I no longer felt so dizzy and disoriented. Now the worst of the sickness seemed to be over, I noticed my mind trying to erase the whole experience from memory as quickly as possible. Perversely, I forced myself to look back at what had passed. Shutting off from memories classed as 'unpleasant' may be a natural instinct in a lifetime of habitually searching for things we label 'pleasant', yet that denies the chance to learn from them.

I wondered at the apparent ease with which I had lost the habitual clinging to my physical body. Maybe this was because it had become no longer functional or attractive enough to generate any feelings of attachment, or perhaps it was just acceptance of what seemed inevitable. What did surprise me was the feeling of tremendous freedom that grew out of this letting go. As the exhaustion of the past days gradually dropped away, this new inner freedom seemed to expand into a total, all-pervading transparency and lightness of being. No wonder 'dancing in the sky' was a phrase the ancient poets had chosen for their legendary and enigmatic Dakinis – it was a figure of speech I could readily identify with, as no amount of heat, dust, or tiredness was now able to weigh down this inner sense of well-being.

I also realised why the Dakini can appear as a beautiful dancer or ugly hag – not just because the meditator, whose vision she is, has transcended outward appearances and can see her inner beauty. She is also a reminder that we can transcend the attachment to outward appearances of ourselves. Never mind whether we look like a healthy athlete or a half-dead corpse, what we are inside does not depend on what we look like from the outside.

For me, all this would soon fade into memory, as opposed to living experience. Just as external circumstances had forced me into a situation of recognition, so the new demands of the world would take their turn. I knew that these spontaneous glimpses beyond the physical world are only glimpses, while stabilisation of these perceptions takes time and application. The outer journey to my own Shambhala was becoming a harsh but effective learning experience, forcing me to abandon habitual perceptions and ideas and see the world from another perspective.

During the next few days the number of people on the trail wearing manufactured clothes from the cities increased, while the homespun-clad farmers were left behind in the hills. The newcomers had the dark Aryan features of the plains dwellers, and I could feel we were entering a different country.

I stood on the crest of a low ridge above Julaghat watching the trail meander down the hillside towards the gorge of the Mahakali river, listening to a sound I had not heard for more than two months. A truck was labouring up the switchbacks of a newly-carved dirt road, engine whining and gears crunching as it struggled round the rutted hairpins. I was about to enter that other world of noise and speed that had been going about its business all the time there had been nothing for us but rivers and animals and wind in the trees. All thought of the exhaustion and hunger of the desert fell away with the realisation of what I had lost. In the loneliness of those wild hills I had come closer to life, and death, and as a result had come to know myself a little better. Mallory's thoughts on challenging a mountain could be true of challenging any wild place on its own terms rather than one's own: 'Have we vanquished any enemy? Nought but ourselves.' I turned and looked back, half wishing I could just fade into the hills again, wanting to hold on to this spacious feeling of freedom for longer before the noisy world crowded in and dissipated it. In the same instant I knew this would be just another form of clinging which would take its place in the cycle.

Besides, going back was altogether impractical; not only were we all short of food and rest but my trekking permit had expired three days ago – not that there had been anyone with the authority to look at it since I had left Kathmandu.

I walked down the hill towards the river.

'You are one day late. The Liaison Officer has been waiting – we have all been waiting – since yesterday.'

The two crisply-dressed young Indians fell into step, skipping to keep up on the rocky trail. I stared at them vacantly, wondering how many guides and attendants the Liaison Officer had brought with her. The Indian Mountaineering Foundation seemed to have taken my estimate of arriving approximately on 12th April rather literally.

The Mahakali gorge dropped away below, vultures wheeling over the twin towns of Julaghat, its two halves joined by the bridge that linked India and Nepal.

A steep zigzag path led down to the squalid streets of the town cramped at the foot of towering cliffs. There was a blare of noise – merchants haggling with customers, radios, horse bells, and the crash of pots as a barefoot woman scrubbed her kitchenware in a muddy alleyway next to a shop selling cosmetics.

At the end of the long bridge a mournful immigration official inspected every page of my passport as if it bore tidings of deepest gloom.

'Madam, to where do you travel in India?'

'Oh, right across the north, I should think. All the way to Kashmir.'

'Ah, it will be a difficult journey. It is not as it was. . . The men, they do not treat the womens well. It is very sadful.'

I thanked him for his concern and followed the young guide to the police station, where we were to await the arrival of the Liaison Officer who had been awaiting our arrival at a hotel in Pithoragarh. She had been assigned to accompany us across India, although as far as I knew, the only special permit that had been granted was for this border crossing, which was not officially open to Westerners. There followed several hours of tedium in dark smelly rooms in the company of various police officers who tapped their feet and made comments about the weather. Eventually I went outside to sit in the sun and work on the map.

The Liaison Officer arrived in the afternoon. She looked strong and solidly-built, with the heavy bovine beauty fashionable among Indian film stars. She was eager to take charge of the situation.

'Now, we will hire porters locally until we reach Uttarkashi. You have already met our cook and guide. They have been advanced five hundred rupees against your account. As that is now finished, you will need to reimburse this and advance them some more. Cash.' She must have noticed my look of alarm, because she continued before I had a chance to reply '. . . and of course they will need equipment, so you should pass over that issued to the Nepalese porters. You can then send them home.'

'But it was all agreed that I would continue to Uttarkashi with the Nepalese porters and meet and equip the Indian staff there. Why the change?'

'Oh, you don't know? Your friend has written to me from Kathmandu and arranged everything for you. It is quite simple.'

From where she was sitting it may well have been, but I felt completely baffled. Why had Fran suddenly changed everything in my absence? It put me in a difficult situation because I was now expected to hand over the Sherpas' equipment which I no longer owned. The Liaison Officer handed me a note from Fran. It didn't say much, except that she had changed her mind about coming to Jumla and had run up unexpected expenses in Kathmandu. She had decided to come out to Uttarkashi by bus and had invited some of her friends from England to join the expedition for the remainder of the walking in India. The way things were looking, they would be making their own 'expedition' without us, as the Liaison Officer did not seem inclined to let us continue unless we followed the new plan.

'Ah, yes. You must send your porters home because they do not have government permission to enter the restricted areas we will be visiting.'

This was exciting news. I had no idea we had been granted special permits.

'Really? Please show me which areas.'

She took out her map and made sweeping gestures at a range of impressive mountain passes barely a mile from the Chinese border. One of the Indian guides who had met me on the trail leaned over and followed the line of her finger.

'Ah. Not quite there. All that is beyond the Inner Line. You only have permission to visit areas within the Inner Line.'

'You mean areas open to all visitors?'

'Exactly.'

I opened my mouth to ask why, in that case, we needed a Liaison Officer, then closed it again quickly. Antagonising her would be no help at all.

Ang and Phurba were looking increasingly worried at the prospect of losing their hard-earned equipment. Intimidated as they were by the presence of so many policemen, they still steadfastly refused to hand over their property. Eventually, Balu was sent home by way of a compromise, and the two Indians, who had arrived without a blanket between them, agreed to return to Uttarkashi. As we were leaving, I mentioned that we had been ill in Nepal. The Liaison Officer edged away from us hastily.

'You can visit the hospital in Pithoragarh.'

It was a long and bumpy ride to Pithoragarh, wedged in the back of the jeep, with the Liaison Officer and the local dignitaries in the front. We waited for half an hour in the hospital while the doctor chatted with the Liaison Officer. Then he remembered his professionalism and bustled over, waving a stethoscope. It took him ten seconds to diagnose dehydration and prescribe three separate antibiotics, to be taken together.

'Are you sure about the antibiotics?' I asked.

'Oh, you don't understand tropical medicine. This is not Europe. Here we give them out like aspirin. Like candy!' He handed out packets of pills, which I cautiously stashed in the medical kit.

The hotel was several kilometres outside town. Looking at its luxurious appointments, it was easy to see where the five hundred rupees had gone.

Balu was looking relieved at the prospect of going home. India had already been too much for him. I promised to take him into town to organise his bus tickets. The Liaison Officer offered to find the jeep driver, but half an hour later, I found her drinking lemonade on the roof garden with the District Magistrate, who waved a welcoming hand at a vacant chair.

'Sit down, sit down. Have some lemonade! This is such a beautiful hotel. You should stay here for a week or two before continuing your journey. Tch! You should not be worrying yourself about this *coolie's* bus tickets! I have all the information you need. He can go by bus, or by train. There! Simple, isn't it? Or he can go to Mahendranagar in Nepal. It's quite close to here.'

'And from there to Kathmandu?'

'Why, he can walk.' His gleaming white smile matched his suit.

The Liaison Officer ordered another round of lemonade against my account and I felt obliged to explain the expedition's current finances and its inability to support this kind of expense. She was remarkably understanding, and suggested that a lot of money could be saved if the Sherpas and I were to move to a much cheaper hotel in town. She would meet us in the morning.

Ang and Phurba spent the evening helping Balu memorise all the bus connections, which Phurba had written on a piece of paper for helpful passers-by to read, as Balu could not. Ang was flashing rupee notes of different denominations for Balu to remember by colour, as he could not recognise the numbers. His money was hidden in his sock, under the sole of his foot.

'Stealing not possible,' said Phurba reassuringly.

'Unless they cut his leg off,' Ang added cheerfully, swiping graphically with his hand. Balu left, looking apprehensive and relieved at the same time.

The Liaison Officer arrived just before noon the following day.

'Now, we really must get properly organised. First of all, I hope you were informed that, according to regulations, I am required to have my own porters. Also you must know that I don't eat rice, just chapatis. And you should buy plenty of salad and fruit, and those little lemons are nice, and we should get some sweets too. . . We should go shopping now. Come, come!'

It rained all day as the bus chugged to the roadhead at Gwaldam. There was no five-star hotel, to my enormous relief. The Liaison Officer took shelter in the corrugated iron shack while the Sherpas and I unloaded the equipment. The manager was despatched to find her porters, and Ang cooked lunch. He presented her with a specially prepared pile of chapatis, but it was clear all was not well.

'No. Take this back. I think today I shall have an omelette with salad and fresh fruit. And please change the milk tea to lemon tea. That will be all.'

By the time they had prepared it she had gone out. Phurba was baffled. It was the first time he had met anyone who did not immediately shovel down everything that arrived on the plate.

I was reminded that the lifestyle of the British Raj was not invented by the British. It was already an integral part of the Indian caste system, and the colonials simply took advantage of a situation that both suited their convenience and had reassuring similarities to the class system of their own country. In spite of Ang's best efforts to maintain the kind of elaborate service the system prescribed, it had been easy for me to dispense with the more superfluous aspects which hampered efficiency and progress. However, I could see how difficult it would be for someone from within the Indian system to renounce the trappings and privileges due to their caste and status, whatever the improvement in efficiency.

By lunchtime the following day, the two local men, who were the only porters the hotel manager had been able to find, were demanding a five hundred per cent pay rise if they were to continue. The Liaison Officer rallied splendidly, telling them to get lost in voluble Hindi, then recruited two more from the nearest village. Next morning she decided to reorganise everyone. Ang was instructed to help her watch the two Indians while Phurba was sent ahead to cook for the six of us. Phurba looked alarmed. His culinary skills only extended to readymix tea and dal-bhat. Salads and omelettes would be totally beyond him. In the end I volunteered to go with him. Although Ang was mortified at being unable to take charge of the kitchen, I began to enjoy my new job as cook, learning from Phurba the art of foraging in the jungle for good fuel and edible plants. Even so, Phurba was amazed at my inability to coax a fire out of damp wood.

'How do you cook at home? Even small children can make fire.'

The Liaison Officer had been taking photographs, and arrived some time later.

'Oh, look! You are in the kitchen making *my* chapatis. I must take a photo.' She clicked away with her miniature camera. 'Oh. I seem to have run out of film. You must give me one of yours. Give me colour slide.'

The route crossed another roadhead at Ghat. Reeking barrels of kerosene were stacked behind the bus station, and I realised it would be more appropriate to visit this area by bus. All the locals thought we were crazy to walk when it was so obviously unnecessary. Right across northern India military roads were being pushed as fast as possible to the Chinese border. The threat of Chinese expansion seemed to increase with each new influx of Tibetan refugees who fled into exile. By the time we reached Ramni the two malnourished Indian porters were casting anxious looks at the snow on the lekh above and demanding to be paid off. We hired two more from Ramni.

The self-appointed spokesman for the two Ramni porters was a middle-aged man with a sharp nose and weasel eyes. The boy with him might have been his son, but as he never said a word in my hearing the whole time he was with us, I never found out. They refused to carry more than twenty kilos each, but as supplies were running low this was not an immediate problem.

The snow was not far above the village, lying in wet drifts among the tangle of fallen trees brought down by recent storms. Here and there snow and earth had been scraped away beneath the trees leaving shallow troughs where long claws had raked the soil for grubs. There were bear droppings on the snow.

Phurba looked round nervously. 'The small bears are no problem but the big bears *eat people*. These are big bears.'

A rock rolled and crashed through the undergrowth and we both jumped visibly.

'Make a noise. Clap your hands.'

We walked on, clapping and shouting in chorus.

'*Oi, bears!* I got *no* honey, *no* peanut butter, *no* candy! *Oi!*'

The locals who had assured us we were crazy to cross the lekh would have been comfortably confirmed in their suspicions if they could have seen us.

We camped in a clearing, lighting a large fire in the hope of scaring away any lurking bears. Great rocks had been tossed aside and the soil beneath raked for grubs. Phurba and I pitted our combined strength against one of the rocks, but we could not budge it. I held out my arms to demonstrate the probable size of the bear. Phurba glanced anxiously over his shoulder and threw some more wood on the fire.

Ang arrived and immediately began frying pancakes for the following day on the snowbound lekh. Unfortunately Phurba poured his second cup of tea into the wrong cup – the one containing the hot oil. It was the last of the oil, so we finished the cooking amid showers of sparks and crackling flames.

'Never mind, it'll scare the bears away.'

By the time I crawled into my sleeping bag I was too tired to worry about the bears.

Although we left at first light, the sun was up before we reached the final climb. Jagged cliffs rose on either side of a snow gully choked with avalanche debris. We had to get across the gully in order to reach the rocks on the far side which would be safe from avalanches. Ang plunged into the deep snow while the rest of us held back; if he set off an avalanche the more available hands to dig him out the better. Even following his trail was hard work. On the far side I looked back to see the Indian porters stopping for a smoke in the middle of the gully. Nothing came down, so I suppose they were convinced they had made the right decision.

The ridge above was now a horrible wet slog through thigh-deep snow, with ominous-looking cracks to worry about every time we crossed a gully. The Liaison Officer proved herself to be a young lady of stout nerves and strong legs, keeping up determinedly as Ang and I took turns at breaking trail.

I caught a brief glimpse of the Nanda Devi range before the clouds engulfed it and the first flakes of snow began to fall. Ang glanced over his shoulder at the deteriorating weather and plunged straight downhill towards the trees. His guess was right; it was hard going through the steep undergrowth and wet snow, but there were no more cliffs. In the absence of a trail, we followed a small stream down through the forest – it was less resistant than the undergrowth and it was already impossible to get any wetter.

The first clearing was hardly a luxurious campsite but it was still a better option than continuing in the wet and cold. Supper was a stew of the last scraping of our rations, but there were no complaints. Everyone was too tired. The Liaison Officer disappeared into her tent with a bowl of hot washing water to change into dry clothes. The rest of us sat round the fire and steamed like the teapot perched above the flames.

'Tomorrow by bus to Uttarkashi?' Ang asked.

I nodded. We had time to walk a short distance from Joshimath to the next roadhead, but what was the point? I was losing interest in this artificial route, and the Sherpas were overworked and overloaded to compensate for the inadequacies of the Indian porters and the needs of the Liaison Officer. After Uttarkashi we would go on to Ladakh without all the paraphernalia of this 'expedition'.

Next morning we walked down to the roadhead through the wet fields. A shepherd looked at us, then at the snowbound lekh above. He turned back to his flock, shaking his head in disbelief.

The Nehru Institute of Mountaineering is an imposing modern building perched on a pine forested hillside above the town of Uttarkashi. There were no mountaineering courses that week, and the rose gardens and concrete balconies lay silent and deserted. Pasang had already arrived from Kathmandu, and had been working for Fran and her friends on a short trek to the snowy lekhs above Uttarkashi. She had returned to Delhi for a few days to meet her boyfriend. Pasang looked much older than I remembered him, more worldly-wise and wary, and his smile did not reach his eyes.

'How are your hands?'

Reluctantly he held them out to show me. Five fingers looked as if they had been melted like candlewax, ending with scarred and lumpy tissue. Ends of bone were sticking out of two of them. 'They took off this one in the hospital just before we came here,' Pasang explained. I noticed how he winced when he touched things.

'You shouldn't be working with your hands like that. They'll get infected.'

He shrugged. 'I need the money. I can't get another job with my hands like this. Maila's finger not so bad – he got work with a climbing expedition.'

Pasang turned to Ang. 'Did you get your letter? The other memsahib said she would send you a letter about your father.' Ang shook his head. Pasang looked worried. 'So you don't know then. . .'

'What?'

'A message came from your village two months ago to Mike Sahib at the Sherpa Co-op. "Your father is very sick. And your sister is dead." '

Ang stared at him, shocked. Phurba looked worried. Which sister? Was it his wife? Pasang was unable to help, as he had received the message in English from Mike Cheney. There is only one word for sister in the English language, unlike Nepalese, which has different words for older sister and younger sister.

The Liaison Officer was sympathetic. 'They are so quiet now. Of course, we would be upset if something happened to our family, so perhaps it is understandable they should be upset too.'

I could not understand why there had been none of this news in the letter I had received from Fran in Julaghat. The whole situation did not feel right at all, and in that moment I made the decision to go back to Nepal with the two Sherpas to see if I could be of any help to the family. I told the Liaison Officer it would be best if she continued the expedition with Fran and her friends. The following day I would be able to collect money sent out from England, and then we could leave.

9

The Spring in the Cave

།དཔེར་ནམ་མཁའ་འདི་ལས་གཞན་དུ་ཅི།

The heat was stifling in the crowded railway compartment. I leaned back against the hard seat. We were lucky to have got on at all. Just to get this far had taken three buses and two trains from Uttarkashi, and we were very tired. We were no match for the experienced crowd milling on the station platform and had been pushed off three times. This compartment had been easy to board, reserved as it was for Army personnel and their families. Just as we were about to be politely removed by a railway representative, a moustachioed sergeant had taken pity on us and said we could stay. Pasang had decided to come back with us, and now had a stomach upset from drinking untreated water. The other two delivered a long lecture on being careful with drinking water, and Pasang moved to the far end of the compartment, out of earshot.

The sergeant was teaching me to write my name in Hindi, much to the amusement of his sari-swathed wife. The corporal sitting next to him showed me how to write it in Urdu, and I struggled with the strokes and pothooks until a sinewy brown arm descended from the luggage rack above and removed my notebook. The hand reappeared, empty, demanding the pen with imperative gestures. That, too, disappeared upside. Moments later both book and pen reappeared, followed by an inverted head.

'Bengali,' it explained, then retreated.

The hoarse cries of the *chai* sellers heralded a station. The sergeant took everyone's orders for tea and lunch, then bawled at the vendors out of the window in his best parade-ground voice.

The food was passed through the window – hot curry and rice, with tea in unfired earthenware cups. We threw the empties out of the window to smash on the ground as the train rumbled its way through open countryside once more.

We took another bus from Gorakpur to Kathmandu. After two months of walking, the return journey had taken 48 hours. Ang and Phurba visited a friend for news. There had been an epidemic of meningitis in east Nepal and nine people had died, including Ang's younger sister Kamali. His father had recovered, but already had TB, which had rapidly become worse because of his weakened state. I bought drugs for TB and next day we were on the plane to Tumlingtar.

We reached the village after two exhausting days of walking. The heat and heavy squalls of rain brought out hordes of blood-sucking leeches that were skilled at working their way into clothes and shoes. I was too tired to care.

It was dark inside the farmhouse, a smell of damp and a feeling of neglect about the place, with the stone mill left out where it had been used, and other utensils scattered about. Everything was covered in dust. The family were huddled round the meagre warmth of a smoky fire. Ang's father was lying on the floor by the fireplace, covered in blankets. He heard us come in and struggled to sit up. He had become very thin. It was hard to believe this shrunken frame of skin and bone could still be alive. I took the bottles of pills out of my pack and worked out the right dose. Then I crawled into my damp sleeping bag, totally exhausted.

It was three days before I could do more than drink tea and measure out the old lama's medicine. I knew that people who had never taken antibiotics before responded quickly to a first dose, but the improvement by the end of the week was remarkable. He was still thin, but coughing much less. Ang and Phurba had spent the week cutting dry wood and the lack of smoke helped.

Slowly life in the tiny farmhouse returned to the routines I had seen on my previous visit. Utensils were cleaned and put away, meals were cooked, and the lame ewe currently resident in a corner of the woodshed had the cut on its leg cleaned each day. It would have been easy for a chance visitor not to realise how recently there had been both illness and death in the family. Then there were the times when everyone was gathered together around the fire, cooking a meal or drinking tea, and someone would start to talk about Kamali. The potato fields she had planted would be ready to dig soon, but she would not see the harvest. The calf she had cared for was growing, but she would never milk it. Then the whole family would be crying openly, remembering her and the part she had played in their lives. Everyone would cry, and talk, until this episode in the remembering was complete. Within a few minutes the grieving would be put aside and they would be back at their everyday chores again. Until the next time.

By the end of the second week the lama announced that the spring *chang-bi* ceremony was long overdue, and he was now well enough to get on with it. I tried hard to persuade him that it was too soon to be walking from one farmhouse to another, but he was convinced that the health of the community was more important. If the local gods were not properly invited up to the high pastures for the summer season, the cattle would probably die.

It took several days to visit each of the scattered farms. The ceremonies seemed to be a cross between a family party and lengthy reading aloud from religious texts. Chang was first offered to the gods then consumed by the assembled villagers in large quantities. The lama had to abstain because of the antibiotics. Perhaps this was just as well. At the second house we visited, I watched in surprise as the elderly lama sitting next to Ang's father slid gracefully off the cushioned bench and under the table, where he remained for the rest of the ceremony with an inebriated smile of contentment on his face. The young monk who had sat on the other side of him glanced solicitously under the table to make sure the old gentleman was comfortable, then moved along the bench into the vacant seat in order to get a better view of the text they had been sharing.

It was time to leave. The passes into Ladakh would have been open for a while, and the sight of a glass of chang was enough to give me a headache. Ang had repaid what his mother borrowed for Kamali's funeral, and was anxious for more work. Phurba had to take his dzos up to the summer pastures.

By the time Ang and I reached Srinagar I had promised myself I would never travel on Indian buses again.

I wanted to photograph the Hemis festival in Leh, but the Zoji La was closed because of the heavy late snows. My wish to avoid buses was automatically granted as, after a two-day wait, the news came through that the Indian Army had managed to hack a narrow opening through the avalanche debris, but only trucks could cross the icy stretches. I managed to find room on the first convoy to depart for Leh. The other passenger on the truck was a heavily-built Tibetan by the name of Gyurme. I wondered why he spoke English with such a strong American accent. When I mentioned I had once lived in Colorado, his face broke into a broad grin.

'Colorado! I know it well. I was there for some time. The CIA shipped many of us Khampas out there for guerrilla training. When we returned we managed to infiltrate into the Resistance bases on the Himalayan border. I was in Lo for several years – '

'Where in Lo?' I was fascinated by the forbidden kingdom of Lo on the Nepal-Tibet border, known in Nepalese as Mustang.

'I was in several of the secret bases in my time there, but I guess I spent the most time just south of the walled city itself. From there we could slip over the border at night to join an attack on a Chinese Army base.'

His expression had become animated; clearly for him the resistance was not yet over. 'In the desert places we'd have to keep going all night – day and night – on foot, to reach target before the ration we could carry ran out. When we could get it, we would drink nothing but strong coffee to keep awake.'

'Did you think you could beat the Chinese?'

'I don't know. Of course you wouldn't carry on the fight if you didn't believe you were going to win in the end, whatever the odds. Maybe if China had not become a world market – maybe if the CIA had not cut off our support, who knows? We Khampas have always been the best fighters in Tibet. It was a chosen group of us who smuggled the Dalai Lama out of Tibet during the uprising.'

'What started the uprising?'

'The Tibetans thought the Chinese were about to imprison the Dalai Lama and it started a chain of events that were bound to happen. Lhasa was like a tinderbox about to go up. Tibetans had been exploited long enough. . .'

The truck lurched to a halt. The back was loaded with crates of eggs bound for Leh and the driver would stop from time to time to fry up part of his cargo. Gyurme yelled over that it was all very well for him – stuffing himself with egg sandwiches – but how about stopping in a village so the rest of us could get something to eat? He glared ferociously across the cab as if he still had half the Red Army in his sights. The driver changed his mind about the egg sandwich and eased the truck back on the road as fast as his delicate cargo would allow.

The Zoji La had been swamped by a series of avalanches. Rumour had it that there was a bus buried somewhere beneath the snow which could not be dug out before August the way things were looking. A gully had been hacked through the ice by the Indian Army and the trucks were slowly grinding through. It took another day to reach Leh.

The festival had already started. Hemis courtyard was coloured with a pageant of masked figures slowly pacing the traditional theme of Guru Rinpoche establishing Buddhism in Tibet. The gentry of Leh were there in their best aprons and jewellery; the women wore high-crowned hats embellished with velvet. I became involved in conversation with a Zanskari woman wearing a long serpent-like head-dress of huge turquoises which reached down her back. The Zanskari dialect of Tibetan was beyond me apart from a few words here and there, and the 'conversation' was held largely in sign language. She was pleased to hear I was going to trek through Zanskar and insisted I should visit her house near Padum. I never found it.

Roerich's search for stories of Shambhala had brought him to Leh on his long journey from Delhi to Lake Baikal in Siberia. He had spent some time here before setting out on the long and dangerous crossing of Karakoram pass north of Leh, which led to Khotan in Western Tibet. Karakoram is a pass that is unlikely to see any crossing for some time to come, as it is in the war zone on the disputed territory between India, China, and Pakistan.

Roerich was fascinated by the parallels he saw between the final battle in the Shambhala legend and the Armageddon of the Christian tradition. He even recorded a number of legends he had heard in the area of Leh about Jesus (often referred to as Issa).

> In the legends which have the estimated antiquity of many centuries, it is related that Issa secretly left his parents, and together with the merchants of Jerusalem, turned towards the Indus to become perfected in the highest Teaching. . .

Villagers going to market; Everest range in the background

Inside a Himalayan farmhouse

Village in the far west of Nepal

Ang on the Dhorpatan bridge
and Phurba in his robes

Measuring out cornmeal

Rhododendron forest

Children in the far west of Nepal

Kali Bahadur

Lal Kumari

The King and Queen of Lo (Mustang)

The stupa at Lori

Chortens at Tangye.

Lo Manthang
and the Himalaya

Yuma, her mother-in
-law, and cousin

Lori Gompa, Mustang

Yonden in the
Black Hat Dance

Trulzhig Rinpoche

Black Hat dancers in Chiwong temple courtyard

The Sand Mandala is offered to the Nagas at Chiwong

Zopa Rinpoche

Meditating sadhu at Shivaratri

The twiggy bridge to Phuktal

The three-tired pagoda temple, with Ganesh behind

The nuns in the temple and reading *peja* in the snow

The precipitous trail the Hidden Valley

Finally Jesus reached a mountain pass, and in the chief city of Ladakh, Leh, he was joyously accepted by monks and people of the lower class. And Jesus taught in the monasteries and in the bazaars, wherever the simple people gathered, there he taught.

I returned to Kargil with Ang to begin the journey on foot through Zanskar to Kulu. The Kashmiris were an alarming contrast to the cheerful Ladakhis in Leh; perhaps it was the will of Allah that the infidel should be given a hard time. I remembered a remark by a young Ladakhi that if ever he really disliked someone he would pray they be reborn in Kargil. I could see what he meant. Ang said he'd rather carry extra food than haggle with recalcitrant Kashmiri pony men – we could re-stock in Padum. If I had known there was only stale rice in Padum, I might have risked the pony-drivers.

Zanskar was a brown and ochre desert; high and cold with spring shoots barely above the dry earth of the small fields. Beyond Padum the trail followed the course of the river, until it would climb to the Shing Kun La which led to Lahoul. Steep russet cliffs rose on either side of the gorge, slashed on the northern side by another gorge running in at right angles. This was the route to Phuktal Gompa, the sacred spring in a cave high on the cliffside half a day to the north. To reach it meant crossing the river.

Ang paused at the bridge and turned to me. 'You go first?'

If it scared even him it must be as bad as it looked. Ropes of plaited birch twigs spanned the gorge for fifty feet. Four braids bound together formed a footbridge four inches wide, with two braids above for handrails. Upper and lower were joined by strands of thinner braids, some of which had given way and were wafting in the breeze. My rucksack suddenly felt very heavy.

'Maybe we should leave it. You can't swim.'

Ang peered apprehensively at the rock and man-eating river that churned ochre waters forty feet below.

'Swimming – no swimming – same. Dead.'

At least there was a new bridge spanning the tributary and a path to the Shing Kun La on the other side. We would not have to cross the twiggy bridge again. I stepped cautiously on to the twig rope, gripping the handrails as the whole thing sagged under my weight. I had to splay my feet and keep upright; once my pack tipped sideways I would fall as I had a year before in Tibet, when I had almost drowned. After the downslope to the halfway point the four strands had lost their binding and my feet started to slip between the braids. I had to look down at my feet, and the sight of the water rushing beneath was not only terrifying but also disoriented my balance. My throat was dry but my hands were sweating. Then the handrails began to sag. They had started at shoulder height but within a few yards they were almost down to my knees, shifting my centre of gravity to toppling point. It was a living nightmare, this bridge, a dream where every bizarre thing could go wrong. I felt a wave of fear as I realised I could not turn round to go back. Suddenly the handrails began to rise again and I was on the other side, heart pounding and my knees like jelly. At least I would never have to venture on to the dreadful thing again.

Ang crossed with the same difficulties, and we set off fast northwards up the side of the tributary, away from the river and its twiggy reminder of terror.

Two hours up the tributary we came in sight of the new bridge. It was gone, except for the two steel hawsers which had supported it; a tightrope act that was totally beyond me. The nightmare hadn't finished with us yet – we would have to recross the twiggy bridge tomorrow. There was no other way out. My hands began to sweat again. The trail to Phuktal was little more than a trampled mark in the dust and rocks of the scree below tall cliffs. A monk wearing a high-crowned felt hat appeared from around a corner where he had been resting. Yes, he said, he was returning to Phuktal where he studied, and would walk with us. Ahead, the trail led past a line of white chortens and then climbed steeply to the mid-point of a vertical cliff of golden rock which fell sheer to the river. Phuktal was perched like a swallows' nest on a series of narrow ledges in front of the cave. We followed the monk through a maze of narrow twisting alleyways between the temples and the cells of the monks. The place was silent and deserted; all the monks had gone to visit their families for a few weeks. Our guide offered tea and tsampa cakes, which we embellished with the last of the Srinagar marmalade. Hospitality complete, he showed us round the temples and courtyards of Phuktal. One wall of the lower temple was badly cracked and in danger of falling into the river directly below it, adding an almost tangible atmosphere of impermanence to the ceremonial hall. Narrow steps led up to the main temple in the great cave with the sacred spring. The water was crystal clear and very cold, the sole water supply for the whole community.

The temple was moulded on to a narrow ledge at the front of the cave. A low doorway led into a low-ceilinged hall with richly-coloured paintings on every wall and carved pillar. The Buddha statues were illumined by a single butter lamp flickering red on the peaceful golden faces. In the dim light filtering through the small window I could see in a corner a heavy stone tablet leaning against the wall. The sides of the stone were chipped and broken, but the letters carved deep into its smooth face were still bold and clear. The script was English, looking strangely alien in this remote Tibetan monastery;

'Alexander Csoma de Koros,
a heroic pioneer,
lived in this monastery.'

Csoma de Koros – the man who first brought news of Shambhala to the West. Suddenly I had stumbled upon a piece of history, a tangible link with the past and the elusive legend of Shambhala. I could see him in my mind's eye, living in one of the cramped, white-painted cells on the cliffside, muffled in heavy woollen robes against the biting cold, poring over ancient texts by the light of a candle. There was no record of where his search had taken him after Phuktal.

I wondered where my own search would take me now that the traverse was almost over, the outer journey complete. Another few days of hard walking and wispy bridges would bring us to the snowbound crest of the Shing Kun La, the pass that marked the southern boundary of Zanskar. Beyond lay the valleys of Lahoul, and the road that would lead back to England. Unexpected events had moulded my final route and these had been an integral part of the whole experience. The Hidden Valleys – as elusive as ever – still beckoned, but I knew intuitively that what I was seeking would not be found in another linear journey from one point to another. Only a superficial understanding can be gained by just briefly passing through, and clearly the dimension in which the Valleys were hidden could not be perceived in this way. My interest now lay in spending more time in some of the places I had already visited, getting to know them and their people better.

I also wanted to learn more of Shambhala itself from Zopa Rinpoche, and would seek an audience with him as often as possible, even though this aspect of the inner journey might take years. Or, as Rinpoche himself would say, 'perhaps many lifetimes.'

On the far side of the side of Shing Kun La, the dusty hills of Lahoul faded into the distance. The river below the pass was spanned by a single steel cable on which hung a wooden box suspended by a pulley, capable of carrying two people. A wiry Lahouli sat in a hut on the riverbank, operating the cranks which pulled the box back and forth across the river. He explained apologetically that only Ang could be allowed across the rickety contraption. It was, he said, because local people were not considered to be particularly important by those in authority. If, on the other hand, a Westerner fell into the river and drowned, there would be no end of trouble with Embassies, police and so on. It took only ten minutes to convince him that I was unimportant enough to be allowed across. After weeks in the desert, I was indescribably dirty and probably didn't look very important.

PART TWO

The Inner Journey

There are more things in heaven and earth...
Than are dreamt of in your philosophy.
William Shakespeare

Shambhala

10

Mountain Gods

།སྤྲུལ་སྣ་ཚོགས་སྣང་བའི་ཡོ་ལང་འདི།

For several weeks back in England, it was bliss to bath in hot water, wear clean clothes and know that my next meal was a reasonable certainty rather than dependent on luck or fate – or even imagination. It was bliss to get up in the morning and not have to cram a damp sleeping bag into a rucksack, to be able to peer outside at foul weather and have a choice about venturing out in it or not. I published some photographs and articles and gave a few lectures, but most armchair and actual travellers are interested in facts and scenery, and I found I soon grew impatient with this aspect of the journey. Few people seemed to understand the kind of experiences I had encountered. I was not sure I really understood them myself; for every question that had been answered, several more had appeared. I soon became as restless as I had been before the traverse.

Six months later I was back in Nepal.

Events had moved on for the Sherpas who travelled with me the previous year. Phurba and his family had moved to Lukla in the hope of starting their own trekkers' 'hotel' business, but with rent and food eating up every *paise* that Phurba earned from casual labouring it was unlikely he would ever raise enough capital. I felt sad that they had abandoned their peaceful farm for urban squalor and the illusion that they were on the way to something better. Ang and his wife had set up a small *chai* shop in Kathmandu, but they lacked experience and the place had more flies than customers. They were already talking of moving on to Darjeeling. I suddenly realised that while for me the traverse had been a unique experience of learning to survive in the harsh environment of these remote mountains, for them it had been just a small step in the process of earning a living. All they wanted was an escape from the stark realities of a precarious existence.

Pasang had found work as a kitchen boy, but Maila had gone to Kangchenjunga with an American couple who hoped to make a winter ascent. He returned with terrible frostbite in his hands and feet. The following year he went to Tibet as Base Camp cook on a British Everest expedition and was killed in an avalanche at Camp I.

I had returned to Nepal to prepare for a sponsored walk for Guide Dogs for the Blind which I was planning with my friend Julie Donnelly. All the time I was working on this project, I was becoming more aware of the effect so many foreign visitors were having on the lives of the mountain people. The Sherpas were paying a high price for prestige and comparative wealth gained from work in tourism, not only in terms of damage to their environment and community, but also in the ever-present risk to life and limb on climbing expeditions. I knew I would not feel comfortable paying someone to share risks I was taking out of choice on a mountain. I was not even sure if climbing mountains was really what I wanted to do any more.

The journey to Everest with Julie was a challenge of a different kind, a test of trust and friendship as much as of physical stamina and strength of will. For me, it was an exploration into Julie's world of sound and touch as together we discovered the tactile qualities of intricate patterns on carved Mani stones and sat around Sherpa fires answering questions about Braille or walking with Guide Dogs. Although I had already visited Khumbu many times in connection with my photography or guiding work, with Julie I learned to see this hitherto familiar place in a new way – almost as if I had stumbled through a door into another world that all along had lain concealed behind a facade of habitual perceptions. Even as I became her eyes and described the soaring mountains and huddled villages so that she could create mental pictures to carry with her, the very act of observing and describing brought an awareness that much of what we think we 'see' is in fact a projection of selected memories. Now I was seeing everything afresh, and suddenly there were dozens of new details that had previously gone unnoticed.

I began to realise that the change in perception needed to see

Shambhala or a Hidden Valley is not just at the exalted level of the Great Yogic Practitioners of legends and guidebooks. It is a gradual process of unfolding, starting from *now.* It is as if we perceive the world in a series of layers, one on top of the other, and suddenly a certain experience or moment of clarity will render the top layer transparent so that we can see beyond it to the next one – and so on through a continuous process. The mistake lies not in being unable to see all the layers straight away, but in thinking that the one we have reached is *all there is* – something that is fixed and unchanging to which we can cling.

One frozen afternoon at fourteen thousand feet I found myself in the comparatively snug warmth of a tiny woodstove in the Pheriche clinic in the company of the resident doctor and a young American trekker bound for Everest Base Camp. The trekker could not understand why Julie was here if she could not see the mountains.

'What's the point of her coming apart from the exercise? Which she could get at home.'

Attempting to answer questions like this made me realise how difficult it is to express to others something that is not part of their actual experience. It also occurred to me that this could be precisely how the writers of the Shambhala guidebooks might feel about my efforts to understand the meaning of their obscure symbolism.

Even though, in the language of the legends, the Hidden Valley of Khumbu has been opened and colonised, it retains a resilient quality in spite of the changes wrought by people and time. This still beautiful valley would unfold as my ability developed to see its deeper levels, even though not all the layers were necessarily in line with my own projections of how a 'perfect' valley ought to be.

The unfolding continued when I returned to Khumbu a year later. I needed to check out damage to the trails inflicted by a huge flash flood along the Dudh Kosi before guiding a trekking group there. I also intended to use the occasion to research the history of the Sherpas, and for this I would spend more time than usual visiting temples and monasteries. In the Himalayan region these are the main centres of learning and local knowledge. In a land where farming and trading have been the main occupations, to be educated is regarded as a full-time career. The educated people are the monks and village lamas. The monasteries are far

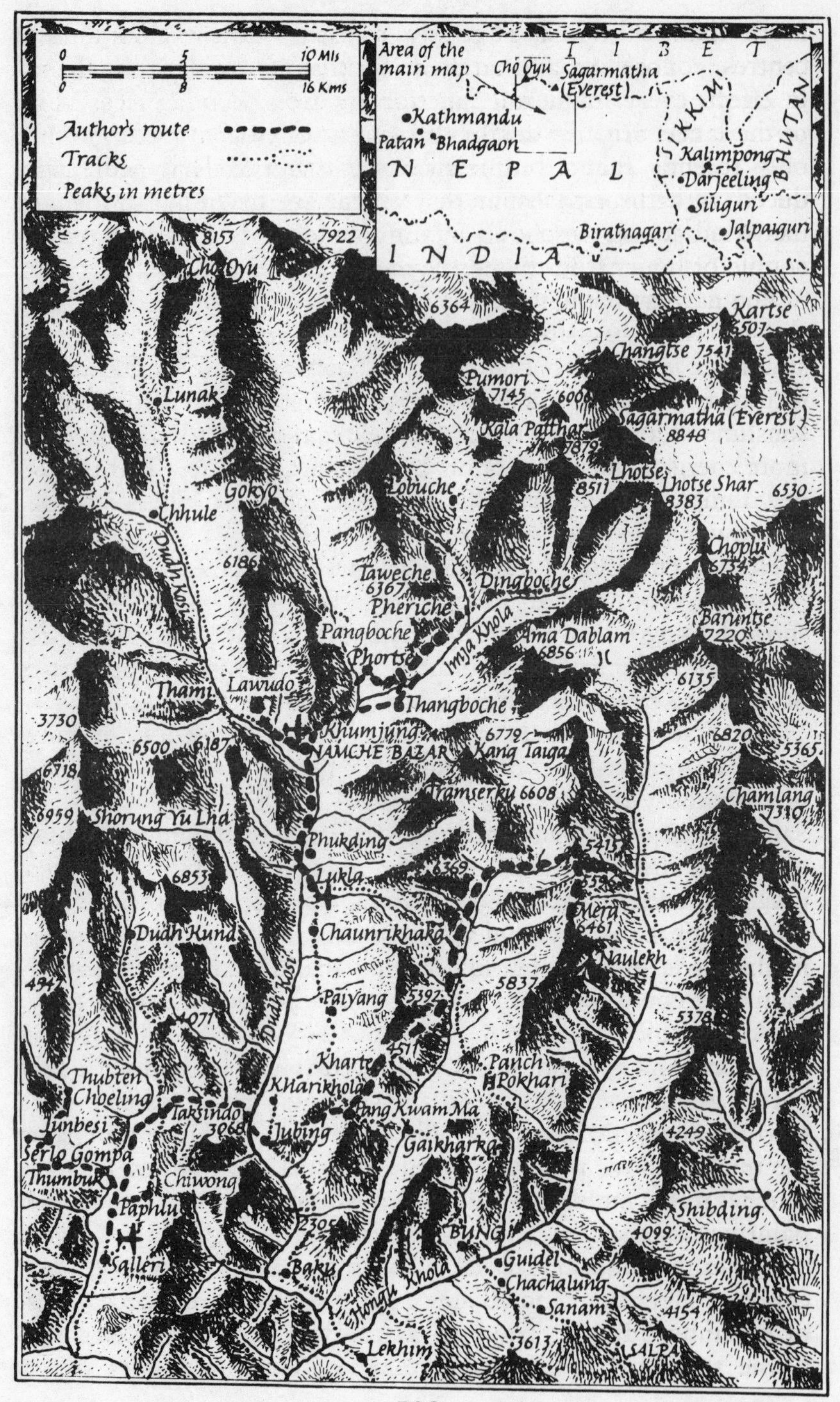
0 5 10 Mls
0 8 16 Kms
Author's route
Tracks
Peaks, in metres
Area of the main map
Cho Oyu
Sagarmatha (Everest)
TIBET
Kathmandu
Patan
Bhadgaon
NEPAL
SIKKIM
BHUTAN
Kalimpong
Darjeeling
Siliguri
Jalpaiguri
Biratnagar
INDIA
8153
7922
Cho Oyu
6364
Kartse
Changtse 7541
Pumori
7145
Kala Patthar
Sagarmatha (Everest)
8848
Lunak
Gokyo
Lobuche
Lhotse
8511
Lhotse Shar
8383
6530
Chhule
Dudh Kosi
6186
Taweche
6367
Pheriche
Dingboche
Chopolu
Pangboche
Imja Khola
Ama Dablam
6856
Baruntse
7220
Phortse
Thami
Lawudo
Thangboche
6135
3730
Khumjung
NAMCHE BAZAR
6779
Kang Taiga
6820
5365
6500
6187
6718
Tramserku 6608
Chamlang
6959
Shorung Yu Lha
Phukding
6369
Lukla
6853
Mera
6461
Dudh Kund
Chaunrikharka
Naulekh
5837
Paiyang
5392
Dudh Kosi
5378
Kharte
Thubten Choeling
Kharikhola
Panch Pokhari
Junbesi
Taksindo
3068
Pang Kwam Ma
Jubing
Serlo Gompa
Gaikharka
4249
Thumbuk
Chiwong
Paphlu
Shibding
2305
BUNG
4099
Salleri
Baku
Guidel
Chachalung
Hongu Khola
Sanam
4154
Lekhim
3613
SALPA

more than churches. They are schools, libraries, community centres, counselling and advisory centres, and retirement homes; in effect, every municipal function focused on one place. Many of the lamas are also doctors of traditional herbal medicine. It is only recently that a business-centred education has been introduced with the establishment of Nepalese medium schools and increased access to schools in Kathmandu. My first stop, only a couple of hours from the airstrip at Lukla, was Rimijung.

The narrow path snaked steeply upwards through pine forest, slithery with dust and pine needles underfoot. The old temple stood in a level clearing barely thirty minutes' walk from the main trail to Everest. An elderly and wizened monk was reading in the sunshine of a small courtyard. He explained that the younger and more energetic members of his community were busy painting the new temple ten minutes away up the hill.

'How many visitors do you get in a year?'

He paused, deep in thought. 'Seven last year,' he said finally.

Only seven out of thousands of foreign visitors had made the short detour to visit one of the oldest temples in Khumbu. I had known of Rimijung's existence for some time, but it had not even occurred to me to go looking for it until now.

The first temple in Khumbu was founded in 1667 by Lama Sangwa Dorje at Pangboche, twenty minutes' walk above what is now the busy tourist route to Everest. Within a few years Lama Sangwa Dorje's two younger brothers had also established temples in Thame and Rimijung. Such were the spiritual powers of Rimijung's founder, it was said that he could stand seven barley grains on top of each other. I could not imagine what practical use this might have, but nevertheless I was curious, and asked the old monk if I could see them.

He mumbled and shook his head. 'No barley.' He explained that Rimijung's decline had been attributed to the fact that the barley grains had subsequently fallen down and gone mouldy. I tactfully changed the subject. Now a new phase was beginning, as the temple above was swarming with workmen putting finishing touches to the building, while several younger monks were already painting murals.

According to local legend, Guru Rinpoche flew from the magic caves of Maratika to the black spire of rock above Kunde, home of Khumbu Yul Lha, god and protector of Khumbu. Guru Rinpoche then foretold that Khumbu would be a Hidden Valley where Tibetans could find a refuge in time of need. Padzin, the son of a god, then discovered and 'opened' the Hidden Valley of Khumbu. He came from Tibet via Rolwaling and the Tashi Lapcha pass and stayed in a cave below Namche, overcoming the bad spirits there. From him, came the Paldorje clan of Sherpas.

Later, the Nangpa La pass from Tibet was opened and more Sherpa families crossed into Khumbu. These forefathers of other Sherpa clans originally migrated from Kham in eastern Tibet and arrived north of Everest in Tingri. (Sher-pa means people from the East.) From Tingri they crossed the Nangpa La in search of fresh pastures for their herds of yak. The area was probably already known as a place of meditation for Tibetan hermits, but the valleys were not settled; this would be in keeping with the conditions of a Hidden Valley. According to the lamas, when a Hidden Valley is inhabited by ordinary people, it becomes 'affected by their karma' and loses its special, magical qualities.

As I descended once more into the Dudh Kosi gorge the devastation wrought by the late monsoon flood became more apparent. A glacial lake high above the Bhote Kosi had burst through its moraine, bringing a fifty-foot wall of rock, mud and water crashing through the narrow gorge. Farms, fields, crops and livestock had sunk into the gaping maw, leaving giant white scars of naked rock reaching barren fingers up into the green hillside. Mercifully the human toll had been low. Warned by the roar of its approach, most people were able to make a desperate scramble for safety. From above, they watched their homes and land disappear for ever.

Sherpas on the trail spoke in hushed voices of seeing the god of the lake rise up in anger and hurl itself in a mass of ice and water at the moraine. Its first victim was the hydroelectric scheme; ten years of foreign aid money and labour which on completion would have brought to an end the Sherpas' dependence on wood for fuel. Some felt uneasy that it would then make them dependent on foreign technology and maintenance technicians instead, but in five minutes the god of the lake made such speculation obsolete.

Removal of the protective forest layer makes such floods and erosion increasingly common in mountain areas where the delicately balanced ecosystem can so easily be upset. Ironically, the lamas had already given warnings of these disasters as the consequence of trespassing into the snow mountains, symbol and abode of the gods. The Reincarnate Lama of Thangboche was particularly concerned about the way that tourism, and mountaineering expeditions in particular, were affecting the relationship between the people and the mountain gods.

'If we go on the mountain and make it dirty with foul smells, the god will become angry and eventually may leave, upsetting the balance of energies in the land.'

The god, or protector of the land, is a focus of spiritual energy for the people who live there. This force keeps the elements and the land in fertile harmony. When respect for the gods is lost, then people once more follow their baser instinct of greed, and cut down too many trees, or from sheer carelessness begin to pollute the streams. Far from being the 'primitive superstition' with which early European expeditions sought to dismiss such beliefs, they represent a stylised and simplified version of an ancient wisdom which provided the laws of basic ecology that kept the Sherpa homeland balanced, productive and fertile for successive generations. It had taken near-starvation in the desert for me to understand the relationships that Zopa Rinpoche had described. Now, with time for reflection, I was looking for logical explanations to support that intuitive awareness I had experienced in the wilderness of west Nepal.

When the gods leave 'in storm, hail, and flood', harmony is lost and the land becomes a desert. Looking at this ravaged wasteland of tumbled boulders and shattered trees, it was easy to identify with the respect the mountain people held for such power. Not for them the packaged luxury of a few weeks of sport and recreation in an attractive mountain area before jetting home to a lifestyle so artificially shielded from the reality of living with nature that many people are simply no longer aware of it. For the Sherpas, it is a matter of life or death. They must live with the mountain and its power; its fragile and precious gift of fertility and its god.

From a Western viewpoint, it does not follow that to climb on a mountain will bring destruction to the surrounding area. From an Eastern viewpoint, there is less of a distinction between an action and its associated state of mind. Changes in mental attitudes bring other actions. Commerce with climbers and trekkers involves more than just a requirement to trespass on sacred mountains.

I reached Namche as the Saturday market was coming to a

close. Ragged porters from the lower villages were counting handfuls of grubby rupees while others were slinging empty carrying baskets on to their shoulders and heading downhill before the freezing high altitude night was upon them. A few local dogs were sniffing round bloodstained patches at the top of the market area – all that remained of the buffaloes which had been slaughtered early that morning after plodding for several days from farms in the lowlands. Although the Sherpas leave the killing to the low-caste Hindus who bring the animals to market, there are still some who feel that, as Buddhists, even to allow it to happen within their village is offensive to the gods, not to mention the negative karma of killing. However, fresh meat is in demand from tourists and popular with newly-affluent Sherpas, and most people prefer to keep their misgivings to themselves.

Below the market area the main trail from the valley looped and curved between steep walls and houses. A line of zopkios, laden with bales of firewood, moved slowly upwards, prodded into greater efforts by a khaki-clad policeman from the National Park. He saw me taking photographs and attempted, unsuccessfully, to move out of sight by scuttling behind the loaded animals. He was clearly embarrassed about being on record with such a large amount of firewood. It was he and his colleagues who enforced the ban on cutting firewood within the National Park, and while the police themselves have plenty of wood brought in from outside, there are many Sherpas who strongly resent the regulations because they cannot afford to fetch fuel from such a distance.

Although the rules were originally meant to conserve diminishing forests, the situation has become unbalanced. Local Sherpas who work for trekking groups have to sit and shiver around sputtering kerosene stoves in their own homeland, while porters bring up to twenty basket-loads per day to the bigger lodges to feed, warm, and provide hot showers for independent trekkers.

Ang Khandi runs one of the best lodges in Namche, with large pine-panelled rooms and two upper storeys of guest bedrooms. In the dining room a large steel-topped clay oven heats a water tank; it is fuelled by successive loads of firewood portered in from the forests a day's journey away, outside the Park boundary.

I settled into a comfortable corner by the fire, holding out cold fingers to be warmed. The menu was more Western than Sherpa, offering rare delicacies such as fried potatoes, scrambled eggs, and carrot cake, as well as the indigenous *dal-bhat* and Sherpa stew.

Several other visitors were already ensconsed, working their way through cups of hot chocolate and heaped plates of jam pancakes. The conversation revolved mainly around how to get the cheapest deals out of various lodges along the Everest route, all of which were competing heavily for a slice of the tourist market. After a few customary exchanges I chatted to Ang Khandi while she kept me liberally supplied with hot chocolate.

Khandi could remember the days of the early expeditions, before there was a National Park. 'When Khumbu was our own place, things were different. Nepali people stayed in Kathmandu; no police up here. Sometimes we see in bazaar, sometimes Tibetan people come. And we have our own wood, our own policeman looking after the wood.'

'What did the wood policeman from the village actually do?'

'That time, we can all cut wood up here – but not too much. Just enough for what we need. Some greedy people take too much, so they have to come to village meeting and say "very sorry" to all the other village people. Because wood is for everybody, and their children after them.'

'That's all they had to do? "Very sorry" – that's all?'

Khandi laughed. 'Nearly all! And they have to bring enough chang to make everybody happy again.'

What an excellent way to pay a fine! Provide enough home brew to get the entire village tipsy enough to forgive you. Unfortunately the idea is not likely to find much favour with our own Home Secretary.

'So why was the Park necessary if everything was so well organised?'

'Two things. Nepali government say, "This is government forest, not Sherpa forest." And many expeditions come, all pay much money for extra wood. Sherpa people have no control over the forest any more. So greedy people make a lot of money selling wood. Soon everyone worried. They were storing wood and selling wood, because everyone afraid nothing left for them. Then National Park comes, and many Nepali policemen come, saying, "No cutting wood." Now we get from outside Park. Very expensive. Not so bad for us, but very hard for poor people.'

More than anything, Khandi's story showed how delicately balanced the system had been, so that even apparently small changes in markets or ownership would result in changes in attitudes which had devastating results. The Park regulations had brought problems of their own, but had at least saved remnants of high altitude forest. Now that the beliefs of the Sherpas are changing, there is no way to go back to old systems that worked in the past; somehow they will have to come up with something completely new. This tiny, once self-sufficient kingdom is evolving rapidly and often painfully into a busy twentieth-century tourist resort. It is impossible to reverse the process and turn back the clock, to lament commercialisation and the passing of a romantic image. Sherpas have quickly grown to like smart clothes and warm living rooms, news on the radio and the possibility of a university education for their children.

From Namche, I took the trail out of the west side of the village. As I passed the temple I heard voices from inside the courtyard. I stepped through a narrow doorway into a crowd of Tibetans. From their exhausted appearance and overheard scraps of conversation I gathered they had just crossed the Nangpa La pass from Tingri on the north side of the Himalaya in Chinese-occupied Tibet. Most of them seemed disoriented, although a few looked more self-assured. Perhaps they had been here before on trading trips. Bags and bundles were stacked against the walls. One man had a dirty bandage wrapped round three fingers of his right hand; he had probably suffered frostbite during the crossing. He was smoking a cigarette, one indication that a Tibetan had grown up within the Chinese system. Only those in the system could afford to buy them, and would also not know that it is considered highly offensive to smoke in a Buddhist temple. I was about to tell him to put out his cigarette when the caretaker monk caught my eye and shook his head.

'Best not interfere with Tibetans,' he said. 'They've had a bad time, and some of them can get rough. They are terrified of being sent back.'

'Who would send them back?'

'Police. If they catch them. That is why I let them hide here. I hear the Chinese shoot them if they are sent back. I hope they will be moving on soon.'

'But they're refugees, they can't be sent back. What about the Geneva Convention and international law – '

The monk stared at me blankly. Clearly conference tables at

the United Nations were a world away from the stark realities of this frozen border area in the mountains.

'Do many of them come over?'

'More and more. Sometimes every day. Then if the weather is bad, too much snow, it stops for a while.'

Things must be pretty bad in Tibet to make people come over the pass in these conditions, I reflected, feeling saddened that the once magical Valley that Guru Rinpoche had hidden was no longer a 'place of refuge for Tibetans in time of need'.

I puzzled over the police policy for most of the morning, hoping the Tibetans made it through to wherever they were going, wondering what kind of pressure the Chinese were putting on the Nepalese government to treat refugees in this way.

Lama Sangwa Dorje, the founder of the oldest temple in Khumbu, had 'flown in an instant' to Thangboche in his search for a suitable site on which to build. The journey took me considerably longer, especially the last long pull up through the pine forest. The vertical rock wall of Kangtaiga towered above; from this angle it is truly the 'horse saddle snow mountain' of its Sherpa name.

The temple stands on a rocky ridge and is framed by snow mountains, with the Everest massif as a final backdrop. Legend has it that when Lama Sangwa Dorje landed here from his spectacular flight, he slipped, and so decided that although this beautiful place would eventually be the site of a significant temple, it would be better to build the first one somewhere else. The rock which bears his slipping footprint and handprint cracked in the heat of the fire which destroyed the monastery in 1989. The half which bears the handprint was moved to the new Cultural Centre.

Legendary characters in the East are more complicated than their Western counterparts because they have so many reincarnations, and Lama Sangwa Dorje is no exception. His fifth incarnation founded Dza-Rong-Phu Gompa in Tibet, on the northern slopes of Everest, relatively close to Khumbu. This made a tremendous difference to Sherpas who had previously had to travel deep into Tibet, sometimes as far as Kham itself, in order to receive Buddhist teachings. As Abbot of Dza-Rong-Phu, the fifth incarnation persuaded a Sherpa hermit finally to establish the temple at Thangboche.

The present Lama of Thangboche is the reincarnation of that

hermit. His life's work has been to maintain the delicate balance between the economic reality of the flood of climbers and other tourists, and his attempts to preserve traditions and culture which had protected the Sherpa community and environment for centuries. He had explained this tradition to me in terms of the relationship between the people and the mountain gods.

'Each place has its god and the people living there pay attention to it. Khumbu Yul Lha is the god of Khumbu; we perform the ceremonies which focus the energy of our spirit on the mountain and its god. The power of the god causes the energy in the earth, the fertility and the supply of water, to flow in harmony with the needs of man. There are many gods, on Chomolungma and Gauri Shanker, on different mountains and in different places. In the practice of Buddha-Dharma, by meditation training, our spirit becomes clear, and clean, and at this point great energy becomes possible for us. It was with this power that the first lamas controlled the gods.'

The Lama's words implied that these protector gods are regarded as powerful neighbours to be placated and respected but are not, ultimately, objects of worship. They were the focus of the shamanistic Bon religion of Tibet which preceded Buddhism. Rather than try to suppress this indigenous form of nature-spirituality, Guru Rinpoche and other early Buddhist teachers incorporated it into the wider view that Buddhism encompasses. In the stylised language of the texts, he 'overcame the Demons, and made them solemnly swear to be protectors of the Dharma'.

In the West, most of us take for granted our academic education with its emphasis on abstract ideas. For people scratching a living in the inhospitable deserts and mountains of the Himalayan region, it is easier to relate to abstract ideas through symbols such as those provided by protector gods. Although most Westerners regard these as superstitions, it is difficult to come up with convincing explanations for why so-called primitive communities have preserved a balanced and healthy environment while the supposedly sophisticated and educated West is causing so much pollution and damage. Perhaps we, too, need symbols and images to help us relate to our family, community and larger environment. Perhaps we need to rediscover our own Earth-Goddess traditions, because while science explains the mechanics of how things function, it does not give inspiration to work constructively with what we know.

How did the lamas have the prescience to conserve resources *before* they became scarce? How could they predict so accurately what would happen when the first trickle of what was to become a flood of foreigners first arrived in these cold high valleys? Perhaps it is worth investigating whether these gods are simply an anthropomorphism, a paradigm for the wisdom of the lama and the shaman that provides a link between people and their environment. Or is there some primordial force or energy prowling these wild places, something that can be perceived by those with the 'wisdom eye' as easily as they could perceive Shambhala or a Hidden Valley? As Western science refines technology to measure more and more phenomena, I cannot help wondering if one day we will find it transferring ancient symbolism from the department of primitive superstition to the department of respectable scientific fact.

The meditation cave of the Lama's previous incarnation is on the opposite side of the gorge, above a cluster of tiny herders' huts. To reach it, I descended a little-known path which snakes and plunges through rhododendron forest. A log bridge crosses foaming ice-melt of the Imja Khola and leads to a long haul up the far side. From high on the hillside, Thangboche appears almost to float above the gorge in a dark sea of pine forest.

I followed a perched trail that contoured the steep tussocky hillside, heading north towards Pangboche. The only trees here were a few high altitude dwarf junipers and my only companions a herd of silky-haired wild goats which were quite unconcerned by my presence. The Buddhist villagers have never hunted them, and with the thousands of tourists safely channelled on the other side of the valley, they had no reason to be afraid of humans.

The first sight of Pangboche is a cluster of tall, full grown junipers around the temple in the shelter of a small valley. An ancient Sherpini with creaky knees fumbled with an enormous key and led me inside. In the main hall she moved aside some of the dark wood panelling below the shrine and proudly showed me an extraordinarily shaped rock set in the cavity behind. She explained that Lama Sangwa Dorje had flown from his unfortunate landing at Thangboche and arrived safely on this spot. He sat down to meditate on the best place to build a temple, and his powers of meditation were so strong that he left the print of his backside in the rock on which he sat. The shape looked exactly right, but the venerable Lama must have been considerably overweight.

As I walked back along the perched trail I looked across at the massive rock walls which separate Khumbu from the Hinku valley to the east, beyond which Khembalung is said to lie. The Mingbo La pass leads through from this side, steep and snowbound. Even now it is only attempted by strong parties with mountaineering equipment and experience. Lama Sangwa Dorje is supposed to have visited Khembalung to collect medicinal plants as he was renowned as a doctor of Tibetan herbal medicine. He may well have used his considerable powers to cross this and the other high passes beyond, which bar the route to Khembalung.

Earthbound, I descended the steep stone staircase which enterprising Sherpa engineers had spiralled ingeniously down an almost vertical cliff face. Skirting the lower slopes of the black rocky spire of Khumbu Yul Lha, the home of the god of Khumbu, I reached Kunde as dusk was falling.

I called on Temba, a talented painter I had come to know well. He was in his usual perch on a broad window sill of the family chapel at the far end of the house, working on a canvas stretched over a wooden frame. He had been deaf since birth, but communicated well with a series of eloquent hand gestures, showing me where he had just painted a yeti high in the stylised mountains of his picture. We sat and chatted with our hands while his mother plied us both with endless cups of sugary tea. Temba is one of the few local artists who paints landscapes instead of bodhisattvas, but in the same traditional style. His pictures remind me of several pictures of Shambhala I have seen, with the same strangely shaped mountains and fertile valleys.

Next morning I cut across the boulder-strewn slopes west of Kunde which lead to Lawudo. The Bhote Kosi (River from Tibet) foamed and growled, unseen, far below in its gorge. Dapple-shadowed sweet smelling pine forest gave way to open winter heath with the flame red spiny bushes of berberis bright against the deep blue space of the gorge. A raven floated below, wings reflecting sunlit snow on the barrier of peaks to the south.

High above the valley shadow the mountain hermitage of Lawudo basked in sunlight. Dusty switchbacks led steeply upwards, giving only an occasional glimpse of the temple beyond the towering shoulder of the hill. Halfway up, I stopped to rest, gazing absently into the space below. A tall English girl slithered suddenly into view, descending the dusty path. We both seemed surprised to find the hillside inhabited by someone other than birds and the wind. She said something about taking a break from her retreat to do some shopping in Namche, but I wasn't really taking in her actual words. It was her eyes that caught my attention; sparkling with a light and energy you rarely see in the world of busyness and preoccupation. She seemed so happy to be alive, slithering and skipping down the scree. I watched the little cloud of dust follow her and pondered that long meditation retreat must have a lot going for it if that was what it could do for you. I never expected to see her again but, strangely enough, I did – some years later in London. She was running a meditation centre and also a housing project for homeless people. Overwork had dimmed the sparkle, but the memory of it was still there, just below the surface.

I turned and continued the long slow plod upwards. A small wooden door led into a paved sunny courtyard, perched above the huge valley as if floating on an island above a deep ocean. The south side of the valley was a vertical wall of rock, throwing a pool of purple shadow in the depths of the gorge.

Samten, Zopa Rinpoche's sister, came out of the small kitchen, her broad features creased in a huge smile.

'So. You have come again. Come, there is tea.'

She wrung my hands in welcome and led me inside to be plied with tea and potatoes. Rinpoche's mother sat in her usual corner reciting mantras, her main occupation since going blind several years before. I answered Samten's questions as best I could between mouthfuls of tea. She was eager for news, as she left this isolated hermitage only occasionally to go shopping in Namche.

'How is Rinpoche's health? Is he still teaching in Europe and America or has he had time to do the retreat he was hoping for? Did you hear if he will have time to visit us here again soon?

When she was eventually convinced that I could not eat any more potatoes, she led me to a small courtyard above the temple.

'Look. Only finished a few months ago, and already someone has done retreat here!' She proudly showed me the new meditation hut that had been built for Western students to use for retreat.

From here, a narrow path led across the hillside to another paved courtyard in front of a huge sloping overhang which formed a natural cave. A white-painted stone wall had been built under the overhang, closing the entrance to the cave except for a small window and a low wooden door. This was the meditation cave of the Lawudo Lama, Zopa Rinpoche's previous incarnation.

Inside, I was able to stand upright under a high rock ceiling which had been painted a deep blue. A carved wooden shrine ran along the back wall, piled with statues, postcards and other pictures of Buddhas and Lamas. In the corner by the small window was the carved wooden meditation box, where Zopa Rinpoche in both his present and previous incarnation had spent his daily round of meditation. There was no bed, only this carved seat; Zopa Rinpoche's previous incarnation had passed beyond the need for sleep, and Rinpoche himself had also reached this state, even when on exhausting teaching tours through several time zones. The cave was light and homely, with an atmosphere that was at the same time peaceful yet full of inspired energy.

The Lawudo Lama was a married practitioner of the Nyingma lineage who spent the last twenty years of his life meditating in this cave. He had been the spiritual guide of many of the local people whom he served and helped. His energy was said to be inexhaustible. When he passed away, some reported seeing auspicious signs, such as a rainbow appearing in a clear sky, usually taken to mean a meditator had attained enlightenment. A year after his death in 1946, a child was born in the nearby village of Thami. As soon as he could talk, he would insist, 'I am the Lawudo Lama', and would attempt to crawl up the steep trail leading to the cave. Eventually, after his fraught mother had retrieved him from the hillside several times, she decided to consult senior lamas in the region. After the traditional tests they confirmed that the child was the reincarnation of the Lawudo Lama.

One time, when I was planning an expedition to follow the Tamba Kosi river to its source in the Rolwaling, Rinpoche had drawn for me a careful map of the high valley, showing the location of a hermit's cave.

'You have to climb up a steep hillside between many boulders, and the cave is under a huge triangular-shaped rock.' He marked the spot with a small triangle. 'I went to that cave when I was spending some time in the Rolwaling.'

'Were you doing meditation retreat in that cave?'

Rinpoche smiled. 'No. Playing most of the time. I was only about seven years old. I was very naughty. When my mother first sent me to learn to read Tibetan texts in our local monastery, I kept running away and coming back home. So she sent me with my uncle to study at a monastery in the Rolwaling on the other side of the Tashi Lapcha pass – then it was not possible for me to run home. I could only return with my uncle, because we had to climb up through water and falling rocks to reach the top of the pass. After seven years in Rolwaling, I went to Tibet with my two uncles. We crossed the Nangpa La pass and walked all the way to Tashi Lhunpo monastery, then to Phagri. My heart was set on going to study at Mindroling, the greatest Nyingma monastery in Tibet, but when we reached Phagri I met a monk from a Gelugpa monastery and decided I would stay and study there.'

'When did you leave Tibet, Rinpoche?'

'When the Chinese took over Tibet, we were close to India and there was no immediate danger. I spent several months in my first meditation retreat, but by the end of the year, when the threat of torture was imminent, we decided to escape. One day we heard that the Chinese would reach our monastery in two days' time, so we secretly left that same night. We had to cross one mountain to reach Bhutan. It was very wet and often we could not see the road, so things were difficult as we slipped and sank in deep mud. We had to avoid an encampment of nomads on the border because we had heard that some of them were Chinese spies. If they had seen us, it would have been difficult for us to escape.

'Finally we reached India and the refugee camp at Buxa Duar. I continued my studies there, and I also made much effort to learn English. I once thought to learn the whole dictionary by heart, not realising this was not the best way to learn a new language! At Buxa, I, and many other monks, caught TB and smallpox because of the climate and poor conditions. In the hospital I found a very nice Indian man who helped me to learn English. When I recovered, I continued my studies.'

Rinpoche met his teacher, Lama Yeshe, in the refugee camp and together the two lamas returned to Nepal and established Kopan monastery on the outskirts of Kathmandu. Rinpoche also honoured a promise made in his previous incarnation to establish a monastery school for local children at Lawudo itself. However, keeping children warm and well fed at 13,000 feet presented logistical difficulties, so the school was moved to Kopan.

Lawudo relapsed once more into peaceful tranquillity, a place of individual retreat for those with the vision and stamina to make it up to this remote oasis in the mountains. My own experience of Lawudo comes very close to that special, magical quality that is described in the guidebooks to Khembalung. Somehow the tranquillity of that place soaks into your very being, until your mind seems to become a reflection of that peaceful stillness.

I used to think that 'me' was located within my skin, while everything outside it was 'other', but spending time in quiet and remote places brings an intuitive awareness that 'I' cannot be so simplistically defined. It is a feeling that goes deeper than the ecological principles of our interaction with our environment; our dependence on trees to produce the oxygen we breathe, or on plants and animals to provide our food. It can be expressed logically in the principle of 'dependent origination', which is fundamental to Buddhist metaphysics. All phenomena, both subjective experiences and external objects, come into existence in dependence upon causes and conditions; these are external causes in the form of physical objects and events, and internal causes such as cognitive and mental events. Like most people, I find images and symbols easier to relate to than abstract concepts, images like that of the universe represented as Indra's Net, with a jewel at each connection reflecting every other jewel in the whole interlinked web of relationships.

It was a conversation with Zopa Rinpoche which showed me that just as the mountain gods were seen as valid within the wider view that Buddhism encompasses, so our own science of ecology has a valuable place within this wider view.

'Just because it is not written in the traditional texts exactly in the kind of specific detail for this particular (Western) culture at this time, it doesn't mean you ignore it. If you really look, if you really understand the essence of the teachings, then it is all there. Therefore you should follow in your daily life as much as you can, within your understanding and awareness of these issues. So for example, when the teachings say you should practise non-harming, then this you should do on every level, as far as your understanding of these interconnected environmental relationships allows. But do not become distracted into thinking you can create a complete solution to all these problems by acting in this way. The Buddhist view of interdependence is vast, more all-encompassing than just the aspect you see in the environment, and the only complete solution to all problems will be when all sentient beings are enlightened.'

As usual, Rinpoche had given me a balance between the ancient wisdom and current everyday practicalities. And although I had not even asked – in words – he had also explained why so many people become discouraged and depressed as a result of their practical or emotional involvement with environmental issues. So often conservation efforts fail because of the power of vested interests, and for each one that succeeds there are so many that do not. If we allow ourselves to become attached to the material result of these efforts, inevitably we are going to become discouraged. If we can see it as part of our practice of something more all-encompassing, then we begin to see the value of the motivation and action as part of our spiritual path. Any practical success we achieve on top of that is a bonus.

This balance also underlined a growing awareness of how often so-called environmental projects are focused solely on the short-term benefits for humans, with no concern for the additional needs of all the other species which depend on a particular area for their very existence – for example, cleaning a polluted river with the motivation only to provide a water supply for a nearby city. Long-term solutions can only come from a realisation that everything is a valid and essntial part of the whole.

Rinpoche's own plans include a huge statue of Maitreya, the Future Buddha, itself a synthesis of a focus of inspiration and practicalities such as a reforestation project and the providing of employment in Bihar, one of the poorest states in India. The Governor of the province made a welcoming speech acknowledging this synthesis:

'. . . Technological and scientific development is getting out of balance with our moral and social performance. And hence instead of exercising control over biosphere we must exercise control over ourselves. . .'

The Buddha taught that suffering comes from craving and attachment, and that if this greed ceases, so will the suffering it brings. This is true of the state of our own minds, and is reflected in the larger environment of which we are an integral part. The Buddha's followers gave up their personal property and lived on alms; the very word which later became translated as 'monk' originally meant simply, 'one who receives a share'. One does not need to study long and complicated texts to see that more sharing and less grasping would lead to a more harmonious world.

11

Mountain People

།དྲག་མི་སྦུབ་ཆུ་ཡི་རི་མོ་བཞིན།

Khembalung haunted me for the next few years – time spent in an ever-quickening blur of 'busyness' establishing a small travel company with Lhakpa, who had been the guide on the long trek to Everest with Julie. Ironically, Lhakpa and I had spent the first weeks of our acquaintance arguing about almost every aspect of how things should run. He was a very different character to any of the guides and sirdars I had worked with before. Although his roots were in the mountains, he had several business interests in Kathmandu as well as years of experience in organising large expeditions and tour groups. He took care of his clients with an urban sophistication. They were not there to dictate to him but to be told, politely but firmly, what was good for them – and I was no exception. No deferential 'Yes, memsahib' for Lhakpa. He would look me straight in the eye, call me by my first name, and tell me how he was going to run things. In most ways, this was a great relief as I had never felt comfortable with the role the Raj had cast for itself, but the result was two experienced, well-qualified professionals, each with a demanding job to do, and both with their own, often very different, ideas of how things should be done. It was just as well that we were able to see the funny side of the inevitable arguments. Somehow, in this process, that safe compartmentalisation of caste difference of which the Nepalese are so aware, became blurred. The working relationship became a romantic one, and within a year we were married, as well as running an adventure travel company together. To my surprise, this was extraordinarily successful and the business grew quickly into a series of expeditions to the most remote and inaccessible corners of the Himalaya. It became a matter of professional pride to be the first to gain access to some of the least explored areas.

At the back of my mind, I knew I was hoping to discover one of the legendary Hidden Valleys, yet something held me back from attempting an expedition to Khembalung itself. Perhaps I was heeding the warnings in the guidebooks, or knew deep down that the time was not yet right. There were few occasions when I could take a break from the scramble of running a business to research new projects and itineraries, and I used these precious windows of opportunity to re-connect with my interest in the Hidden Valleys.

Meanwhile I tried to put into practice my environmental ideas. There had to be ways in which tourism could replace declining traditional trade without causing so much damage. Awareness of the situation should lead to positive input. We began by sponsoring small tree plantations in marginal areas, took groups of trekkers to festivals and supported a project to give hill children access to higher education.

Climbing expeditions still presented ethical problems until I discovered Mera Peak. Regarded by most Sherpas as 'high altitude trekking' rather than serious climbing, it is without the dangers of avalanches and cornices that are typical of most of the comparable peaks. It reaches an altitude of 21,612 feet and stands at the head of the beautiful and uninhabited Hinku valley, a whole mountain range away from the crowding and commercialism of Khumbu. Lhakpa's family knew the mountain well, as their village, Pang Kwam Ma, perches high on a rocky ridge that forms the watershed between the Dudh Kosi and Hinku. What better reason could there be for planning expeditions there?

The Hinku valley is also one of the approaches to Khembalung.

I stood on a rocky outcrop above Pang Kwam Ma watching the light fade on the cluster of white-painted farmhouses and the snow and rock peaks of Kwangde and Karyolung beyond the cloud-filled valley of the Dudh Kosi. Banks of cloud were spilling over the forested ridge and the pass above the village, surging up from damp forests east of Hinku and trailing in ragged streamers into dark rhododendrons on the steep hillside.

The expedition Sherpas had finished pitching tents in front of the house belonging to Lhakpa's parents, and were repacking the high-altitude equipment which had been hastily bundled together at the Paphlu airstrip only two days before. The plane had arrived late, so precipitating the rush to get started. I had felt nothing but relief to have arrived at all. Of all the terrifying experiences on offer to those who use mountain flights regularly, landing at Paphlu is quite the most nerve-wracking. Due to wind currents, the plane flies straight towards the huge cliff below Chiwong, executing a last-minute banked turn which all but brushes the tops of the pine trees with a left wingtip, then flings itself at a runway constructed of uneven dirt and stones. Compared to this, climbing mountains seemed reasonably safe.

By the time darkness fell, all the equipment had been repacked into thirty-kilo loads for porters to haul up the ridge the following day, with ice axes and crampons well separated from gas canisters and climbing ropes. As I watched this demonstration of efficiency and professionalism, it was hard to believe that scarcely thirty years ago no Khumbu Sherpa would have dreamed of climbing mountains for a living, or for any other reason. These days, most people's idea of a Sherpa is a slightly updated version of Tenzing brandishing a flag at the summit of Everest – as if such mountain dwellers had never done anything else.

After their migration from Tibet, the early Sherpas augmented their high altitude subsistence farming by trading between lowland Nepal or India and Tibet, using the 19,000-foot Nangpa La as a crossing point. The closing of the border by the Chinese in 1950 and dwindling trade prospects coincided with the opening of Nepal to an increasing number of European mountaineering expeditions. Poorer Sherpas who did not own land in Khumbu often migrated to Darjeeling in search of labouring work, and early Himalayan climbers employed Darjeeling Sherpas to carry loads on their forays from India into Sikkim and Tibet. It soon became clear that the Sherpa's experience on trading journeys in rugged terrain and his toughness and stamina made him ideal for the job of carrying large amounts of equipment up a mountain.

Khumbu families, although mainly landed middle-class farmers, were soon lured into climbing by the buying power of foreign currency which offered, in local terms, extremely high wages. The early climbers considered the use of bottled oxygen essential for Europeans to succeed in reaching 8000-metre summits. The assault would suffer from the law of diminishing returns if those hired to carry it needed to use it for themselves, so Sherpas became an integral part of this equation. Some expeditions ran into problems when their Sherpa employees, faced with the reality of actually going up the mountain, expressed strong reservations about trespassing on the home of their gods. This irritating 'superstition' could usually be overcome by the expedition leader paying out more money – and no doubt the Sherpas soon learned the profitability of having pangs of religious conscience only at appropriate times and places.

Lhakpa was always guarded about his reasons for giving up the big expeditions in favour of trekking. He showed little interest in religion but talked in a general way about the risks involved. Somehow I doubted this was the whole story. He was not the cautious type. Only a few weeks before this expedition to Mera Peak he had insisted on clinging to the outside of an overloaded jeep crashing its way down the dry riverbed near Pokhara – and had fallen under the rear wheels. No sooner had x-rays revealed – miraculously – no broken bones than he was back in trouble again, parting company with his mount in a high speed horserace with a friend. He was ambitious as well as adventurous, and although he had several business interests in Kathmandu it was generally accepted that, provided you survived, a series of big expeditions brought quicker returns – if you were strong enough to make it to the summits. Lhakpa had already done that, and still he had quit.

Living and working with Lhakpa was like living on adrenalin for most of the time. There was always some new escapade in which to become involved, and the access we each found to the other's culture opened up many new possibilities. Rarely did I stop for long enough to become aware of the frantic speed of our existence. Spanning time zones as well as cultures, life was exciting so long as we could keep up with the pace. There was nowhere – in Nepal or Britain – where we could both settle and feel happy and secure. We were seeing less and less of one another, but while we both had the energy for all these new adventures, we did not look too hard into the future.

It was getting cold outside, so I went into the house in search of tea. Lhakpa was already ensconsed, regaling his parents and sisters, as well as several other friends and relations who had drifted in, with tales of remote expeditions and the traffic congestion in Kathmandu. His father had been to 'Nepal' (as he still called Kathmandu) only once, thirty years before.

I had the usual difficulty resisting the privilege of being treated as an honorary man, invited to sit on the carpeted bench by the window. These prestigious seats in the household were reserved exclusively for the men. The window glass was tacked in loosely with small nails, so that an icy wind squeezed through the gaps in a latticework of draughts. It was much warmer and more comfortable to sit in the humble places on the floorboards around the fire, where Sherpa women were allowed to sit.

Lhakpa was cheerfully downing the cupfuls of chang pressed on him by an enthusiastic elder sister.

'I went to a big party at the Sheraton with Dawa. He had *so* much money to spend! Very lucky man. They reached camp 6, and the client was too tired to go for the summit next morning. So he pays Dawa *one thousand dollars* to dress up in his clothes, take the camera to the summit, take pictures of himself looking like the client, then come straight back to camp 6 again. Okay, so he has some trouble getting the client off the mountain next day, but one thousand dollars for a couple of pictures!'

Everyone was laughing. Most Sherpas see little difference in hauling the clothes to the summit with or without the client inside them.

'You had plenty money when you came back from Jannu,' said his sister, prising his hand from the top of the cup and filling it again. 'But you had a broken leg as well, so no wasting your money at the Sheraton!'

Lhakpa made a wry face. 'Jannu. Never again.'

I was intrigued. 'Because of a broken leg?' He'd broken two ribs the year before, falling through the flat mud roof of a Tibetan house on which we had pitched camp, and landing in their kitchen – as much to the Tibetans' surprise as his. This had in no way diminished his enthusiasm for camping on flat roofs, or any of the other activities which seemed to me to invite further injury, such as riding on bus roof-racks and abseiling down crumbling cliffs without a helmet and on belays which were the climbing equivalent of a wing and a prayer.

He shook his head. 'Not just the leg. The way it happened. We were leaving camp 6 for the summit. There were three of us carrying oxygen for the three clients who were about fifteen minutes ahead of us. We could see them going up the ridge above the avalanche which came down on us – wet snow mixed with blocks of ice. There was nothing I could do. Anyway, I blacked out.

Maybe I was near the edge of the avalanche because when I woke up I was half buried in the ice. I was lying on my side and my leg was broken and I couldn't move.'

'How did you know it was broken?' asked his sister. Everyone in the room was listening with rapt attention, although they must have heard the story before.

'Because it hurt! And I could see a lot of blood soaking into the snow. So I just lay there.'

'Why didn't your friends dig you out?'

'Dead.' He stared morosely at his cup. 'I couldn't hear anything. Couldn't feel anything moving on the end of the rope. So I lay there all day, thinking soon I'll be dead too, but by the end of the day it hadn't happened. Then the sirdar came up from base camp with some of the other Sherpas and they carried me down. It took weeks for the leg to mend.'

He rolled down a red woolly sock to reveal a patchwork of scars just below the knee. 'See, there was a bit of bone sticking out here, and another bit there – '

My stomach was beginning to turn somersaults, and I changed the subject. There was something in the story that didn't quite make sense.

'Why didn't the climbers come and dig you out if they were so close when the avalanche came down?'

He shrugged. 'It was good weather. Good chance. They went to the summit.' He didn't seem surprised, and I began to understand why Sherpas liked to have their own 'friends' along on expeditions.

The attentive audience encouraged Lhakpa to go on with his stories. 'Trekking peaks are okay. Short, straightforward, and I'm in charge of the way things get done. So long as the group do as they're told.' He took a long swig from his glass and the ever-watchful sister bustled over and filled it before he could get his hand across the top.

'There was one time when they didn't and it was a disaster. We were crossing Tashi Lapcha from Rolwaling. As usual, we had trouble with the Rolwaling porters. They carried to the bottom of the pass, refused to go across, took their wages and went home. So I fixed up with the Sherpa staff that we'd ferry the gear over to Thame – there wasn't much – and hire more porters on the other side.'

Even now, Tashi Lapcha is one pass I have no ambition to cross.

Lhakpa was still talking. 'We went up to Parchemo Base Camp at the top of the pass and put up the tents. I told the group to stay there and rest while I went back for the gear. I said I would guide them up Parchemo the next day. Hours later, when we got back with the loads, I could not believe what had happened. They had gone straight off to climb the peak and a rope of three people had fallen. They were just carrying in one man with a broken leg and one beautiful French lady was dead. So I had to go straight off to Namche to radio for a helicopter. Namche is three trekking days from where we were. I thought I could do it before morning so I took a torch and ran down the pass.

'I walked all night and when I reached just beyond Thame I suddenly found myself in the middle of a herd of yaks. They were everywhere – running all over the hillside, on the trail, everywhere. There was no moon and suddenly one would appear in front of me in the light of the torch, take fright and leap off into the bushes on the hillside. None of them had their bells on, so I couldn't hear them coming.'

'What did you do?' asked Lhakpa's sister as she poured more chang.

'When I got to Namche I radioed for the helicopter and crawled off to PK's lodge for some tea and breakfast. I was absolutely finished. There was a friend of mine already in there and he looked exhausted too. "Oh, I've had a terrible night," he said. "I was taking my yaks up to Tibet on a trading trip and I hadn't bothered to get a permit – you know how much baksheesh they want for permits these days – when suddenly the police came after me with a torch, coming really fast. I left the yaks and ran for it. I hid in a cave until they'd gone. Then I had to try to round up the yaks again. It was terrible! There was no moon and I'd taken the bells off, so I was running around in the dark. Couldn't see anything, couldn't hear anything – I was at it all night." '

Lhakpa grinned. 'Well, I thought I'd better tell him. "That wasn't the police, that was me. I was running down to Namche to radio for a helicopter. I wondered where all those *cheterika* yaks had come from." He wasn't angry. We had another drink together and laughed at the joke on ourselves. Then I had to go back to base camp to evacuate the rest of my group.'

We were joined by a tall, middle-aged Tibetan from the farmhouse next door. Rhi Tsering was married to the sister with the jug of chang, and he was soon being liberally supplied as well.

He would join our group the following morning for the rest of the journey to Mera. He herded yaks in the upper reaches of the valley in the summer and knew the area well, as did the rest of the Sherpas on the team. However Rhi Tsering had been in the high pastures only a few months before, and knew exactly where all the caches of delicious high-altitude potatoes were buried. The yak-herders often store surplus from their summer crop in deep pits to protect them from frost, so that they have some for the start of the next season while the new crop is still growing. Nobody minds if they dig down to the bottom of a pit the following spring to find, instead of potatoes, a tin full of rupees and a note saying, 'I've eaten your potatoes, here's the money.' At least, that was what the Sherpas assured me when, several days later, they ate the potatoes and left the tin of money in the pit before filling it with earth again. Presumably the money had to make an extra trip home for more supplies worthwhile, but as I was not up there when the herders arrived at the highest pasture, I could only speculate.

I was half-dozing in the warmth of the fire, my nose tingling with the smoke and the occasional whiff from the basket of red chillies strung to dry in the heat above the flames, when a familiar word in the mumble of conversation in Sherpa made me sit up.

'Did you say Khembalung?' I asked Rhi Tsering.

The soft lilt of his Tibetan accent was a subtle contrast to the chatter of the Sherpas.

'Yes, I went there once. Long time ago.'

'You went all the way to *Khembalung*?' It couldn't be possible. Could it?

'Long time ago,' he repeated. 'My cousin Urkien was going across from here to Makalu with an expedition and he asked me if I wanted a porter job carrying supplies. I was quite young and I'd never had that chance before. There were hardly any expeditions and treks in those days.'

'Which way did you go?'

'We went up Hinku valley to Mera La and crossed the pass. Then we cut eastwards across more snow passes, then through valleys with very thick forests where none of us had ever travelled before. It was a long way, and we ran out of food. After seventeen days we had no strength to walk any further. Those of us who had leather boots took them off and boiled them in water until they went soft like a kind of glue. We ate that, and somehow managed to walk on and reach the Arun. It was horrible stuff. Stuck to our mouths so that we couldn't even talk to each other!'

'So you went right through Khembalung?'

'Yes, we did. We call the whole place Khembalung and that's where we went. The secret part is somewhere there I suppose, but I didn't see it. That's only for great lamas, not ordinary people like me. Hardly anyone has been across that way, and after what happened to me I do not want to go again!'

I thought of the warnings in the guidebooks and the gung-ho expeditionaries tramping across the unseen frontiers of the guardian deities. Perhaps they had been lucky to get out at all.

Lhakpa's father had been listening intently to Rhi Tsering's story. Now he edged closer into the group around the fire, the flames casting a ruddy glow on his wrinkled face and deep-set eyes. He had been the most powerful shaman in the area until a few years before. Although he was now retired, his bearing still displayed the authority to which he was accustomed. When he spoke, everyone listened.

'I went up that way once, when I was a young man. There used to be a small gompa high up on the other side of the Mera La. It had been abandoned and was falling into ruin, so some of us decided we should go and fetch the statue from it and bring it back here to put in our village temple. Four of us – all strong men – crossed the Mera La, and we found the Guru Rinpoche statue in the ruin. We wrapped it carefully in cloths and then we carried it back over the pass and got it safely past all the crevasses and snowfields. But as we brought it down through the upper yak pastures, instead of our task becoming easier, the statue grew heavier and heavier, until the four of us could not even lift it from the ground. We were puzzled, and a little bit frightened, so we began to unwrap the coverings. The statue was weeping, tears flowing down the painted face. I was sure it was about to speak to us.'

There was a long silence in which nobody moved. Then Lhakpa's father continued.

'It was clear that Guru Rinpoche did not wish to leave the valley – and besides we couldn't carry him any further. So we built a shrine in a cave on the mountainside, and put him in there. It is called Druk-phi-Puhk, the Cave of the Dragon, because there is a great dragon flying across the cliff opposite the cave. We made offerings of burning juniper branches, and then we came home. After that, whenever I went up the valley with my yaks, I would burn juniper in the cave.'

Khembalung suddenly seemed to be much closer than before. It had always been a fascinating myth, but something abstract and unreal. Now it was emerging as a real place, visited by several people – albeit with great difficulty. Lhakpa's father, perhaps because of his shamanic experience, seemed to have a sense of that mysterious dimension that led to the inner levels of Khembalung, but his story was finished as he wished to tell it, and he would not divulge more.

People were starting to drift back to their homes. I too began to think that my sleeping bag would be warmer than my place between the fire and icy draughts from the door. Lhakpa nudged my arm.

'Do you want to stay here some more? The *Lha-wa* is coming to see my mother. Either go now, or stay to the end.'

I shivered involuntarily as prickles of apprehension crept up my spine. The powers of the shaman had been fascinating to research and observe from a distance but a Western education and background does little to prepare you for living with it.

Two years before, in England, Lhakpa had started having long, painful and debilitating headaches that no painkiller would alleviate. He would withdraw into himself, as if he knew what was happening but could not communicate it to me, or to any doctor. Finally he started talking about it, explaining that his father was about to give up his duties as shaman.

'He is old. His body is not strong enough to walk with the gods, and they are leaving him.'

'So what has that to do with your headaches?'

'They want me.'

I was appalled. It is risky enough in Asia when someone begins to make a connection with the gods – or with whatever it is they are in communion. Several times as a young man Lhakpa's father had disappeared for days on end, and would afterwards have no recollection of the time he had been away. More than once the family had to call on the services of the shaman from the next village in order to locate him, so that someone could be despatched to fetch him home again. Finally, he had to undergo a period of intense training with several experienced *lha-wa*, in order to learn the rituals which would bring this strange condition under control. Without this, he would almost certainly have met his end on one of his amnesic forays into the wilderness beyond the village. There were stories of a few who had not gained control of the condition in time, and had fallen off a cliff or into a river.

But in provincial Buxton?

It was unthinkable. Heavy lorries, railways, and muggers were but a few of the reasons why even one session of wandering off without knowing who or where he was would probably have been Lhakpa's last. And where in twentieth-century rural Derbyshire was I supposed to find an experienced shaman to give him the appropriate training?

'No,' I had insisted. 'Definitely not. Cancel that idea. Tell them to go find somebody else.'

Lhakpa was as indignant as the headache would allow. 'This is *not* my idea. It is *theirs*.'

I consulted various 'experts' on shamanism, all of whom were of the opinion that the gods in question were local to the Himalayan region, and their territory could not possibly extend as far as the United Kingdom. This did nothing to alleviate the headaches. Either the gods were waiting to pounce as soon as Lhakpa returned to Nepal, or such definitive logic does not apply to the mysteries of shamanic trance. The headaches grew worse, Lhakpa became more and more miserable, and I became increasingly worried. I began to realise the vast unknown I had entered by becoming involved in a relationship with someone who usually seemed so familiar and down to earth but who would always belong to a world that contained another dimension, one that from a Western viewpoint simply *cannot* exist, and yet does. It was my first hovering premonition of the disaster to come, but I quickly pushed it aside.

In desperation, I packed Lhakpa into the car and took him to see an eminent Lama who was on a visit to England from Dharamsala. As suddenly as they had started, the headaches stopped, and never returned.

A few months later we received a letter from Lhakpa's brother, saying that the gods had chosen a young cousin who had become the new shaman.

However, for the purpose of curing his wife's stiff and aching back, Lhakpa's father had called upon an older, more experienced man from the next village. He looked quite ordinary when he arrived, soberly dressed in tweed jacket and cap not unlike any farmer in rural England. It was only after he had finished the generous helpings of rice and vegetables offered by the family that he began to unwrap the cloth bundle he had brought with him.

I edged into a position where I could see better, still unsure whether I had stayed out of curiosity or because I needed to know what might happen to Lhakpa when the gods were in the house. I was glad the expedition members were all safely in their sleeping bags in the tents outside.

I had heard that one of the local *lha-wa* used the skeleton of a snake, which would appear as a real, wriggling snake when placed on the body of the sick person, while another could make an egg bounce up and down on the tip of his *phurba* (ritual wooden dagger). This man took out among several small ritual objects a five-faced crown made of intricately carved and painted pieces of wood. The five sections were joined with loose strings; these the shaman draped around his shoulders like a mantle.

When he had arrayed himself in his ritual clothes and set up a small shrine to the gods on which he piled offerings of barley, rice, and chang, the *lha-wa* sat down in front of it and began to intone in a strange, undulating chant that seemed to contain no recognisable words. Someone handed him a long-handled temple drum which he beat rhythmically with the chanting. The tempo increased to a crescendo, when suddenly the man's body twisted and shook – and the crown stood upright upon his head. The chanting eased and quietened, and the crown collapsed and fell neatly on to his shoulders again. This performance was repeated three times, while I struggled to find a logical explanation – elastic, wires, magnets – anything that could possibly achieve the result by mechanical means. There was none, and I found myself becoming mesmerised by the pulsing drumbeat and the whining, keening chant.

All at once, everything stopped. The drum was quickly removed from the shaman's hand as he began to speak. His voice was completely changed, and he was speaking in Tibetan. Rhi Tsering the Tibetan moved forward and took on the role of translator, as none of the Sherpas could speak Tibetan as fluently as the god who was speaking through the medium. I discovered afterwards that the *lha-wa* himself in his normal state of consciousness spoke very poor Tibetan. Five gods in turn arrived to have their say, each with a different voice and personality. The fifth and last one had a strong predilection for good chang, insisting on more each time the cup was refilled and drunk dry. It seemed rather unfair that the god should taste all the chang but the unfortunate *lhawa* would have to endure the hangover the following morning.

The essence of the instructions for Lhakpa's mother was that she had somehow managed to upset the local *Naga*, the serpent spirit of water, guardian of the village biological balance, and her back would only recover after she had performed several ceremonies of apology and cleansing at its sacred places by spring and tree. Fortunately these could be done on her behalf, as she was in too much pain to get up from the bed in which she lay. When we returned to the village two weeks later she was bustling round the house supervising the chores just as she had always done. Meanwhile, as soon as her 'prescription' had been concluded there was an excited shuffling forward of the other people in the room, eager to have a glimpse of their personal future before the shaman came out of the trance. This was done by pressing a pinch of rice to the forehead and handing it to the shaman, who tossed it violently in the air and then pronounced the appropriate future for the donor. Most of this concerned the welfare of children, animals, and crops, and was too long term to be able to check with any certainty.

When my turn came I found my hand shaking, and passed the plate of rice hastily along to the next. The future hovered dimly on the periphery of my own vision, and I knew I did not want to see it more clearly.

We left the village early the following morning and struck out left from the pass, following the spine of the ridge northwards towards the mountains. Walking near the back, I could see the line of porters ahead and started to cut off what seemed to me an unnecessary loop in the trail, but Lhakpa called me back.

'Not that way. Over here.'

'Why not? It's quicker.'

'Over there is where we burn the dead people.'

I gave the stock reply without thinking. 'You're not afraid of ghosts are you?'

Lhakpa shivered. 'I saw too many up here once.'

It was the first time he had ever admitted to being afraid of anything. Cremation grounds are the traditional places for hermits to contemplate the impermanence of human existence. I had always assumed they pondered upon a few remaining ashes and used their imagination to meditate on the frailty of this human existence and the need to stop wasting it in frivolous pursuits in order to get on with some serious spiritual practice. I had not thought of it in terms of a daily confrontation with hordes of lingering ghosts. The few other cremation spots I had passed in the course of my travels had never given me any cause for concern – in fact the view was often particularly fine from these hilltops. I might have felt differently on my own in the middle of the night, but I hadn't tried that.

'Are you sure you really saw anything?'

'Too much. My fault really. We were up here for a funeral puja and my friend told me I could ask one of the lamas to show me the spirit world. I was quite young, and I was quite interested in seeing new things, so I just asked. And the lama stood up and made an arch with his arm like this – ' he demonstrated by holding his arm away from his body in a downward curve like an arched doorway – 'and he told me to look through the door into the other world. So I did. It was terrible. There were all these *people* coming up the hill behind the lama. Some of them looked quite reasonable but others were horrible – they had all kinds of bits missing, and some of them had plants growing out of their mouths and others had smoke all around their heads – '

'Come off it, Lhakpa – you're just trying to scare me.' I was already heading back towards the detour in the route.

'You asked, so I'm telling you,' said Lhakpa, striding out as if to show he was at least less scared than I was. 'Anyway, I noticed that all these people were trying not to turn sideways towards me and suddenly I saw they were kind of flat, and they were trying to hide this from me. They were getting really close, and I started to back away – and the lama noticed and snapped his fingers and shouted "Phat!" and they all scrambled and pushed each other and ran away.

'After that I was too scared even to go outside for a pee in the dark. I kept making my brother come out with me. My Dad thought I was going crazy and asked what was the matter. When I told him, he was quite angry. He said, "Young people like you shouldn't be watching scary things like that!" He told me to go and talk to our village lama about it.'

With difficulty I suppressed a comment about lack of parental control on video nasties. Lhakpa would not have appreciated it.

'The lama explained that the reasonable looking ghosts were the ones that had died quite recently and the messy looking ones had been around a long time. Ghost bodies are different – when they get old bits just fall off. They get untidy. And they don't like people seeing they are flat.'

'What about the trees and the smoke?'

'Those are people who smoked a lot when they were alive. Then the tobacco plant grows back out from where it was all sucked in, and the smoke stays around their heads so they can't see properly. He told me if I said lots of mantras the ghosts wouldn't do me much harm anyway.'

'So did you feel better after you talked to him?'

'Not really. I felt worse.'

'Why?'

'I was smoking twenty a day at the time! All I had to look forward to was *that* after I died. I tried to stop a couple of times but I really started wanting one again, and that was it.'

'And then along come Julie and I and start lecturing you about the state of your lungs. I thought you made the decision to give up pretty quickly. . .'

Lhakpa marched off ahead and I walked on in silence. Rhi Tsering was waiting for me over the next rise. He had been appointed 'back Sherpa' that morning, so it was his responsibility to round up stragglers.

'Do you stay away from the cremation ground, same as Lhakpa, Rhi Tsering?'

'Mostly. Just say many mantras.'

Not just for ghosts. I thought. His rosary was hardly out of his hands except when he was eating or pitching tents.

'Lhakpa had some trouble up here when he was herding yaks,' said Rhi Tsering.

'What happened?' I was half convinced I was about to hear the story of childhood trauma that had precipitated the illusion of seeing ghosts later on; Eastern mystery solved by Western psychology. I should have known better.

'Lhakpa, he was up here with his father's yaks, and there was another boy called Ang Kitar. And one day, Ang Kitar disappeared. Lhakpa had to come home all alone and tell our family. The search party went back, and there was that particular smell . . . we knew he had been taken by the *tel-mang*.'

'What's that?'

'They are like small brown . . . not quite monkey, not quite bear . . . they live in jungle places away from people. If you see them first, it's okay, but if they see you first, they steal your mind.

You don't know where you are or who you are. So we had long time and much work to find Ang Kitar. We went very far from here, through the jungle until we came to a lake the colour of blood. There was a cliff by the lake, and the boy, we saw him on a ledge halfway up the great cliff. It was not possible to climb either up or down to him, so two of us had to go home to fetch a climbing rope so that we could get him back.'

'So how did the boy get up to the ledge?'

'*Tel-mang*,' said Rhi Tsering softly, as if that were explanation enough.

It was as if people out here danced to a different tune. You can see the dance, but you cannot hear the music, so you make your own interpretation – and it all seems to fit until you stumble on pieces that suddenly reveal themselves. I found myself glancing over my shoulder, half expecting to catch a glimpse of a little brown furry creature trying to steal my mind.

We walked for three days through wild and uninhabited country, more beautiful and lonely with each day further into the mountains. Above the mossy tangle of deciduous forest were open meadows surrounded by dark pine trees and splashed with the reds and pinks of rhododendrons. The air was sweet and heavy with the scent of tiny pink daphne flowers which grew in profusion – it was too far for the paper-makers to travel up here to collect the bark for their trade.

An old man twisting rope from slivers of bark stopped to chat in the afternoon sunshine. His yaks grazed nearby, close to the rough stone shelters which protected them at night from prowling leopards and other predators. Later in the spring they would make their way up to the high pastures at the very foot of the glaciers. There were few home comforts in the shelter for the herder, who was watching my appraisal of his dwelling with curiosity. He picked up the rope and began twisting again, holding it firm between bare toes while his strong knobbly fingers twisted the stubborn bark into place. His face was brown and wrinkled by the high altitude sun, his jacket patched homespun wool. He seemed so much a part of this lonely valley, unlike us intruders with our city-made nylon quilted jackets and vibram-soled boots.

The following day we reached the Cave of the Dragon, perched above the valley where the grass and juniper dwindled and the black rocks broke through the thin soil like heavy bones pointing upwards. Opposite, across the green sweep of the valley, a massive rock wall towered vertically to the heavy snowfields above. A white vein of quartz curved sinuously across the dark upper slabs, poised like a snake about to strike, or a dragon flying across the cliff – towards Khembalung. Outside the cave, strings of tattered prayer flags whipped in the sharp breeze, cold despite the thin sunshine. A crude wooden door had been built into the low cave entrance. Inside, the statue stood in the centre of a stone ledge, with a row of offering bowls and an unlit butter lamp ranged in front. The painted eyes of Guru Rinpoche gazed through the doorway at the lonely valley where he had chosen to remain. The Sherpas laid sprigs of burning juniper on the stone slab, then we left the cave to its isolation and moved on towards the pass.

A few days later we stood on the crest of the Mera La, but we saw nothing. Swirling mist obscured the mountains beyond in drifting curtains of sunlight and shadow.

'Maybe one day we'll go all the way to Khembalung,' I said.

Lhakpa laughed. 'You can eat boiled boots if you want to, but I'd rather have my *dal-bhat*.'

Rhi Tsering grinned and added a comment of his own in Tibetan. I did not catch the words – they were probably unrepeatable – but I understood the emphatic agreement.

I fell silent, staring into the shifting ribbons of light and wondering what lay beyond. I made up my mind that I would go to see Trulzhig Rinpoche, the High Lama of Solu Khumbu, and ask his advice about attempting to find a way through the mountains. I knew he had a worn copy of an old Tibetan guidebook to Khembalung – a strange blend of geographical directions and spiritual symbolism which would take the skill of a High Lama to interpret. At least the Rinpoche would know if the dire warnings of the danger of trespass could be avoided in some way.

In fact, I was back on Mera with another climbing expedition before I managed to see the Rinpoche. It made little practical difference because the schedule only allowed time for the actual ascent, not for diversions into unexplored valleys. This time the sky was a brilliant clear blue, with the jagged edges of the mountains etched white against the distance, right across to Kangchenjunga. Khembalung was as elusive as ever; it could lie anywhere in that sea of peaks and valleys, white and shade.

12

The Kingdom of Lo

།དེ་ཆུ་ཡི་རང་བཞིན་ཆུ་ལས་འབྱུང་།

Tsering Gombu riffled through the heavy sheaf of papers and scratched his head in perplexity.

'This is what the lawyers gave us,' he explained, 'but they seem to make everything so complicated.'

I was not surprised that Kathmandu lawyers were far more absorbed in detail than their English counterparts, and I could tell it would take a while to reshape the draft into something both legal and useful as a basis for a co-operative. I could also tell that Tsering Gombu would much rather be back in the deserts of his homeland, riding off on another trading trip to Tibet, or overseeing his farm.

It was more than three years since Tsering's wife Yuma, a princess of Lo, had adopted me as her sister. This ceremony of acquiring an extra brother or sister is a part of Tibetan tradition and carries the same obligations as those involved with a blood relative. I discovered that I was now related to the entire Royal Family of Lo, including the King himself. It took a while to get used to the invitations in almost every town to drink tea, eat dinner, borrow horses and visit other Tibetan aristocrats to whom I was, apparently, also related.

That first expedition to Lo* had been the result of years of negotiations with the Nepalese government. As the first foreigners to enter this Restricted Area for more than thirty years, we had a unique opportunity to get to know many of the people who lived

*Described by Audrey Salkeld in her book, *People in High Places* (1991)

there. Even though on the next few expeditions I was preoccupied with looking after clients or academics conducting research, I was also able to spend some time with several members of my newly-adopted family.

Until then, all I had known about Lo, or Mustang as it is called in Nepalese, was hearsay gleaned from a few Lo-ba friends who spent their winters in Kathmandu. According to them, Lo is a feudal Tibetan kingdom ruled by a Dharma-Raja, or religious king, who lives in a magnificent palace in the centre of Lo Manthang, a great walled and gated city far to the north of the Himalaya on the borders of Tibet. Perched above the steep valleys and rivers are fortified towns and Buddhist temples, while in the cliff faces are labyrinths of interconnected caves and secret shrines. There are no roads, electricity supplies or modern buildings. There are hardly any trees save for desert thornscrub and dwindling juniper forest in a few shady valleys. Lo was traditionally divided into seven areas, each under the jurisdiction of a member of the Royal Family, who collected the King's taxes.

Although the kingdom lies on a desert plateau just inside the Nepalese border and has the same language, religion, culture, and architecture as Tibet, it has been a part of Nepal since 1795, when the 'Gurkha' kings of Kathmandu conquered the western kingdom of Jumla and unified what is present day Nepal. Lo had previously been defeated by the Raja of Jumla and obliged to pay an annual tribute, which was transferred to Kathmandu after the defeat of Jumla.

Lo was allowed to remain a kingdom within a kingdom, and then in the early 1960s the Nepalese government designated it a Restricted Area when the Tibetan Khampa freedom fighters, backed by the CIA, used this northern province as a base from which to carry out raids on Chinese strategic targets in Tibet itself. When the CIA withdrew their support for the Khampas, China put pressure on the Nepalese government to remove these troublesome fighters from their desert stronghold. No guerrilla bases remain in Mustang, but there had been no Western visitors since the French anthropologist Michel Peissel visited the kingdom at the time of the Khampa activity.

When news leaked out that the Nepalese government, hoping to earn extra foreign currency, was planning to open Mustang to tourism, I felt an obligation to help my unusual 'family' to protect their country from environmental damage and the danger of being taken over by sophisticated commercial interests in Kathmandu. Forming a co-operative seemed a good starting point.

Anyone who has never attempted to get a disparate group of mediaeval Tibetan aristocrats to organise themselves into a committee and deal with the mountains of paperwork presented to them by high-powered Kathmandu lawyers would have difficulty imagining just how complicated and long-winded a process this could be. There were times when I felt we were simply going round in circles.

Finally we drafted proposals for a locally-run co-operative designed to protect the natural environment, architecture and culture, including paintings and artefacts. Before anything could be formally implemented, the draft had to be shown to the King of Lo for his approval. Although officially only a constitutional monarch within the Nepalese democratic system, his influence was still considerable and his patronage essential if the Lo-ba were going to work together on any project. Royal assent was by no means guaranteed, for His Majesty did not always approve of the more radical ideas of some of his younger relatives. There were one or two on our newly-formed committee who had already been keeping a polite and respectful distance for the last couple of years in case they fell any further into disfavour. These domestic feuds would have to be healed if we were to progress, and the nervous looks that were being passed around at the very suggestion indicated that this was not going to be easy.

Legal negotiations in Kathmandu finally over, Tsering Gombu suggested that he and his friends return to the capital, Lo Manthang, to present our ideas to the King. They would go on ahead and meet me with horses at the nearest airstrip of Jomsom. On horseback, we could make the return journey to Lo Manthang in less than two weeks, and I would be back in time to take my scheduled group to the Mani Rimdu festival in the Everest region.

The lush dampness of Pokhara seemed a mocking reminder of the dust and dryness that was waiting on the other side of the Himalayan rain shadow. Scarlet gladioli and purple bougainvillaea splashed deep rich colours against orange marigolds and green parrots among heavy jungle foliage, heightening awareness of the empty desert that would take their place so quickly the next day.

The tiny aircraft lurched, dropped, and recovered in the churning air currents of the Kali Gandaki gorge. The snow-capped summits of Annapurna and Dhaulagiri towered on either side, as we bobbed like a cork on an invisible turbulent sea. The thin line of the river threaded its way between cliffs and valleys covered with tropical jungle which soon gave way to dark pine forest as the mountain rain shadow swung into view. There was more lurching and bumping as turbulent air was exchanged for the rough dirt runway at Jomsom and the plane screeched to a halt in a cloud of ochre dust.

I spotted Tsering Gombu waiting in the crowd by the airstrip – or more accurately spotted his smile. He grabbed my bag and headed for Om's Home, the best hotel in town. It was run by a friendly Thakali innkeeper known as Vishnu, who seemed to be on good terms with most of the visiting Lo-ba despite the legendary rivalry between Lo-ba and Thakali.

The last time I had been in Jomsom the entire establishment had been taken over by a film company from Bombay shooting scenes for a four-hour epic called *The Hero*, having decided that Jomsom was a reasonable look-alike for the badlands of Afghanistan. Most of the cast were clad in sinister black leather jackets and dark glasses and galloping through the stony streets on rented horses, trying to look as much like Afghan bandits as their portly build would allow. Now, at the beginning of winter, the dusty town seemed almost deserted.

Tsering's uncle, Gyalwo, was feeding the horses tethered outside. Although not much older than Tsering – probably in his late thirties – Gyalwo rarely travelled beyond the borders of Lo and kept to a traditional style of dress more typical of his father's generation. He wore his hair wound around his head in two long braids entwined with strands of red silk. A wide-sleeved Tibetan chuba was slung casually over one shoulder. Tsering Gombu himself followed the style of most men who travelled abroad to work or trade, wearing ordinary jeans and a quilted ski jacket. I wondered idly, as we worked our way through several cups of tea in Vishnu's dining room, whether the effect of allowing tourists into Lo would be that the young – isolated for so long – would in future want to wear Western fashions like the visitors, or whether they would revert to exotic Tibetan style for the benefit of the tourist trade.

Several of Gyalwo's friends from Lo Manthang who were on

their way to Kathmandu for the winter to look for work were drinking tea in the dining room. Most of their conversation centred on the possibilities for business opportunities once Lo was opened to tourism. Since the border with Tibet was closed by the Chinese, the Lo-ba had lost their already diminished salt trade for ever, and new suppliers from India had quickly filled the deficit. Now the only trade was in sheep and goats brought down from Tibet for the Kathmandu market, and the carpets woven by Tibetan refugees in Kathmandu brought north to sell to the Tibetan nomads. This was not enough to supplement the subsistence farming of buckwheat and radishes, and most Lo-ba men were forced to spend their winters in Kathmandu or Calcutta to augment their incomes. Small wonder the promise of a new tourist industry right on their desert doorstep brought new hope of restoring trading prospects closer to home. I could not resist the wry thought that there might have been similar speculation among the gods and Nagas of a Hidden Valley when they heard a prophecy that some great *mahasiddha* would soon come and open their Valley to the outside world. Although I had not heard any legends referring to Lo as a Hidden Valley, the qualities I had encountered on my previous visits seemed to echo descriptions in the guidebooks.

The main concern of the Lo-ba was that outside entrepreneurs from Kathmandu would move in and take over control of the tourist trade. Vishnu himself had elaborate plans to start a helicopter service and a chain of luxury hotels. It was inevitable that a sophisticated Thakali would come up with a far more grandiose scheme than the Lo-ba themselves could conceive of, or would want. I wondered how they would take to this kind of intrusion. I noticed that little thought was given to the environmental effects of most people's ideas, whether grandiose or not. Perhaps a certain amount of damage has to be done before enough people realise the need for protective measures.

In the absence of helicopters, horses were the fastest means of transport beyond Jomsom. Gyalwo saddled ours which were still waiting patiently tied to the wooden rails outside the hotel, and packed our kit into ornate leather saddlebags. I had come prepared for several days of hard riding Tibetan-style and tied my sleeping bag over the saddle for extra padding. Tibetan saddles are made of wood and despite a beautifully woven Tibetan carpet underneath to protect the horse, and a tastefully matching piece of carpet on top to protect the rider, in my experience an extra layer of padding is essential.

The ugly sprawl of Jomsom's government buildings was soon behind us and it was barely an hour along flat riverbed to twisting streets and covered alleyways in Kagbeni. A party of overweight Hindu pilgrims from Bombay plodded breathlessly along the undulating trail that ran beside the river. They were going to find it even harder on the steep uphill stretch to their destination at the shrine of Muktinath, at 14,000 feet – another 4,000 feet of climbing. They would make their traditional offerings of rice and marigolds at the one hundred and eight waterspouts and the sacred inner spring with its mysterious blue flames. Then they would struggle thankfully down again to a kinder altitude at Jomsom. Only a few of the really determined *sadhus* (wandering holy men) would make the far longer and more difficult journey to Damodar Kunde, a lake regarded by Hindus as sacred to Shiva, which lies beyond the deserts and high passes of Lo.

My resident's visa precluded the necessity of a special permit, but there was no one at the border checkpost to cast even a glance at my passport. For a while we followed the main trail high on the east bank of the Kali Gandaki, crossing several small ravines by means of rickety wooden bridges. One of the ravines dropped steeply to the crumbling cliffs overhanging the river where we had almost lost our Liaison Officer a few months before.

The first I knew that anything was amiss was when one of our Sherpas had come running back down the trail to announce that the Liaison Officer's horse had fallen off the bridge and down the ravine. Naturally assuming the rider had been attached to it at the time, I ran down the trail to look for him, fearing the worst. Fortunately, his tolerance of hard Tibetan saddles had run out shortly before the bridge and he had been leading his mount on foot. When I arrived at the ravine, he was standing on the bridge looking very shaken, still clutching the reins which disappeared under wooden support trusses. All that could be seen of the unfortunate horse was its head jammed in the corner between the truss and the rocks of the ravine, and one rear hoof twisted up behind it at an impossible angle, caught between two timbers. Sherpas and porters were swarming around the bridge and the ravine, trying to loop lengths of rope under the creature's belly. I stood frozen, trying to make the decision to tell them to stop before one of them was kicked over the cliffs by the terrified animal's flailing hoofs. All at once everyone started shouting, and at the count of three, each grabbed a rope, or any part of the poor creature's anatomy that came to hand, and heaved. The horse appeared back on the bridge, flicked its tail, and wandered nonchalantly off down the trail, with no sign of a scratch, let alone the broken leg I was expecting.

Our sirdar let out a sigh of relief. 'I'm glad we got it out. The owner would charge me double its price if we damage it.'

This time we crossed all the bridges without mishap, but not without a twinge of vertigo as images of the horse slithering towards its doom superimposed themselves on each ravine as I crossed. I was relieved when Tsering and Gyalwo swung left to take the short cut straight up the riverbed. This involved crossing back and forth over the river as it meandered in loops over the flood plain. Even on horseback it was not long before wetness of the feet extended to well above the knee.

Behind us, the great rock and snow wall of Nilgiri soared above the clustered buildings and red temple of Kagbeni, a seemingly impenetrable barrier barring the route south. It was hard to imagine how the first intrepid Tibetan explorers found courage to keep going to the foot of these huge mountains, and determination to fight their way down the Kali Gandaki through jungles and gorges to tropical lands beyond.

After a couple of hours I could see the fortifications of Tsuk ahead, above sandy cliffs beside the river. Only a couple more crossings and I could look forward to peeling off soggy socks and thawing my freezing feet while wrapping my hands around a steaming mug of tea. I arrived at the next crossing a little ahead of the other two and hesitated.

'We're at the wrong place – it's too deep here.'

'Go on – go on! It's okay,' encouraged Tsering Gombu.

I turned back to the river. Great waves undulated over a deep section on the far side as the water swung hard against a shingle bank. I was already half-turning to get out of the shallows when the other two urged their horses in with a yell and a splash. Mine took the cue as if it had been prodded with burning embers, and with a sudden leap it too plunged into the icy water. There followed a frantic series of images and sensations as waves seemed to rear up above us and an icy torrent surged over horses and riders alike. I felt certain we would be swept away. Tsering and Gyalwo were whooping and yelling and suddenly we were heaving and scrambling up a steep shingle bank on the far side. Rather to my surprise, I was still attached to my horse, and was soaked only to the waist. It was a short canter to Tsuk across flat pebbles in a chill evening wind. It seemed strange to reflect how insignificant my wet socks had suddenly become now that everything else was soaked through.

Tsuk comprised two fortified clusters of houses separated by a tributary of the Kali Gandaki. We headed for narrow streets in a grove of willows directly above the river, and tethered the horses in the walled courtyard outside Ram's house. Being related to both Tsering and Gyalwo, Ram was another of my newly-acquired relatives. Most Lo-ba take Hindu names for travelling 'abroad' to Kathmandu where people find Tibetan names difficult to pronounce. Ram had grown accustomed to using his, and I never found out his Tibetan name. He welcomed us in and plied us with salt tea and apples while we sat and steamed by his fire. Ram, as a member of the aristocracy, owned several walled orchards on the outskirts of the village.

'Ram, why don't you take some of these apples to Kathmandu? They're much better than the woolly Indian ones in the market.'

He laughed. 'We tried! We put them in boxes and loaded them on the empty mules that were coming back from Lo Manthang. And we wrapped and padded them *so* carefully – and those darned mules bashed and banged them on every rock between here and Pokhara. By the time we unloaded them we had apple soup – you couldn't even make jam with it! So we gave up. What we don't eat, we make into arak.' He waved a dusty green bottle. 'Have some – *Shea – shea*!'

The others grinned and nodded assent, and we switched from salt tea to fierce apple brandy. I soon forgot how cold my wet clothes were.

Next morning Ram wanted to show me the salt spring. My head was telling me that bouncing around on horseback was not what it needed just at the moment, so I readily agreed to a walk instead. We followed a tributary up the huge gorge that led eastwards from the Kali Gandaki, great golden walls dwarfing forty-foot-high chortens flanking the trail. A short twisting path took us to the neighbouring village of Tetang, where Ram proudly introduced me to the old caretaker who kept the key to the gompa.

The temple was perched on a rocky outcrop overlooking the

gorge. It was too dark inside to see much detail beyond that haphazard dusty charm that seems to be the hallmark of Himalayan temples. As I was leaving, my eye caught an uncertain lurking shape in the corner by the door. Curiosity overcoming my dislike of murky corners, I ventured closer, eyes straining in the deep gloom. Gradually shadowy shapes coalesced into an almost recognisable form – or rather two forms, crouching, pressed together, backed into the corner. Grey-white bandages oozing dark stains were swathed around the mummified forms of two snow leopards. It was impossible to guess how old these things were, or why they inhabited a half-forgotten corner of a dusty temple. I was glad to get back outside into the bright sunlight of the walled courtyard, pushing the repulsive lurking images back into their shadows and the dustiest corner of my memory. I shivered involuntarily as the old caretaker pushed the heavy wooden door closed.

Meanwhile Ram had become involved in a sociable drinking session with some friends in the village and delegated the caretaker to take over as salt spring guide for the morning. We followed the tributary further up the gorge, drawing closer to a great golden wall that filled the head of the valley. By the time we were walking right underneath the cliff I was half convinced the old man was going to lead me on some terrifying hidden pathway up the crumbling vertical face that towered hundreds of feet above us. Suddenly I saw that the river issued from a narrow cleft in the sheer rock wall – and the old man was heading straight for it. Minutes later, he disappeared inside and, despite my misgivings, I followed him.

A narrow shingle bank ran alongside the river, but petered out after a few yards. The only way forward was to wade through freezing ice-melt as the river completely filled the narrow chasm. The vertical walls were barely six feet apart and in some places it was almost possible to run a hand along each wall as I walked. It was cold in here, only a gloomy light filtering down from hundreds of feet above. The cleft was not completely vertical and curves in the rock wall blotted out any glimpse of sky. The only sound was rushing water and the swooshing of our half-frozen feet as we waded upstream. It seemed that this subterranean tunnel was leading into the very heart of the mountain – or the underworld – or both.

After a while the cleft widened, and at last a thin strip of blue sky appeared, edged with sunlit flutings of golden sandstone. A thin arch of rock hung gracefully far above like a mocking gateway to an unreachable world of light and warmth. With a clutch of remembered vertigo, I recognised the arch as one I had seen hundreds of feet below when I had looked down from the cliff path that led to Tangya, on a previous expedition. From here, the arch looked as if it must surely be at the summit of the mountain, not hundreds of feet below it. Now we picked our way over sand and boulders dotted with strange pale bushes and creepers that somehow managed to gasp out an existence in this cold gloomy cavern. The sound of water was louder here, echoing round overhanging walls and broken only by the amplified sound of pebbles kicked against rocks. After another half an hour the gorge widened further, and at last some real sunlight filtered down, transforming the gloom into dappled patches of light and shade, with brilliant colours of red-gold rocks and young willow trees rippling in the wind. All around were pinnacles of rock, like a giant protective wall encircling this tiny valley. I sat on a sunny boulder and stretched cold limbs in warm sunshine. No legendary hunter or herdsman could have felt more euphoria than this on emerging from their respective subterranean tunnels into a Hidden Valley. As far as I was concerned, this place did not need magic trees or invisible palaces to justify the sense of relief I felt on finally arriving.

Two small white piles of salt lay beside three shallow evaporation pans that had been constructed on a flat area of valley floor. Water led into these from a spring that emerged partway up the cliff face by means of an untidy assortment of hollowed out tree trunks (how far had these been carried in this treeless desert?) and odd bits of black plastic pipe. All I could see in the half dry pans was brownish mud with little encrustations of salt rime around cracks in the surface. I turned to the caretaker.

'There's hardly any salt here. How do they collect enough to make those piles?'

He frowned, then realised what I meant. 'You can't see it. We have to take off a four-inch layer of mud first – and the salt is underneath that. There are two qualities – the white pile is the first scraping, which is clean, and the grey pile has some mud mixed with it. Those piles are one year's work.'

They were small piles for a whole year of labour, testament to how precious and essential salt is on these remote farms. Small wonder that Mahatma Gandhi chose the salt tax as the key to unlocking India's independence.

Above the piles of salt, a bamboo ladder led up to a tiny cave in the rock wall. The caretaker explained that this was where a local holy man had meditated for many years in retreat and had discovered the salt spring which he had 'given to the people of the village'. I climbed the rickety ladder and peered inside. The cave was almost filled by a beautifully painted statue of Guru Rinpoche, but the hermit must have been a midget to have lived in this tiny hole barely two feet by two. A rocky scramble above, salt water dripped into a miniature pond on a ledge by the scooped opening of a wider cave. Maybe there were more habitable caves further up the cliff, but the steepness of the face repulsed my best efforts at rock-climbing and I retreated with curiosity unsatisfied. Maybe the hermit could fly.

Suddenly I realised that we were being watched. Three figures were sitting motionless in the shade of a cluster of small willows. I could not imagine where they had appeared from in this tiny enclosed valley and moved closer so that I could see them more clearly. An elderly man was sitting on a richly-coloured rug, flanked by two attendants. His bearing was regal and authoritative, and he acknowledged my presence with a mere inclination of the head.

'So, you are interested in our salt?' He seemed mildly amused – probably by my antics on the rock face. Something in the inflection of his voice made me realise that he was no chance bystander but was here for a purpose.

'Are you the proprietor of the salt?'

Again, that almost imperceptible movement of the head. 'I am the licence holder, yes. I have come, as I do each year, to check on production before we move it out from here. I am head of the Serchan family, from Tukche.'

The Serchans were the most powerful Thakali family in Tukche; this man was indeed an important person in this region. I wondered why control of the salt lay with Thakalis instead of the Lo-ba from Tsuk. Although I knew the decline of the economy of Lo had begun when control of the salt trade with Tibet had passed from Lo Manthang to Tukche, I had not realised that this control extended to local salt production as well.

The patriarch was asking more questions, and I emerged from my mental flight into economic history to answer several at once.

'Yes, I have worked out here for some years. That is why I can speak Nepali. Originally, I am from England.'

The Serchan became positively animated. 'From England? London? Do you know *David*?'

I was about to dismiss the question as naive when something stirred in my memory, something to do with the recent history of Lo. . .

'Do you mean David Snellgrove?'

'Yes! So you do know him! David Snellgrove. He was here – ah – some time ago. I helped him with his book. He sent me a copy.'

Snellgrove's book, *Himalayan Pilgrimage*, is an account of a seven-month exploration of the northern Himalaya, including Lo and Thak Khola, with a particular focus on documenting Buddhist temples and libraries. I recalled that the chapter on Tukche does indeed mention the eminent Serchan family, while also lamenting the decline of Buddhism in Thak Khola, indicated by the state of disrepair of temples and lack of any philosophical knowledge on the part of the lamas. Snellgrove attributed this to an increase in secular education for wealthy families which made them deride the old religion as incompatible with modern and progressive ideas, and also the spread of Hinduism as a result of increased contact with Kathmandu. However, Snellgrove did observe that no Hindu temples had yet been built, and I had noticed on my last visit that this was still the case. In fact the Buddhist temples had been repaired and tidied up, and in one I even found a puja taking place which involved a number of monks. It was beyond me to speculate what had caused this apparent revival of Buddhism, and as I was unsure to which camp the Serchans now adhered I decided not to pursue this line of questioning with the patriarchal licence-holder. I left the regal entourage and carpet in its unlikely desert setting and braced myself for a return journey in the freezing river.

Next morning Ram insisted I borrow his horse for the ride to Gemi. It was a sturdy bay animal with an uncanny skill at bashing my knees against passing rocks the minute my attention wandered from active restraint. The creature didn't come with a name, so I called it Sod. Its one redeeming asset was a lively keenness to move, so I was freed, to my great relief, from the necessity of constantly whacking it with the end of the reins.

A few minutes out of Tsuk and we had to cross the Kali Gandaki

The Kingdom of Lo

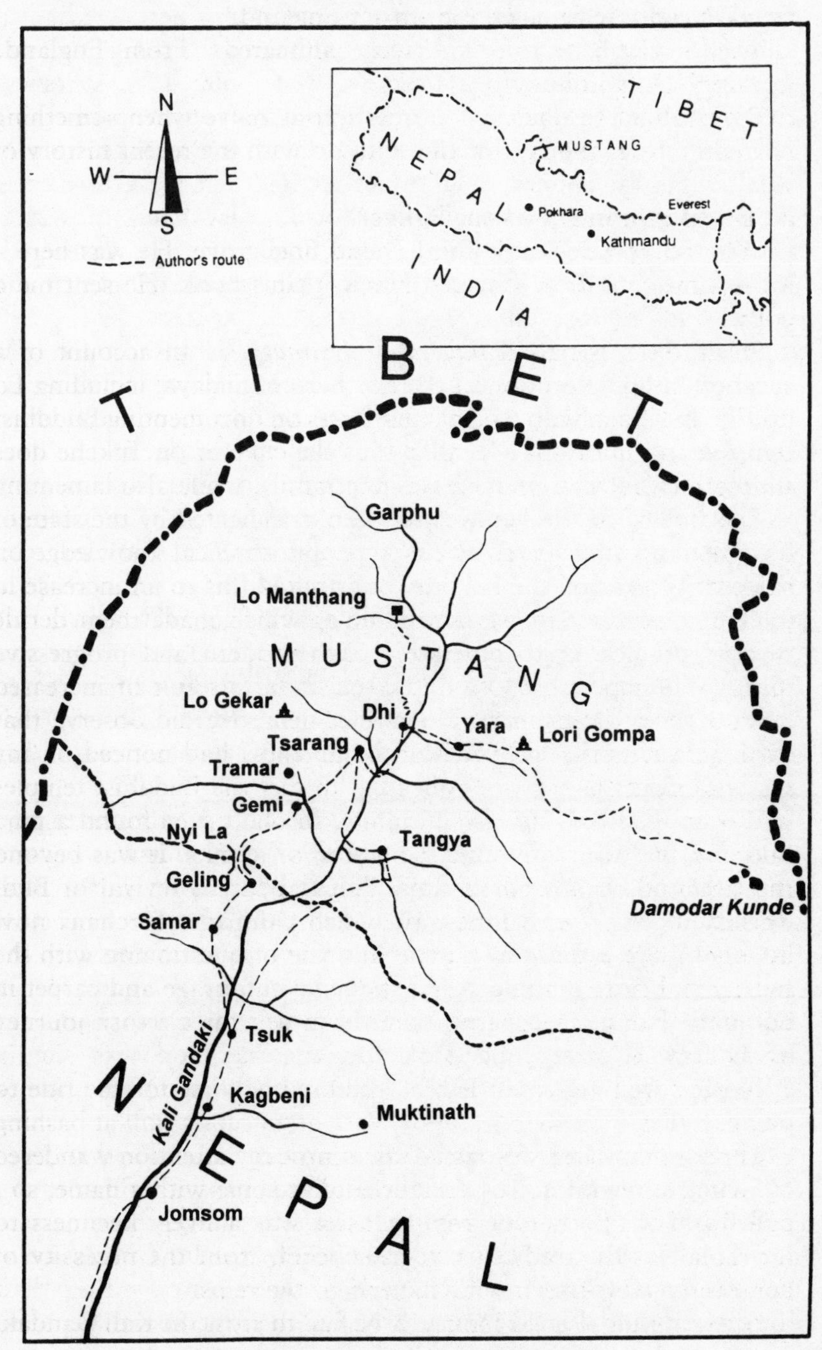

The Kingdom of Lo (Mustang)

just below a massive fallen rock which blocked the gorge, making the river appear to emerge from a tunnel. From here, we had to climb the west bank to reach Samar. Although the village of Tsele is barely ten minutes from Tsuk, we were obliged by politeness to stop off at the house of Tsering's relatives for a cup of tea. It was clear from the size of the house that this was an extremely wealthy family. They were 'in transport' and had augmented their large teams of mules on the Pokhara to Lo Manthang run with a fleet of trucks based in Pokhara which linked their operation with Kathmandu itself. A framed colour photograph of one of the trucks hung on the wall, draped in a white khatak.

From Tsele, the road twisted and looped back on itself as it climbed almost vertical crumbling golden cliffs which dropped dizzily into a shadowy ravine. This section had been much improved by Khampa guerrilla forces in the 1960s, to facilitate supply lines to their secret bases beyond Gemi and Tsarang.

The ravine on the left was so deep and narrow that it would have been possible to yell across to people standing in the terraced fields of Gyakar on the far side, but it would have taken an hour to climb down into the ravine and up again. The cliff to which this twisting road clung so desperately was also ridged with ravines, so that it was impossible to tell how much farther it was to Samar. Several times I came round a corner, expecting to see the red-earth pinnacles that give Samar its name, only to see yet another series of ridges and ravines ahead.

We stopped only briefly in Samar for salty noodle soup and salty tea, and then continued on towards Gemi. I began to notice the rather odd behaviour of Ram's horse, which from time to time would suddenly veer off the trail and stop dead in front of certain houses. Quite a difference of opinion would erupt between the two of us before it could be persuaded to move off again. It was not until later I discovered that these were houses which had home-brewed chang and arak for sale and Sod was simply exercising well-ingrained habits, thinking he was on yet another pub crawl.

Three hours later we passed the scattered houses and temples of Geling sprawled across a shallow hillside below, and began the pull up to a 13,000-foot pass that leads to the northern part of Lo. This was the traditional jurisdiction of the Lo Gyalpo when he was an absolute monarch in his own country, rather than the constitutional local monarch he had become in the Nepalese political system. I had met him several times in Kathmandu and sensed that he still carried an enormous power and presence with his people that went far beyond his official political capacity. I was looking forward to meeting him in the capital, in his own palace, and seeing at first hand how he still ruled this tiny forgotten kingdom.

At the crest of the pass we paused while our horses panted for breath after the long hill. Away to the east, the Damodar Himal raised crests of snow-covered peaks along the horizon, while to the north there was nothing but an endless sweep of barren ochre desert broken by countless crumbling ravines. A line of distant low brown hills marked the border with Tibet, while the Kali Gandaki remained hidden, deep in its gorge below a tangle of cliffs and pinnacles. It seemed impossible that anyone could scrape a living from this lifeless expanse of stones and thornscrub, let alone evolve a sophisticated civilisation with temples, libraries, stately homes and palaces.

I was glad Gyalwo's house in Gemi was of the sophisticated variety. My right knee was sore from the occasions on which Sod had taken advantage of my mind wandering and admiring the view to give it a sharp whack against the cliff wall. I sank on to one of the lavishly carpeted benches that lined the walls and propped my back with a convenient cushion. I even managed to persuade Gyalwo's wife to serve me boiling water instead of salt tea as I 'had a cold and was taking medicine'. This was the only ploy I knew to avoid drinking the never-ending supply of salt tea that is an integral part of every Tibetan household without causing offence to the host. Not that I particularly dislike salt tea – unless the butter is extremely old and rancid – but there seems to be a Tibetan philosophy that if a little is good, then more is necessarily better, and this seems often to apply to the application of salt. By the time I left Samar that afternoon, I had been nursing a dehydration headache which had nothing to do with Ram's apple brandy and everything to do with the amount of salt that was in every bowl of soup, stew and tea I had consumed since leaving Jomsom. The only answer was to go on a diet of plain water until the headache went. Gyalwo and Tsering were greatly amused.

'This tourist business is going to be so profitable if all they want to drink is water,' observed Tsering Gombu.

Gyalwo's wife was concerned about my health.

'You cannot go riding all day if you are unwell,' she admonished. 'Here, I have some really good medicine will cure your cold in no time.' She reached up to a shelf above the fireplace and took down a small china bowl with a lid. Carefully, she poured some of the contents into a clean cup and passed it over to me. I looked at the yellow liquid, trying to convince myself it didn't smell of what I thought it did.

'Is this what I think it is?' I asked Tsering Gombu.

'Big Lama's piss.' He nodded cheerfully.

'*Shea-shea*!,' said Gyalwo's wife.

So much for clever ploys to avoid offending one's host. I had managed to get myself into this one very neatly. My mind ranged this way and that, trying to think of a ploy to extricate myself from the results of the previous one, but no bright ideas presented themselves. Everyone was watching me expectantly. Oh well, maybe big Lama's pee had undiscovered medicinal properties and could eradicate dehydration headaches in mere seconds.

It didn't taste as bad as I expected, but it did absolutely nothing for the headache.

Next morning I visited the temple in Gemi. It had improved considerably on Snellgrove's observations of neglect and use for drying onions. I saw a large pile of new *peja* (religious texts) which had recently been brought in from India. Plans were being made to build more shelves to accommodate them, and the caretaker was justifiably proud of the efforts that the community had made to get the project this far. In his book *Mustang, a Lost Tibetan Kingdom*, Michel Peissel observed that trade with the Khampas based near Gemi had done much to revive the flagging economy in the early 1960s. I wondered if anything had occurred to keep up that revival in the intervening years. Peissel had survived a tense and apprehensive interview with one of the local Khampa leaders only a short distance from here, and discovered that the folded hills around Gemi concealed many secret guerrilla camps operating more or less independently of each other. Apart from the impressive cliff road to Samar the only other tangible legacy of the Khampas' stay is the much depleted juniper forests around Samar and Gemi which they used for firewood to cook their food.

I left an offering of rupees on the shrine and hoped that future foreign visitors would contribute towards the efforts at temple upkeep. Then I hurried outside to where Tsering and Gyalwo were waiting impatiently with the horses.

The trail to Tsarang dives into a ravine just beyond the village, then hauls up to a low pass flanked with rows of blood-red fluted cliffs. According to local legend, Guru Rinpoche slew a terrible demoness on this hill and it is her lungs that form the serried rows of cliffs, streaked red with her blood. A huge Mani wall holds down her intestines, its stones striped in the Sakya colours of white, red and grey; natural earth straight from the hills of this rainbow-coloured desert. In the centre of the flat plain below the cliffs stands a lone white chorten, marking the way to the sacred temple of Lo-Gekar, 'Pure Virtue of Lo', on the spot where Guru Rinpoche flung the demon's heart. The horses bore right, away from the chorten towards the pass that leads to Tsarang.

From the pass, thin lines of other trade routes were barely visible in the shimmering desert light. Away to the west, the steep trail from Gemi to Tsharka snagged up a line of hills that divided Lo from the neighbouring kingdom of Dolpo; a dry, hard route even by the accounts of a party of Dolpo-pa I had met in Tsuk, who had crossed the 20,000-foot passes only a few days before. Mysterious passes and new valleys always filled me with a restlessness and longing for new adventures, but if even the locals said it was tough – well, maybe it was time to think of somewhere a bit more accessible. The locals insisted that every route I had taken so far in Lo was 'very easy, not very far', and this rarely proved to be the case.

To the east, only a tiny part of the trail from Tangya to Muktinath was visible. This was mainly a pilgrim route to the 'water that burns' and the shrines of Muktinath. The high route from Tsuk to Tangya was also just visible, weaving along the narrow ridge above countless rows of pinnacles which I had named the 'sword forest' when I had taken that route before. That path was so precarious, so exposed, that it made the cliff road up to Samar look like a major highway by comparison. More than once I had felt the faltering of confidence that we were indeed on the right route, despite the reassurances of two Lo-ba brothers who had been hastily signed up as local guides that morning in Tsuk. They had been returning home to Dhi with their newly-purchased spotted cow and jumped at the chance of subsidising their journey by throwing their lot in with ours. They were given several expedition tents and two large bags of potatoes to carry, with the additional responsibility of showing us the way. The brothers easily slung the tents on top of their own loads, but they made the cow carry our potatoes.

The Damodar Himal raised its white peaks beyond, while to the north lay the barren sweep of the high plateau around the walled city of Lo Manthang. Tsarang was still hidden in a fold of the desert.

Most of the descent was not steep, and we were able to ride. Only in a few places did the gradient drop more sharply, and we had to walk to ease the horses. Tsering Gombu insisted I weighed so little that it would do no harm if I rode these sections as well, but I had no particular objections to parting company with the infamous Tibetan saddle for a while – and in any case, Sod had developed a new trick of dropping on to both front knees when my attention wandered. It seemed he had worked this one out all by himself after a few frustrating hours without any available boulders at knee height, and several times had almost succeeded in pitching me over his head in a spectacular somersault which Tsering and Gyalwo found enormously entertaining.

Morning was slipping into afternoon by the time Tsarang appeared, set in a flat plain surrounded by rounded, empty mountains. The huge gateway chorten framed a cluster of white-painted buildings dominated by the deep red walls of the temple and the massive grey-white hulk of the fort which dwarfed other buildings like a scale version of the Potala Palace in Lhasa. A latticework of irrigated fields surrounded the town. We rode through the gateway chorten and into Tsarang.

13

The Walled City

།ལར་ཆུ་ལས་བྱུང་ཞིང་ཆུ་ལ་ཐིམ།

A scattering of spiky-haired children stared briefly as we approached, but soon lost interest. It had been both a novelty and a welcome relief to find this happening in each place we visited – such a contrast to the hullabaloo caused every time our previous expeditions had been spotted and everyone able to walk had turned out to see the show. A small party of Lo-ba on horseback does not arouse anyone's curiosity, and as I was wearing Tibetan clothes and my hair was protected from dust with a scarf, it was easy at a distance to mistake me for a local. My skin was caked in dust after only a few minutes on the road and it was impossible to tell whether it was a different colour from anyone else's. Being of slight build, I looked no taller than the Lo-ba when sitting on a horse. It is size that is the most distinguishing feature of the European in this land of hard work and lean rations which limits the height of all but a few wealthy aristocrats.

We tethered the horses in the courtyard of Tsewang's house. He was expecting us, and tea was already brewing on the fire. Tsewang proudly carried the name Bista, originally a Chettri name, reserved exclusively for the Royal Family. His mother, a gentle but regal woman of middle age, was the King's sister. Tsewang's father and sister Maya were also currently in residence, as was the King's brother, the Shabdrung of Dolpo, here on one of his rare visits to his sister before heading with his retinue to Kathmandu for a family wedding. He was a heavily built man, tall for a Lo-ba and very similar in appearance to his brother the King. It took an effort of imagination to realise that he and his entire retinue had come over the difficult high passes from Dolpo.

In spite of the thirty years that had passed, it was still possible to recognise the Shabdrung from the photograph in Peissel's book, taken when he was Lama of Tsarang. At the time Peissel had met him, he was engaged in solitary meditation retreat as a penance for the unreligious life he had been living, which had included abandoning his monastic vows and taking a wife. When she died, leaving him a single parent with a four-year-old son, he had taken vows to spend years in meditation. Such was the intensity of his practice, he had subsequently been recognised as the reincarnation of the High Lama of Dolpo, and had gone over there to take up his new position. His brother, the King, had adopted the enchanting child of Peissel's photographs as his own son and heir, for he had no children of his own. The Shrabdrung had remarried and this time succeeded in combining family with his holy life. On this visit he was accompanied by a delightful girl of about ten, her hair slipping around her shoulders in hundreds of long thin braids.

Tsewang was interested in the business potential of tourism. Like several in the Royal Family he had received a university education in Kathmandu, spoke good English, and understood intricacies of business and politics better than many of his less educated friends. He had been unanimously elected as chairman for the co-operative and his enthusiasm and experience helped the disparate group to work together.

As soon as enough tea had been drunk to satisfy the rules of hospitality, Tsewang showed me round his house. A servant cleared away the teacups and began preparing supper. The house was large even by Lo-ba standards, with two storeys and a flat roof bordered with a dark band of stored brushwood. It was built in traditional Tibetan style, with a central courtyard in which horses were tethered, surrounded by stables and storerooms. Stone steps led up to the first floor, which comprised a covered balcony running around the square of the courtyard giving access to the rooms of the living quarters. One side had been extended and contained a complex of interconnecting guest rooms, a dining room and a spacious kitchen. A notched tree trunk ladder led up from the balcony to the flat roof, where broad woven mats were spread out, covered with apricots drying in the sun.

A low table had been set at the far end of the roof and one of the local priests was ensconced, beating a large temple drum and conducting an elaborate ritual for the well-being of the household.

A small girl was acting as his assistant, following his instructions as best she could, moving small red *tormas* from the table to critical points at the periphery of the roof. The low wall of dried brushwood, Tsewang explained, was more of a status symbol than a regular firewood supply, as it was used extremely sparingly. Most of the fuel burned in Lo is dried animal dung.

The tree trunk ladder was not as easy to negotiate down as up, the more so since it was unattached at either end and tended to wobble alarmingly at the slightest loss of balance. A short distance from the base of the ladder was the door to the inside toilet – a typical desert home dry variety with a hole letting on to a room beneath which could periodically be cleared out into the fields as fertiliser. This one had two holes in the floor, as if the intention was that it be used by people visiting it in pairs. At least the outhouse beneath was devoid of occupants; I had received an unexpected surprise on visiting one Lo-ba loo when a sudden movement underneath the hole made me realise I was not entirely alone. A second look confirmed my suspicions – I had just peed on the head of a large cow in the outhouse below.

A heavy wooden door led from the balcony into the family chapel, a beautifully ornate room with detailed wall paintings and a carved wooden altar piece on which were placed some elegant statues of Buddhas and Bodhisattvas. Carved wooden tables were ranged in front of carpeted wall seats. These would support heavy Buddhist texts during a large house puja when a number of lamas would come to read scriptures. The proceedings on the roof above were presumably a fairly routine affair, not requiring the full ceremonials of the chapel.

Tsewang was outlining which rooms he wanted to convert to 'hotel' accommodation for foreign visitors, pointing out that there was enough space to take a group of sixteen or so without building anything new. The difficulty he and other Lo-ba faced was lack of experience in maintaining the high standards expected by the kind of visitors who would be able to afford the expensive government permit fees. Ambivalent though I felt at the idea of turning one of the last unspoilt places on earth into a tourist attraction, I understood the economic realities of a desert kingdom whose trade had been wrecked by political changes on its northern borders. If local people were able to control the trade, they would have a far stronger motivation to protect the culture and natural environment than a herd of outside entrepreneurs. All they needed was training and capital – and needed it fast, before the herd moved in.

The late afternoon windstorm was getting up, throwing an occasional cloud of grit and dust on to the balcony from the roof above. The lama finished his ceremony and retreated down the wobbly log ladder, while Tsewang and I returned to the living room for more tea and pickled radishes. Elegant country houses certainly had the edge on flappy gritty tents once the wind started. It howled and spat outside the small glass window, but made little impression within these thick stone walls.

The servant ladled fresh water out of a large copper tank in a corner of the room to top up the teakettle – another advantage houses had over tents. Water is carried from spring or river in buckets or firkins, and emptied into these large water tanks. In a few hours grit and sediment settle to the bottom, leaving clear fresh water for drinking. This luxury is not available on camping expeditions where the cook team arrives in camp and immediately sets about boiling enough water to feed guests and crew. On one memorable occasion on my last trip, the evening wash-water did not appear at its regular time, and a few plaintive questions were asked. Clutching a welcome cup of tea I wandered down to the kitchen and tackled the cook.

'What's up with the wash-water then? Do you have a problem?'

Cookie shuffled and looked at his feet. 'Ah, well. We did do it, yes, *diddi*. But when we put it in the bowls it was all black and gritty, and we felt embarrassed taking it round to everybody looking like that. So we didn't.' He looked up and smiled disarmingly. 'But it was all right, it didn't show in the tea!'

I thanked him for his concern and returned to the group, still happily drinking tea outside their tents, and reassured them that the water would simply be a little late, and might arrive after dark.

It surprised me that Tsewang's family could keep grit out of the radishes and apricots, apple slices and sugar-barley that had been dried up on the roof.

Tsewang was enthusing about the team of ladies he was organising – the best singers and dancers in Tsarang – who would soon be a performing arts group ready to entertain passing visitors. Although I felt a twinge of disappointment that perhaps soon the beautiful traditional songs and dances would be reduced to mere performances for tourists, as has happened in so many parts of the world, common sense indicated that this might well be the only way that they would survive at all. The Nepalese schools in Lo taught only Nepalese language, song and dance, and already many younger people did not know the traditional art forms of their forefathers.

Next morning Tsewang showed me the walled garden belonging to the family home. It was in a scrubby state of disuse, and he explained that it had fallen into neglect when Lo ceased to be a major trading power on the salt route to Tibet. However, the high adobe walls were still intact, and the irrigation channels only needed digging out and repairing. Tsewang had been working out the possibilities of bringing the garden back into production again. Hearing his enthusiasm, I began to see a picture of Lo blooming once again into a series of rich oases, fruitful havens for travellers and traders like islands in the harsh desert: houses being repaired and repainted, artists and artisans being retrained, temples being endowed and ceremonies sponsored. Perhaps it was romantic nonsense, and trade in tourism was inevitably destructive and could never replace trade in salt or wool or mutton. At the same time, the choice was not ours. It was simply a case of seeing what happened in the Kathmandu corridors of power and hoping the Lo-ba could make the best of whatever that turned out to be.

We walked across to the fort, avoiding the temple as the mastiff on guard was even more ferocious than those in the houses. I was pleased to have got this far without being chewed and saw no reason to push my luck. I had already seen the magnificent assembly hall with its Maitreya statue, albeit by torchlight as no daylight seeped into that darkened room.

Tsewang was laughing at my efforts to keep as far away from the dog as possible. His sense of humour always seemed to bring out the slightly outdated American slang he had learned from imported films in Kathmandu, which made an intriguing mix with his otherwise impeccable English.

I recovered my dignity over the encounter with the dog and changed the subject. 'Do you remember the last time we visited the temple?'

Tsewang laughed. 'That was pretty funny. I'll bet that guy never wore shorts in a temple again.'

'Actually I don't know. The others were so embarrassed they wouldn't go in any more temples with him, so he had to go separately and somebody else took him in. There always seems to be one in every group.'

The character in question had caused a deal of entertainment as well as annoyance by his antics. On the occasion of the gompa visit, he had washed every pair of trousers and hung them, dripping, on a makeshift line. Even though the whole group knew that they were supposed to be respectably dressed to visit temples, he had made it clear that he had no alternative but to turn up in shorts. I apologised to the caretaker in Tibetan, who had smiled tolerantly and mumbled words to the effect that it was 'his problem, not ours'. We had, as always, been pursued across town by the usual crowd of urchins who had never seen blond hairy western legs protruding from shorts before. It was not long before they discovered that if you pull the hairs, a little bit of leg sticks out in a fascinating little spike of lily-white skin – and the more you pull, the more it sticks out. Soon they were all pulling and tweaking, little squeaks of delight and excitement conveying their pleasure at this new game. Their victim's attempts to detach them merely added to the fun, and they followed their source of entertainment all the way round the temple. I was sure the caretaker was mischievously dallying and taking his time over the conducted tour.

Tsewang unlocked a huge antique padlock on the door of the fort. The structure was in a serious state of disrepair. Large sections had already crumbled away. Nevertheless, it was possible to scramble up several storeys, provided you did not exercise any imagination about the imminent danger of the whole thing collapsing beneath your feet. In the central room of the building was the thing I had risked life and limb to see – the huge copy of the Tibetan canon. The thick pages were heavy with gold lettering, and the book itself seemed very old, judging by its worn edges and corners. Tsewang assured me that it was still used regularly by monks during the annual prayer ceremonies. He seemed impervious to the dangers of the place. Perhaps he was the one who volunteered to fetch the book out every time it was used.

In the room above were statues of fierce deities and a suit of mail armour that might well have dated back to the days of Ghenghis Khan. A shrivelled and blackened human hand hung on the wall, a grim reminder of the harsh punishments of the old days. Not all changes are for the worse, I reflected, slithering down more wobbly logs. Lo seems a gentler place these days.

Tsewang still nursed the hope of funds turning up from somewhere to repair this piece of their architectural heritage before it finally crumbled into dust, but it seemed unlikely.

Back in the courtyard of Tsewang's house, we discovered that Sod had managed to wander off in the confusion of so many strange horses being saddled and bridled as the Shabdrung and his retinue were also preparing to leave. I felt guilty about Ram's best horse, but Tsewang seemed unconcerned.

'Don't worry, it's bound to show up somewhere when it gets hungry.'

Or thirsty, I thought, remembering its liking for ale-houses.

Tsewang well knew my aversion to whacking horses to make them move, and smiled kindly. 'You must take my horse, cousin. He goes like the wind, all you do is ask. I'll take the spare horse. I don't mind giving it a prod or two.'

Such generosity made me feel spoiled, as if someone had offered the loan of his Rolls-Royce in exchange for an old van. 'I can't take your beautiful horse, Tsewang.' I knew how proud he was of the magnificent animal.

'Look at it this way,' Tsewang pointed out. 'If you don't, we won't arrive until after dark.'

There was no arguing with that logic. We mounted, and the great black beast set off, 'going like the wind'. It was not the first time I had ridden a horse from the royal stables, and the difference between them and the tired and bored hacks hired out for riding or for pack duties was enormous. Sod had been an amusing mix of both – full of energy and with a smart burst of speed when the fancy took him, but with an erratic style and a distinctly warped sense of humour. I hoped he hadn't got himself into any serious trouble on his solo excursion. Whatever would I say to Ram?

We dropped down a series of steep gullies, walking the horses, until we reached the Kali Gandaki once more. This was not the quickest way from Tsarang to Lo Manthang, but Tsering Gombu wanted to return to his home in Dhi to collect his wife and daughter before continuing to the capital.

Yuma had been expecting us since yesterday. She and her in-laws were in a bustle of activity, tidying the house ready for guests, and preparing for the journey to Lo Manthang. After visiting the King, the family planned to follow the Shabdrung to Kathmandu, for the wedding of the King's grandson to the half-sister of the King of Bhutan. Most of the gossip was about the wedding, the social event of the year. Yuma and her cousin had hauled out the family finery, and it was carefully draped over carpeted benches in the living room. We couldn't resist the excuse to dress up. There were long serpent head-dresses embroidered with lumps of turquoise the size of fat plums, and ceremonial shawls with gold brocade on the corners. The last time I had seen clothes and jewellery like this, it had been at a wedding hundreds of miles to the west, in remote Zanskar, in a village on the far side of the terrifying twiggy bridge on the way to Phuktal Gompa. It seemed strange that the same style should suddenly pop up again in this desert kingdom so far away.

The whole household seemed to be mobilised in organising for the wedding. Storerooms were bedecked with larger than usual ranks of homemade sausage and black puddings – local delicacies unavailable in tropical Kathmandu. The use of domestic meat seems to be the usual Buddhist compromise in these cold deserts, where goats are the only means of converting the parched thornscrub into food suitable for humans. To have proscribed even this would have caused most of the population to die of starvation. For all the Lo-ba reliance on meat from their herds of goats, I had not come across any evidence of fishing, or hunting wild animals. Local custom has it that these Buddhist observances had been introduced to Lo by the great fifteenth-century lama Ngorchen Kunga, known locally as one of the 'Three Holies' of this tradition. According to his biographer in one of the *Mollas*, or historical records of Mustang, Ngorchen Kunga was responsible for making Lo a great religious centre, 'The same as the excellent country of India during the lifetime of the Buddha.'

It was good to see Yuma her lively, cheerful self again. She had become terribly depressed after the death of her mother, to the point where Tsering Gombu was so worried about her that we had taken her to Kathmandu for treatment. Her irrepressible energy and infectious giggle had returned in a remarkably short time as if they had never deserted her. Now she was clucking round the newly-built living room, trying to decide what colour paint she should buy for the walls while she was in Kathmandu.

'Tsering, how did you get the mud walls so smooth, ready for painting?'

'Star beer bottle! And lots of rubbing.' He grinned a little self-consciously as he produced an empty bottle and demonstrated the technique on the wall.

'What about the paint in the gompas – did all that have to be brought from Kathmandu?'

'No. Most of it used to be made locally, from coloured earth and rock. Then it would be mixed with leather that had been boiled to a sort of glue, to make it hard and shiny when it dried.'

'Are there still people in Lo who can make paint?'

'Only a few. It's easier to get it from Kathmandu these days.'

Gyalwo came in carrying a horse blanket. 'Your cousin said he'd found a strange horse in his field with a bunch of fillies. I went over and checked, and found Ram's horse.'

So Sod had taken himself off to visit a girlfriend in Dhi. Nothing that creature did would surprise me any more.

Yuma needed another day to get things ready, so I spent some time visiting Lori Gompa. According to the sparse history available on Lo, this is one of the few Drukpa temples in a region where almost all are Sakya. The story goes that one of the kings of Lo established it because he had a Bhutanese wife and wanted to make her feel more at home by introducing the tradition of Buddhism from her native country. Lori is situated a short distance from the pilgrim route to Damodar Kunde, sacred triple lakes where Shiva is reputed to have taken a bath. It is a much harder journey than to the shrines at Muktinath, and sees only a few of the hardiest pilgrims. They are rewarded by a vast choice of ammonites, the sacred stone of Shiva, scattered across the riverbeds. Pilgrims and tourists on the popular route to Muktinath have carried away almost every ammonite that comes to the surface.

The valley leading eastwards from the Kali Gandaki at Dhi is flanked by tall fluted cliffs pocked with great clusters of cave entrances. There had been similar clusters, equally inaccessible, in the cliffs above Tsuk, and in several other locations in Lo. Their very inaccessibility made them a mystery, subjects only of speculation and local stories. Almost certainly some had been cliff villages, habitations of the earliest settlers of Lo. Living in cliffs was relatively safe from bandits once the ladder to the lowest cave had been pulled up. Somehow these caves in the Yara cliffs seemed different. Perhaps it was just the local stories, or perhaps it was the scattering of half-eroded but accessible caves just below Yara, but it seemed to me that here was the last remains of a great place of spiritual learning.

The half-ruined caves contained very little – anything that could be removed was long since gone – but there were fragments of pot sherds in some corners, and patches of religious paintings on the walls. The larger, more inaccessible groups of caves were too large and complex to have been much practical use as a domestic village. Literally dozens of caves clustered together, all interconnected on the inside, and all relying on just one lower cave to give access to the ground. Ideal for a place of retreat, but awkward and inconvenient for daily domestic use. Tsewang had said the local people made no attempt to go in there, for these were 'holy places' and it would bring bad luck to desecrate them. Another friend had once showed me a few leaves of an old *peja*, a religious text, written and illustrated carefully by hand, that he said had originally come from one of the caves.

If my intuition were true, why had so many spiritual seekers gathered in this inhospitable valley of pinnacles when Lo Manthang had always been regarded as the centre of culture and learning? No plausible reason presented itself.

Above Yara I met a large group of villagers, mainly women, marching purposefully uphill with shovels slung across their shoulders. A little further up, I passed another group already at work, digging out collapsed leats leading from the stream in a series of ingeniously engineered canals to water terraced fields around the village. This system of mutual co-operation, sharing labour and distributing precious water on a rota, used to be commonplace throughout the high Himalayan region. The arrival of the twentieth century, market forces and competition very quickly undermined this delicately balanced community support. The result is apparent in such places as the Everest region, where the old system has disappeared but no really effective new community process has yet evolved to take its place. There the Sherpas are all competing against each other, unable to re-establish the reciprocal relationships needed to form a co-operative like that planned by Tsewang and his friends. In Khumbu, competition and wood-burning keeps prices low, and the natural forests and soil cover suffer as a result. The few trees left in Lo would disappear within six months if a free-for-all system were introduced here. If the tradition of co-operation could survive, it might be the key to avoiding the wholesale ecological and social damage that had taken place elsewhere.

The pilgrim route to the sacred lake of Damodar Kunde climbs a steep slope south east of Yara. It had taken us a couple of expedition attempts to reach the lake itself, three days' walk beyond Yara.

The first time our guide had simply got lost and had marooned us on a barren and waterless hillside for the night. This was no great disaster except for the poor cookboys who were faced with a long haul to fetch the water, but for the rest of us it was a morning view of freshly fallen snow and the massive north side of Dhaulagiri floating above a cloud-filled valley. The second attempt was better guided, to the hut known as Gyuma Tainty, a pilgrim shelter installed, I was told, by the Nepalese Government's Department of Pilgrimages. I wondered how they managed this, when at the time of our expedition nobody in the Nepalese Government seemed to have the slightest clue where Damodar Kunde was. They had probably despatched a message and some rupees to Lo Manthang and left the locals to get on with it.

On our first excursion into this unknown country we had taken several locals as porters. In the evening it was cold on the exposed hillside, and the locals did what they always do when herding goats on a cold hillside – they set fire to a thorn bush and sat round it warming their hands. My environmental conscience felt heavily compromised. If large numbers of groups came through, and their porters fired the brush, it would cause lasting damage. However, as guests in someone else's country we could hardly start telling them to behave differently just because they were with us. In any case, they would simply have smiled politely and moved off round the corner to continue their hand-warming out of sight. On the next expedition I was relieved to find that no lasting damage had been done to the scrub, and was careful to avoid a similar situation on subsequent expeditions. But camping groups are not environmentally sound for a desert region such as this. They are too difficult to monitor, and most Liaison Officers are more interested in warm hands than healthy hillsides.

Above Gyuma Tainty there is a great expanse of empty desert, devoid even of thornscrub. Local information said there was a 20,000-foot pass to cross to reach the sacred lakes, and that it could be managed in a day. Descending from the pass, I had suddenly seen the detail that had been missing from the local information – that the pass was split by a deep canyon. It was a long descent to cross the river, then up switchbacks on the far side. The steep slopes were striped gold and black where wind and maybe occasional water had turned the black weathered side of the stones over, revealing a gold underside. Not a plant lifted a leaf or spike, not a bird sang or a mouse squeaked. The desert was empty, silent, and vast. It was exhilarating to walk alone in it, to see nothing but silent empty stones shimmering like silk in the heat haze, yet I was safe in the knowledge that the rest of the party was only a short way behind. The Indian pilgrim I had met returning from the shelter had been truly alone in this wasteland, where one slip and a broken ankle would mean a slow death from thirst and cold. Inspiration to reach the sacred waters of Shiva must be what gave him courage and confidence on such a journey. Or maybe he had little imagination.

It was already dusk when we arrived at Damodar Kunde. Snow mountains bathed pink in the last rays of sun encircled a valley of dusky purple shadows. A small white chorten stood on a hillock above the lakes, while all around were low bushes and tufts of grass alive with tiny birds and rodents. Heavy-horned wild sheep grazed spiny tussocks on the far side of the lakes. The rustlings and squeakings in the grass seemed so alive after the sterile desert. This beautiful fertile valley was so unexpected, hidden between the snow mountains and the dry hillsides. I had never heard legends of a Hidden Valley in this remote corner of the Himalaya, but it perfectly fitted many descriptions of other Valleys.

Another hour above the village I entered the narrow canyon of Lori. The tiny temple stood on a low hillock on the flat valley floor, surrounded by layer upon layer of tall golden pinnacles reflecting sunlight back and forth until the whole valley was filled with a golden luminosity. The old caretaker monk was polishing butter lamps in the walled courtyard. The temple door was open, and he waved me inside. The wall paintings were shadowed and difficult to see, so he lit one of the lamps and brought it over, pointing out the painting of the founding Lama of Lori. He was depicted wearing an unusual gold bun-shaped hat, the like of which I had seen neither used nor painted on lamas before.

To my surprise, the monk motioned me back outside. Thinking he was busy and not wishing to disturb him further, I hurriedly left an offering on the shrine and scuttled back into the courtyard. The monk was waiting for me, squinting into the sun and pointing to one of the pinnacles that towered above the temple. He spoke a strange dialect, and it took several attempts before I could understand what he was saying. He finally succeeded in explaining that the Lama had been a great meditator, so highly realised that he could fly, and that the slender pinnacle had been one of his favourite meditation spots, especially when things became busy and he needed some peace and quiet. Then one day he flew away from his pinnacle in rather a hurry, leaving his hat behind. And there it was, a golden bun-shaped hat, or stone, perched atop the pinnacle for posterity.

I saw the unusual hat again, just once – the officiating lama at the wedding of the King's grandson was wearing it.

Evidently the caretaker was not particularly busy, for he offered to show me another temple nearby. I looked around this valley of pinnacles and caves, but could see nowhere another temple could be concealed, unless by magic. After tales of flying lamas and fossilised hats, even that would not have surprised me unduly. The old man creaked his way up a steep path in the cliffside with remarkable speed, and before long we were well above the temple, looking down on its flat mud roof. The path crossed the fan at the base of a ravine, then doubled back on itself, re-crossing the ravine on a shaky arrangement of crumbly logs. Suddenly I noticed a small red-painted building just above us, so skilfully blended into the russet cliff face that I had not noticed it in the scramble up the hillside. It was rudely furnished inside and in a state of disuse. Disappointed, I was about to turn back when I realised the old man had kept going, and I followed him through a labyrinth of tunnels, corridors and log ladders leading deeper and deeper into the mountain, but always upwards. The tunnels must have curved back upon themselves, because at one point I came across a tiny window set in the rock wall and realised we were way up inside one of the huge golden pinnacles that overlooked the temple. It seemed very small and far away now, set in its luminous pool of light, encircled by golden pillars of rock.

On we went, until I had lost all sense of direction. In some places the floor had collapsed, and the ladders were almost rotted away. I began to feel that the whole structure was creaking and tottering like the old caretaker's knees. At last we entered a tiny shrine room and the caretaker lit the butter lamps in front of a statue of Guru Rinpoche. The walls were covered with ancient thanka scrolls, beautifully painted, some dark with age and soot, some with their brocade mounts almost worn away. In the corner of the room was the square carved meditation seat of a yogin, still lined with blankets and cushions. Clearly, this was the main retreat cave of the founding Lama when he was not using airy pinnacles to escape the attentions of his devotees. I wanted to stop here for a while, to take in the details and try to imagine a life of meditation halfway up a pinnacle of rock, but the old man dived into a small tunnel at the side of the room, and I quickly followed him lest I should become totally lost inside this maze of tunnels and crumbling floors.

After a few yards I was able to stand up straight again. I was in a vaulted cave almost filled with a delicately painted stupa which rose above my head to lose its spire in the gloom of the domed and richly decorated ceiling. The quality of the art and workmanship in the other temples was nothing compared to this. It was so huge, and fine, it did not seem possible we were in a cave inside a remote desert cliff. Suddenly I realised this was the stupa of the relics of the Lama himself, and I had the answer to my question. This was why so many seekers and scholars had overcome the hardships of the desert to study and practise in this place. The inspiration and teaching of this great practitioner had drawn them here, just as the artists who had painted his last resting place had been inspired to create such works of art even though they would never be seen in this secret cave except by the determined few who made their way up here.

It was no longer early by the time our party had got itself organised next morning. All the bits and pieces for the wedding had to be carefully packed in separate saddlebags; Tsering explained that he would register them at the Jeela headquarters in Jomsom before taking them to Kathmandu, to ensure that no one thought he was taking the priceless family antiques and jewellery to the city to be sold. We led the horses through the narrow streets of Dhi with the beehive-shaped shrines still smouldering the last of the juniper offerings to Thab-Lha, god of fire. Then we halted again under the willows on the flat sandy area by the riverbank. A proper farewell ceremony had to be conducted by Tsering's parents to ensure good luck on the long journey to Lo Manthang and thence to Kathmandu. This involved symbolic offerings of barley and incense and many cups of home-brewed chang. Tsering Gombu's mother draped silk khataks round our necks until we were all swathed in the soft white scarves wafting in the morning breeze. We mounted, Tsering hauling his seven-year-old daughter Yangdzin into the saddle in front of him, and I made ready to set off. But no, the ceremony was by no means complete until we had drunk many more cups of chang, which I felt sure would be incompatible with several hours' hard riding through the desert if we were to reach the walled city before nightfall. It took a while before the jugs and firkins the family had carried from the house were all emptied and we finally moved off.

The road from Dhi to Lo Manthang twisted up behind the village in a series of abrupt hairpin bends before plunging into a virtual tunnel formed by overhanging flutings in the rock wall. We were actually climbing between the pinnacles of the great cliffs of the Kali Gandaki gorge – cliffs that looked vertical and impassable when viewed from the river. Even as I scrambled up the tunnel, the sheer steepness of the road made me wonder how horses – or humans come to that – ever made it down again in one piece.

The horses stopped, panting for breath, on the apex of an exposed hairpin. The rock wall fell away here, leaving a sheer drop to the base of the cliff. We were looking almost straight down on the village; we could have seen right down their chimney-pots if they had had any. As it was, the pattern of the Tibetan architecture revealed itself clearly; narrow twisting streets between high-walled compounds cut out the force of the late afternoon windstorms and made the place comfortable to walk in, even though the wind howled outside the village walls – a technique the Chinese have failed to learn in their colonisation of Tibet. Their building style follows a rectangular grid pattern, and most of their towns have become dust-bowls. The flat roofs of Dhi formed a mosaic marked by the dark rim of brushwood stored around the edge of each roof, and the shadowy square opening in the centre above the courtyard. The pattern was echoed beyond the village in a latticework of fallow barley and buckwheat fields with their irrigation leats and carefully balanced retaining walls of mud. A row of five white stones lay in each field for good luck, bright against the dark earth.

The dim tunnel was carpeted with a fine grey dust, formed from countless hooves of horses and goats trampling the dry pebbles. It rose around the horses' legs in a filmy cloud that soon filled the gully as we climbed. At last the rock walls opened out and we were on easier ground, though the path continued upwards towards the skyline where dun rock met intense blue. A boy was driving a herd of long-haired brown and white goats up a broad sweep of pebbles. Tsering Gombu waved a proud arm towards the animals.

'All my goats!' he announced, and called across to the boy in Tibetan to let us through.

It took a while for the horses to make their way between the milling animals, until we came over the shoulder of the cliff and were on a ridgetop that led away northward to Lo Manthang. The scene was both daunting, and one of breathtaking beauty. It seemed impossible that a route could make its way through this wild chaos of rocks and pinnacles, stained red, gold and mauve in the desert sun. Deep chasms split the formations, leading to unseen rivers far below.

Tsering Gombu seemed unconcerned by this magnificent, terrible vista. He spurred his horse to a gallop along the ridge, Yangdzin yelling and whooping with delight like a kid on a roller-coaster. Tsewang and Gyalwo followed, and so did I. Tsewang had once again ceded his beautiful black stallion to me, and the animal leaped into the wind with an eagerness that belied the steep haul up the cliff road from Dhi. I have always loved riding as a sport since childhood, yet there is something about deserts that makes it a necessity, an essential part of being alive that is hard to describe. Footbound, I feel fettered as if crawling through treacle in the vastness of it all. The barrenness of the open spaces and the savage jagged beauty of the cliffs and plains create a deep yearning in the soul to be flying free across this wild landscape, to hear the drumming of hooves on the dry ground and the wind keening through the spines of the thorn bushes. The terrifying cliffs and ravines seem less threatening, even though the danger is greater at speed, simply because I have become part of the danger, have accepted that it is there so that it just becomes part of the exhilaration of movement, part of the vast landscape, part of myself.

At last we had to slow down to cross a hillside of soft shining sand. We led the horses as their hooves slipped deep into the dry slope and runnels of sand went skittering down to lose themselves in the depths below. Yuma caught up, having traversed the ridge with a little more decorum as befitted a princess of the realm.

'I was afraid for you,' she said, shaking her head with disbelief that I should enjoy such a wild ride. 'I thought you would fall.'

'One day she will race with us and she will win,' Tsering Gombu teased, laughing heartily, knowing it would be a while before I could compete with the Lo-ba aristocracy on their own ground at their best sport. At first he too had felt concerned and responsible when I had exchanged the first slow plodder with Ram's lively little beast. However, after several hours of watching the altercations between Sod and myself on the cliff road which culminated in Sod's total failure to dislodge me from his back, he had given up worrying and relaxed back into his own enjoyment of riding.

It was a day I wished would never end, as we galloped along a series of exposed ridges above a red-gold sea of ravines and pinnacles. Even as the sun began to dip in the west, throwing pink shadows across the desert, something in me wanted to go on riding into the night, past the city if necessary and on into Tibet itself, following the half-forgotten route that once linked up with the famous silk road to China and the court of Kublai Khan. For a Westerner, there is no logical explanation for this impractical desire to push on into the deep desert despite thirst, dust and exhaustion, but for a Tibetan it is simple. 'Oh, you must have been a Tibetan nomad or an Arab in a past life,' they will say, 'And you are just remembering old adventures still imprinted on your mindstream.'

Suddenly we were on the crest of the last pass and looking down through a fissure in the rock to the walled city of Lo Manthang, its white walls and towers catching the last rays of sun against the dusky shadows already creeping across the 'Plain of Aspiration' that surrounds it. Nothing had changed here for centuries. We were riding into a mediaeval city with three huge red temples, a palace for its king, and a city gate that is still locked each night. No matter that this would not keep out the Chinese tanks massed across the border only a short distance away should they decide to invade; the country has not really acknowledged that the twentieth century exists, because within these borders it simply does not. I felt sad that this would soon change, despite the excitement of Tsewang and his friends.

To the north of the walled city the ruined fort of Ketcher Dzong stood on the summit of a smooth barren hill, dominating the city. It was built in approximately 1380 AD by Ame Pal, the first King of Lo, who subjugated all the chieftains of Lo and unified the kingdom. The present King was the twenty-sixth in the direct lineage of Ame Pal.

Descending from the pass and crossing the river, we reached the city gate, where we dismounted, as should all respectful subjects of the King, for only he is allowed to ride within the city walls. The horses' hooves clacked and echoed as we led them across the deserted city square to Surendra's house. Surendra is Yuma's brother and runs the only hotel in town – and the Post Office. The latter is announced by a small red sign tacked above the front door, and as for the former, well, you just have either to know, or ask. Surendra appeared at the top of the stone staircase as we led the horses into the courtyard.

'Welcome, welcome! There's tea and chang ready in the kitchen, but don't put the horses in here – I've already got visitors and the stables are full. Try across the way.'

We turned and retreated through the low wooden doorway. 'Across the way' turned out to be the King's palace itself which stood on the other side of the square. Tsewang led the horses through another doorway to the right of the main portals.

'Are you sure he's not going to mind?' I asked as we tethered the animals at the side of a straw-filled courtyard.

'Oh, the stables are huge,' Tsewang reassured me. 'All Uncle-la's horses are in the main part – he's not even using this bit. I'll tell one of the grooms to take care of them.'

We drank tea at Surendra's in the company of a group of muleteers who had just offloaded a consignment of rice and cooking oil in the city. They were planning to set off on the return journey to Pokhara at daybreak. Tsewang returned from seeing to the horses to announce that we had an appointment to see His Majesty the following morning after breakfast; he had run into the King's secretary as he was crossing the square.

Lo Manthang lies at an altitude of 12,000 feet, and at night in November it is cold. We stayed clustered round Surendra's fire, unwilling to make the move to cold blankets and sleeping bags. Most fuel in Lo Manthang is dried animal dung, as there is less wood available than in the Dhi or Gemi areas where some of the wealthier families have begun to import Chinese-made wood-stoves which they use just to warm the rooms even when there is no essential cooking to do. It is a custom which will devastate the remaining juniper forest if it becomes fashionable. Perhaps the new wealth and fuel regulations which tourism would bring were coming just in time for the fashion to switch to kerosene heaters or solar panels instead. Traditionally, only the King had the luxury of a woodstove.

I asked Tsewang if he knew of any other forests used up by the Khampas.

'I'm not sure about all of them, but there were some forests up by Yara and some big *magars* (military camps) in the hills above, and I think that's how all those trees got used up.'

'How did the Lo-ba feel about the Khampas being here?'

'Don't forget I was just a child then. I didn't get involved with any big political discussions. But generally, we felt sorry for them. The Chinese had ruined their country, killed their families, driven them into exile – and all that was left for them was to fight to try to get their country back. Sure, they cut down trees and sometimes helped themselves to livestock, but generally they were disciplined and their leaders were men of honour. When they could, they traded for what they needed, and they worked hard on the transport routes.'

'Did you meet any of them?'

'I met Wangdu, their leader, a few times. He became a close friend of my father and visited the house sometimes. He was a great man, a hero. I admired his strength and integrity as well as his courage. It was a tragedy that he was killed, but a man like that could never surrender.'

'What happened to him?'

'When the Nepalese government asked the Khampas to give themselves up, many leaders swore they would rather die than surrender. Ten thousand troops were preparing to march on Lo. His Holiness the Dalai Lama tried to avoid more bloodshed by sending a taped message, urging his followers to give themselves up, and this was relayed to all the bases here. Some leaders killed themselves rather than either surrender or disobey their Lama. Wangdu was devastated by the choice, but ordered his men to follow His Holiness' instructions.'

'If he surrendered, how come he was killed?'

'They were betrayed. The amnesty wasn't respected, and as the Khampas moved their caravans of weapons south, they were seized by Nepalese troops. Wangdu and a group of his best men fled north into Tibet, trying to dodge the Chinese soldiers and reach India by the western passes. They were ambushed, and Wangdu died in a hail of bullets. Only a handful of his men reached India to tell the tale.' Tsewang paused, reflectively. 'It didn't have to be like that. It would all have come to an end naturally. The Khampas were getting older and more exhausted with the constant fighting, and a small country like this couldn't support all those extra people indefinitely. There was already a lot of overgrazing by the extra herds and so on.'

After hearing so much rumour about this period of Mustang's history that had been hushed up almost to the point of entering the realm of myth, it seemed strange to be hearing the account from someone who had actually lived through it.

Next morning, after a hurried breakfast, we tidied ourselves in a manner (I hoped) suitable for an audience with the King and crossed the square to the arched entrance to the Royal Palace. Stone steps led up from the entrance, followed by a wooden staircase and a large antechamber. Suddenly a huge black Tibetan mastiff hurled itself to the end of its chain, snarling and barking all manner of menacing threats. Its appearance was made all the more ferocious by the heavy red ruff around its neck, not to mention the murderous glint in its eye. The chain was, in fact, two feet shorter than the distance across the room, allowing us to slither nervously along the wall, within inches of the slavering fangs. I prayed fervently that the chain was a strong one and well anchored to the far wall.

In the next room, also empty of furnishings, hung the dog's predecessor, stuffed with straw and dangling from the roof beams by means of two leather thongs.

After more staircases and corridors, we were ushered from an open balcony into an anteroom by a servant. A few moments later the servant returned and motioned us through a doorway into the audience chamber. I hung behind the group, rearranging for the fifth time the ornate silk khatak draped over the bottle of Black Label I had brought as a gift for the King, and watching the others closely as they presented their offerings to make sure I did not commit any breach of protocol. In turn, each bowed low, extending the gift draped in its scarf with both hands before them. The King accepted each gift with dignity, and motioned for us to sit down. Some of Tsewang's friends from the co-operative who lived in Lo Manthang were already here, seated on the rug-strewn benches around the walls.

There was an awkward silence for a few moments. Suddenly black smoke erupted with a bang from the woodstove burning in the centre of the large room. I jumped visibly, barely suppressing a squeak of surprise. The King broke into peals of laughter, soon joined by the rest of the group.

'Do not worry, it often does that,' said His Majesty. 'You will grow accustomed to it.'

The ice was broken, and the usual polite small-talk began, as a maidservant brought round tea and little plates of herb omelette and pickled radishes. I was still not Tibetan enough not to feel impatient at the seemingly endless pleasantries and protocol. I found myself gazing round the room, taking in the carved wall cupboards with panels of glass in the doors – glass that had been painstakingly carried all the way from Pokhara. Inside the cupboards were displayed elegant china and bottles of malt whisky and brandy – presents, no doubt from previous visiting subjects. On one shelf was an old sepia photograph of a middle-aged couple in the formal costume and elaborate hairstyles of Tibetan aristocrats. I had heard that the Queen was of a noble family from Lhasa, and these were almost certainly her parents. I wondered how they had fared in the purges of the Cultural Revolution.

The Queen herself, a tall, pale-skinned and very beautiful woman, sat in a sheepskin-covered chair on the right of the King. She wore a plain dark-blue Tibetan dress and a striped apron, a quiet contrast to the rich brocades and jewels I was to see her in later at the wedding in Kathmandu. Even the King did not bother with formal finery for everyday occasions; a grey woollen hat was pulled over the long pigtails wound around his head and he wore a knitted sweater and riding breeches tucked into high leather boots as he intended to ride out to Garphu later that day.

Suddenly I was jolted from my mental wanderings by the realisation that the conversation had started in earnest, and one or two of our party were beginning to look distinctly uncomfortable. Tsewang was explaining his plans and asking His Majesty if he thought them worthwhile. The efforts at diplomacy were falling short of the mark. I realised this when the King's personal secretary turned to me and explained.

'You see, His Majesty had been discussing with many important people this very possibility for some time, but now it seems your group has gone ahead and formed your own organisation outside what we had planned for Lo.'

My heart sank. *Outside* the Royal plans for Lo. Clearly the King did not approve and was marginalising this group of unruly nephews before they caused any problems.

'But of course, we haven't *done* anything yet,' I ventured

nervously. 'It was just an idea. We came to seek His Majesty's approval and advice.'

The others nodded and added confirmation of their own, and the conversation resumed in similar circular fashion. Gradually it began to dawn on me what my role was in all this. Because I was an adopted relative, it was acceptable that I should be included in these discussions; nevertheless everyone was acutely aware that I was a foreigner, and as such, could be excused large breaches of protocol that would have been unforgivable in any of my Lo-ba companions – such as simply not taking no for an answer and starting the discussion up again just as we were about to be peremptorily dismissed. The repeated going-over of the outlines and plans also gave the more rebellious of His Majesty's subjects the opportunity to tone down some of their more radical opinions and make efforts to get back into the Royal good books.

An hour went by, and although we had not been summarily evicted from the Royal chambers, we seemed to be getting nowhere. I found I was sitting on the edge of my seat, trying to find the opening that would resolve the situation, when suddenly it was all over. Everyone was smiling and sitting back in their seats, drinking from half-forgotten teacups and the conversation flowed off in every other direction once more. The official summary of the situation was that it had all been a misunderstanding of the term *Baragaon*. The Royal plan had included only the Seven Areas of Lo, the traditional jurisdiction of the King which extended no farther south than Gyeling. The area of Samar, Tsele and Tsuk was outside its scope. We had included this area because it was currently within the region restricted to foreigners and would have become a sort of no-man's-land had it not been included within the jurisdiction of the co-operative. The King and his secretary had thought we meant to include the whole area around Kagbeni and Jomsom as well – Thakali country, and of course the unspoken implication was that this would not work at all. I felt it unlikely that members of the same family would really have such difficulty communicating basic geographical information, but it was a skilful diplomatic summary for the fact that His Majesty had given everyone a good grilling and was finally satisfied that his junior representatives were going to function in a manner that would not bring disgrace to the respectable court of Lo; the times ahead would be difficult enough as it was.

The Queen had left the room quietly some time before. I

thought she had become bored with the proceedings, but now she returned, followed by the maidservant, carrying plates of buckwheat pancakes which they set before everyone in the room, starting with the King. I felt we must surely have been given the seal of approval if we were being treated to the Queen's own pancakes. They were delicious and far less gritty than the variety served by mere commoners, but alas, they came on the same system as the butter tea – in never ending relays as soon as you had finished one. Eventually I was forced to admit defeat and leave half a Royal pancake on my plate. The Queen was very nice about it, but I hoped my immunity from breaches of protocol extended as far as the ultimate rudeness of leaving food unfinished.

Hoping to divert attention from my appalling table manners, I asked the King what his hopes were for Lo in the future. Did he approve of his country being opened? His reply was thoughtful and diplomatic.

'Who can say if bringing in many foreign people will be a good or a bad thing? In many places it has brought much disturbance and damage, but it can also bring good things, too. Here, in Lo Manthang we have no hospital, only a small clinic with one doctor who goes home to Kathmandu in the winter. We need a hospital here, properly equipped, and functioning all year round, so my people do not die for lack of modern medical care. And we also need an electricity supply. These are benefits the modern world can bring. Perhaps tourism can generate the funds for these things, perhaps not. We shall have to wait and see.'

I felt he was preparing himself for many long and exhausting discussions with politicians in Kathmandu. I wondered if the rumours were true that he was considering stepping down before long, so that his adopted son could take over the leadership of his people. 'Raj Kumar', as he was affectionately known by his Nepalese name, had received a good university education and was director of a large carpet export business in Kathmandu. His experience of the modern world, and of Kathmandu, would be a great advantage when dealing with city politicians and businessmen. The four-year-old son of the Tsarang Lama of Peissel's photograph had changed, and learned a lot in the intervening thirty years. His own four-year-old son looked remarkably like that old photograph.

We left the palace in good spirits. No doubt there would be

problems ahead, but they were as yet unseen and we could indulge in optimism. The rest of the day was spent visiting relatives and temples.

The larger of the two older temples in Lo Manthang is in fact only the central part of an even larger building, the outer walls of which have long since collapsed. Even so, what is left is impressive. Massive carved timbers supporting the roof must have been carried for days to this treeless desert city. The wall paintings, although damaged by water seeping through cracks in the roof, are of fine quality, evoking a time when Lo was a great centre of trade and culture, before the economic decline began. Even so, the *Gompa Sarwa* or 'New Temple' was the most interesting for me, for it contained most of the movable statues and was in regular use by a community of monks. They were sitting around two sides of the courtyard when we arrived, drinking tea. I assumed they were having lunch, and was grateful when one of the monks came over and offered to show me around the inside of the temple. As he pointed out various statues and paintings of divinities, I noticed several painted masks hanging on one of the walls.

'Which *cham* are these for?'

He seemed surprised that I knew anything about them at all. 'They are for the *Deje* festival which is held in the third month of our year. These are the masks for the *Khandroma*, the Dakinis.'

I looked more closely at the fearsome masks. If advanced meditators care not at all whether dakinis appear as goddesses or hags, the masks must surely be for the vision of some truly great mahasiddha who had completely transcended outward appearances. These hags were really ugly.

I asked more questions, and the young monk tried to explain, but my knowledge of the classical terms was insufficient to glean more than a muddled idea of the meaning of the Deje. We had arrived back outside in the sunny courtyard as I finished speaking. I was in the process of compiling a guidebook to the Mani Rimdu festival in the Everest region, which I hoped would help raise funds for the monastery. I tried to ask the monk if he thought it would be a good idea to start a similar project here, but I could not be sure he had understood my haphazard Tibetan.

'Excuse me one moment.' He turned away and spoke to the assembly of monks in rapid Tibetan. I could not follow what he said, and assumed he had changed the subject. Suddenly all the monks raised their hands, nodding in assent. He turned back to me.

'I have put your proposal to the meeting, and it has been passed unanimously. I will make an appointment for you to see the Abbot tomorrow for the translation.'

I had walked into the middle of an al fresco AGM of monks, not a lunch party at all.

The following morning Tsewang and I were ushered into the presence of the Khenpo of the Monastery of Lo Manthang, the Venerable Tashi Tenzing Rinpoche. Despite his important position, the Khenpo received us warmly, without formality. His account of the meaning of the festival was clear and detailed without the convolutions that often accompany explanations of esoteric texts. Tsewang was clearly enjoying the job of translating as he was deeply interested in the history and culture of his own country, generally accessible to few beyond the community of monks. Tsewang himself was eager to establish a Tibetan medium school in Lo Manthang; as he saw it, this would be the only way that the value of the old traditions and philosophies would continue into the next generation now all the schools were Nepalese – and on top of that, Western ideas were about to pour in.

The story of the Deje is, in essence, the same spiritual struggle as depicted in Mani Rimdu, where symbolic 'demons' are overcome by a heroic *Bodhisattva*. The Khenpo explained each aspect of the dances in careful detail.

The young monk who had arranged the audience showed us out.

'His Eminence has chosen me to take the role of the Bodhisattva in the Deje this spring. I am even now preparing for the three-month meditation retreat which is essential training for this.'

Tsewang and I walked back through the narrow streets to Surendra's house in silence. I was thinking how fortunate I had been to spend even a short while in this fabled and forbidden land, where disputes are still settled by the wisdom of a religious King, and the focal point of the community festival celebrates the victory over harmful states of mind. Small wonder the city stands in the centre of a 'Plain of Aspiration'.

We left Lo Manthang the following morning. A chill dawn wind stirred the prayer flags and the horses snorted and tossed their heads in the cold air. The city gates were behind us now, as we turned the horses south, across the desert towards the distant snow mountains.

14

Mandala

།དགྲ་ཉོན་མོངས་ཡིན་ཚུལ་མ་ཤེས་ན།

It was three days before full moon. Cold light silvered the path before me and filtered ghostlike between dark shapes of the trees. The lights of the temple complex glimmered faintly above, marking the spot where my long climb would end and a warm fire and a cup of tea would be waiting in the monastery kitchen. I had arrived at Chiwong in time for the Mani Rimdu festival, and this time I was determined to pluck up the courage to ask Trulzhig Rinpoche about Khembalung.

The kitchen was warm and noisy after the moonlit silence of the wooded hillside. The evening meal was over and empty pots were being heaved outside to be scrubbed. Yonden was sitting with a group of monks at a wooden trestle, drinking tea. He waved me over, and one of the cooks set a cup for me almost before I sat down.

Yonden smiled. 'Back again, just in time, eh? Trulzhig Rinpoche arrives from Thubten Choeling tomorrow.' He looked tired, despite the welcome. As leader of the sacred dances and main organiser among the monks, his work schedule would have been non-stop for the last couple of months in preparation for the festival. He was young – only in his mid-thirties – for this level of responsibility and lacked some privileges of age which would ease the pressure for an older man. This tea-break had probably been a meeting as well, until I had arrived.

'Look, don't let me interrupt your business. We can talk afterwards if you've time. My group doesn't fly in until tomorrow.'

Yonden laughed, despite the tiredness. 'Not to worry – business finished! We are already talking about my new idea. We need a better education here – a proper school. I am trying to work out how to get a qualified teacher from one of the monastic universities in India.'

Yonden always had been full of ideas, but this was his most ambitious yet. He seemed able to balance his responsibilities for organising the monks with his scholarly interests in more complex aspects of Buddhist philosophy, and still maintain a cheerful good humour. He had also taken responsibility for a number of poorer boys who had been accepted at Chiwong over the last few years. I had known Yonden a long time and sometimes wondered where he found energy for it all.

'How are you going to keep the teacher warm enough so that he doesn't go straight back to India?'

They all laughed. I was well known for being swathed in a down jacket as soon as the sun went down. Winter at ten thousand feet is one thing in afternoon sunshine, but quite another when there isn't any.

Yonden launched into his plans for a teacher's house, as well as a new schoolroom for classes. 'You see, we need a proper education programme. Right now, there is instruction in reading and conducting the pujas, but no one qualified to explain the deeper meaning of Buddhist philosophy.'

It was easy to forget how hard some communities out here have to work to gain access to the same level of instruction that we take for granted in the West.

'Where are you going to find the money for all this?'

Yonden frowned. 'We were discussing that when you came in. We will go round the villages asking everyone for donations. What else can we do? Monks are not supposed to work for money; that would mean neglect of their spiritual duties here.'

'What about the Mani Rimdu notes we talked about last year?'

'What about them?' Yonden looked puzzled.

I smiled as I reminded myself of the number of exasperated friends who commented on my unnerving habit of jumping from one subject to another, assuming they had managed to follow my intervening thought processes by some kind of telepathy.

'You remember we talked about my idea of asking Trulzhig Rinpoche to check my notes so that they could be published to raise money for the monastery? Well, at the time we were both thinking it would take several years to complete, but we could produce something more quickly, in time to help your education project. Could you arrange a longer interview with the Rinpoche this time? My travel company has enough money now to pay for printing this year – then all the proceeds could go straight to your project.'

Yonden engaged in a rapid translation into Tibetan for the other monks, two of whom spoke little Nepali, then beamed at me. 'Wonderful idea! But you will need someone who can translate straight from English to Tibetan, to make sure the quality is good enough for a book.' (My knowledge of the honorific form of Tibetan was insufficient for long conversations with Lamas, so I usually spoke Nepali with Yonden, who then translated into Tibetan.) 'I think American Dennis is coming tomorrow. You could ask him.'

Dennis is an American monk who has spent most of the last twenty years at Thubten Choeling, much of that time in meditation retreat. He is one of life's great eccentrics, his bushy beard contrasting with his shaved head, his broad frame looking incongruous swathed in maroon robes and dwarfing his slender, clean-shaven Tibetan companions. The following afternoon it was easy to spot him, standing head and shoulders above a gathering crowd of Sherpas and Tibetans. He had shaved his head only the day before, having just finished a three-year retreat during which time his hair had grown long. His newly-shaven pate was now feeling the cold, and he was constantly pulling a droopy maroon woollen hat further down over his ears.

'Why Mani Rimdu?' Dennis asked. 'There are so many real interesting texts at Thubten Choeling. . . Anyhow, no problem, just let me know when you fix up your interview. Trulzhig Rinpoche won't arrive until this evening. There were so many people wanting to see him down in the villages.'

Normally the journey from Thubten Choeling to Chiwong would take four hours but for such a revered figure as Trulzhig Rinpoche it could take up to three times as long, with people from villages along the way coming out to see him. It was an hour after dark when the first retainers and porters came in sight, emerging from the forest as dark figures whose shadows danced with the swinging of their lanterns.

The Chiwong nuns had been waiting for three hours by the entrance gate with offerings of food and incense. Then the milky shape of the Rinpoche's horse appeared and he dismounted with an ease and grace that belied his seventy years. He paused, acknowledging the welcome and offered scarves. Then a great procession with wailing horns and clashing cymbals issued forth from the temple gates, gathered him up and carried him along in a tide of sound and colour until all was swallowed up into the temple and the night was silent and empty again.

I stood outside for a while, leaning on the stone parapet, looking down on the lights of the village hundreds of feet below the vertical cliff on which Chiwong stood, letting the darkness and silence of the night soak into me. It was impossible to say whether it was the enormous, powerful ceremony or Trulzhig Rinpoche's presence, or some strange combination of both that had created the almost tangible energy in the air. It would be hours before I would sleep tonight. I went for a walk by the light of an almost full moon.

The following day I arrived with Dennis, clutching a white silk *khatak* and an offering, outside Trulzhig Rinpoche's audience room. We slipped off our shoes and shuffled through the doorway with a crowd of visiting Tibetan and Sherpa families, some of whom had clearly come from Tibet itself. A few more minutes of patient shuffling brought us to the front of the room where the Rinpoche was sitting.

Dennis explained that we had come to ask him to check the accuracy of my notes on Mani Rimdu. The Rinpoche smiled and motioned us to sit on one of the low carpeted benches at the side of the room. The wooden floor was deeply polished by the feet and hands of the constant stream of visitors making prostrations and offering scarves. A broad latticed window overlooked forested hillsides below Chiwong and the zigzag path that led down to the Paphlu airstrip.

Trulzhig Rinpoche sat on a low carpeted throne, radiating a kind of benign amusement at the goings-on that surrounded him; an amusement nevertheless infused with a warmth and compassion that seemed to pervade all the crowding, prostrating and shuffling in the room. Throughout the entire interview with us, the Rinpoche continued to give each bowing visitor a smart pat on the head with a sacred amulet. His assistant handed out blessing strings and long-life medicine.

As Dennis began to translate my notes, the Rinpoche's amusement turned into great chuckles of laughter. He looked at me, shaking his head in both sympathy and merriment.

'He says you've got it all wrong,' said Dennis.

I hadn't needed his translation or an advanced understanding of classical Tibetan to figure that out; the Rinpoche's amusement had been eloquent enough. I had compiled my notes from the few books written by Western authors on Mani Rimdu, some of them lavishly illustrated with photographs. I had assumed the authors had used reliable sources, but evidently this was not the case.

'Rinpoche is going to start again, right from the beginning,' said Dennis.

'Thank you,' I said in Tibetan.

The Rinpoche beamed, clumped a Tibetan nomad on the head with the amulet and, to my delight, began with his life story.

'I was born in Tibet, in a place sacred to the goddess Tara. When I was four years old I was recognised by the abbot of Dza-Rong-Phu monastery as the reincarnation of his own heart lama. I was taken as a child to be educated at Dza-Rong-Phu, on the north side of Chomolungma. Thirty of my previous incarnations were in India. One of them was Ananda.'

I hastily scribbled notes from Dennis's translation as the Rinpoche began speaking again. Ananda was one of the Buddha's closest disciples who had helped to persuade him to allow women to join his group of followers – a radical step in the patriarchal society of ancient India! The Rinpoche continued:

'Seventeen of my previous incarnations were in Tibet, including Rechungpa, one of the main disciples of the poet and mystic Milarepa. Also including Lalung Pelgi Dorje who ended the reign of terror of the evil king who was systematically killing all religious practitioners in Tibet.'

It was the first time I had attempted to take down a life story which included forty-eight incarnations. If the Rinpoche went into each one in detail, my little booklet was going to be the size of an encyclopaedia. I was already familiar with the story of Lalung Pelgi Dorje, but had not realised that Trulzhig Rinpoche was the reincarnation of this heroic and almost mythical character. Lalung Pelgi Dorje gained access to the evil king, Langdharma, by performing the Black Hat Dance at his palace. He had concealed an arrow in the wide sleeves of his ceremonial robe. Out of compassion both for the victims and for the king who would in future incarnations suffer all the pain he now inflicted on others – and fully prepared himself to endure the consequences of his own action (karma) – the monk drew the hidden arrow from his sleeve and killed the king.

'In 1959, when the Dalai Lama fled from the Chinese occupation of Tibet, I also fled south from my monastery at Dza-Rong-Phu, and crossed the Himalaya to Khumbu.'

The Rinpoche spoke softly, still smiling at the stream of visitors offering scarves. There was no trace of resentment or self-pity in his voice as he recounted what must have been a harrowing journey across the snowbound Nangpa La. The exhausted party had finally descended into the upper valleys of Khumbu and were welcomed by Sherpa monks at Thame, near the Lawudo cave. They stayed there for a little over a year before moving further south to Chiwong.

Many Sherpas who had travelled to Dza-Rong-Phu for teachings already knew Trulzhig Rinpoche and his fellow monks. Some of these joined the growing band of disciples as more Tibetans crossed the high passes, fleeing not only from Chinese soldiers but also from the famines that were sweeping Tibet in the wake of the Cultural Revolution. Soon the need for more space led the group to establish their own retreat at Senge-Pukh, the 'Lion Cave', at the head of the valley a few hours' walk from Chiwong. Senge-Pukh was already a retreat cave for local hermits, but was too small for the still-growing group of followers that inevitably gather round an inspired teacher. Thubten Choeling was built on a larger site a little further down the hill from the Lion Cave, and the number of monks and nuns studying and meditating there grew to more than three hundred. Now Thubten Choeling is the largest monastery in Nepal, while Dza-Rong-Phu in Tibet lies deserted, no more than a bullet-scarred ruin.

Trulzhig Rinpoche's poetry reflects his acceptance of suffering and exile as a part of the ebb and flow of life.

> Arriving now in the wilderness
> In an uncertain place of solitude
> Accompanied by unbiased spiritual friends
> I have drawn forth this song of separation
> For the fulfilment of myself and others.

For now, at least, he had no more to say on this episode in his life and continued with his explanation of the festival.

'The three days of public festival here at Chiwong are actually the culmination of a 19-day sequence of secret ceremonies and empowerments which take place at Thubten Choeling.' There was a pause while a particularly large Tibetan family presented several babies and squirming toddlers to be blessed by the Rinpoche, and I took advantage of the respite to catch up with my notes. Dennis was looking tired. I hoped my offer of dinner would not come too late to revive his flagging energy; I knew he had skipped lunch to make this translation session.

When the Rinpoche continued it was to explain all the sacred dances of the Mani Rimdu at such a speed that had it not been for the pause for translation I would never have been able to keep up. Then, with a smile and a polite nod of the head, he presented us each with a red silk blessing string and indicated that the interview was over.

Dennis steered me outside to where we had left our shoes. 'Rinpoche is due to start a puja now. See you at dinner.'

He left, and I was outside, blinking in the thin sunshine before I realised that I had not asked my questions about Khembalung. There had been hardly a pause in the Rinpoche's commentary and it would have been rude to interrupt even if I had not been so absorbed and had managed to remember. It would have to wait until the next opportunity for an interview.

'Why,' said Dennis, scooping up the last morsels of his second helping of vegetable curry, 'why is everyone so interested in Mani Rimdu? Meditation is where it's at – Mani Rimdu is just a public festival.'

I grinned apologetically. 'I suppose meditation just isn't much of a spectator sport. You actually have to do a lot yourself before it means anything.'

'Exactly,' said Dennis. He tugged the drooping maroon hat another quarter inch over his ears and prepared to leave.

That evening I walked back to the temple. It had been crowded with Sherpas and Tibetans making their customary offerings when I had brought my group to see the Sand Mandala earlier that morning. Now it was quiet, the stirrings and soft voices of the pilgrims only an echo on the incense laden air.

A lone monk sat on the cushioned floor by the veiled pagoda which contained the Mandala, continuing the non-stop compassion mantras which the Chiwong community had been pouring into the Mandala for the last weeks. He held the end of a rainbow-coloured cord which led to the Mandala and the bowl of long-life pills set at its centre, his mantras a rhythmic intonation which seemed to ebb and flow with the shifting shadows thrown by the dozens of butter lamps around the room. For the last weeks the meditations of the Chiwong monks had taken tangible form as the Mandala had been carefully created, grain by grain, from coloured sand. It represents the palace of the Lord of the Dance, a form of the Buddha of Compassion, the central figure of the Mani Rimdu.

By visualising the power of their mantras flowing down the thread into the Mandala, the monks focus their energy on the Mandala and the pills it contains until the vision of the Buddha in the centre of the palace becomes a vivid inspiration for their every action. Tomorrow, Trulzhig Rinpoche would distribute the 'spiritual medicine' of the pills to the village people who were too busy earning a living to have time to meditate. It is generally accepted in Himalayan culture that those who don't have the calling to become monks condense their spiritual practice into repeating mantras, making offerings and having faith that the monastic community would perform rituals on their behalf.

Two days later, waiting in the crowded courtyard for the masked dancers to appear, I could see that for most of the audience jostling for a good place on the balconies and steps this was a great gathering, a festival, a picnic – a time for devotion to their Lama and an opportunity to show off their best clothes and jewels. For a few, such as the small group of nuns clustered around a wooden pillar, it was a gateway to another world. Although they could not explain the ceremony intellectually when I spoke to them later over cups of salty tea, they had watched throughout with rapt attention, totally absorbed in another dimension as real to them as the dust and stones on which they sat.

The symbolism of the dances unfolds layer by layer, much as the outer, inner, and secret levels of a Hidden Valley are said to reveal themselves as the mind becomes able to perceive them. On one level, they represent a re-enactment of historical events – the coming of Buddhism from India to Tibet and the process of adapting and incorporating the indigenous shamanistic Bon beliefs and practices.

The Tibetan king, Trisong Detsen, had married two Buddhist princesses, one Nepalese and one Chinese. His early attempts to introduce Buddhism to Tibet met with inevitable opposition from the existing establishment. The king appealed to the Indian Buddhist saint Padmasambhava to 'overcome the demons' which were causing the problem. Padmasambhava, later known to Tibetans as Guru Rinpoche, or 'Precious Teacher', was a tantric practitioner powerful enough to influence ingrained attitudes and beliefs. Because of his ability to adapt his teachings with such versatility to people with different abilities and outlook, Guru Rinpoche is popularly referred to as having eight different manifestations – six peaceful and two wrathful. In the Mani Rimdu dances Guru Rinpoche appears in his wrathful demon-bashing emanation, heavy-bodied, with red eyes and snarling fangs. Every movement represents the powerful 'magic' of Guru Rinpoche as he paces out his mandala, or sphere of influence, and horns and cymbals resonate with the harmony of the elements.

On a deeper level, the dances play out the inner drama of the meditator on the quest for enlightenment. The 'demon' here represents the fundamental source of all problems, the inability to perceive that no matter what our innate sense of ego-grasping tells us, there is no inherently existing self to be found anywhere inside or outside our ever-changing mental and physical components. In the Mani Rimdu dances this particularly problematic demon is represented by a small rag figure which gets symbolically beaten into submission by two skeleton dancers who represent the impermanence of each human lifetime.

While this inner struggle is being enacted in the courtyard, Trulzhig Rinpoche ritually gathers and entraps all demons and burns them in a bowl of fire. The ashes are buried under a flagstone in the courtyard. This spiritual spring cleaning generates an invisible Mandala of protection around Chiwong and the surrounding countryside, mirrored for those who understand its significance by an inner Mandala to protect the mind from destructive thoughts and emotions.

In tantric meditation, practitioners identify with an image of an enlightened being in order to develop those enlightened and compassionate qualities in their own minds. They use these powerful symbols to develop the intellectual recognition that 'self' is merely a convenient label imputed on an ever-changing flow of mental and physical energy, into a deep intuitive understanding. In Mani Rimdu the dancers appear wearing the outer form of these enlightened symbols to benefit the assembled spectators who do not have time or instruction to engage in meditation themselves. Trulzhig Rinpoche explained, 'The dances can only be performed at Mani Rimdu and not for ordinary entertainment.'

Giggling Sherpinis were showering me with peanut shells from the balcony above my head, a lost toddler was howling for its mother, and two plump Tibetan mums nursed their infants and exchanged gossip about distant relatives. It all became part of the mandala the Rinpoche was weaving around this misty hilltop, the crowds crammed into the courtyard, the mischievous children, the old men and old women, the teenagers flirting surreptitiously with each other, the monastery dogs sniffing round the flagstones for leftover offerings, while the skeletons of impermanence celebrated the burial of cremated demons.

I had travelled to Bhutan the previous year for the Paro Tsechu. It is a far grander spectacle attended by Royalty, Government Ministers, Penlops, Dashos and other assorted aristocracy, as well as hundreds of Bhutanese citizens and crowds of wealthy tourists. The dancers were more numerous, the costumes more elaborate, and the dances went on for several days. And yet the underlying symbolism of the mystery play remained essentially the same, and at this much smaller gathering of Mani Rimdu it was somehow easier to take in the wholeness of it all, to suspend that critical separateness that is the bane of the Western mind and just for those few hours enter another dimension of reality.

The dakini dancers appeared, reminding me that I clearly had not transcended outward appearances because I noticed I was glad they were not of the Ugly Hag variety. Although every culture uses symbols to express ideas that can be explained in words, there comes a point at which they can stand for something beyond words, in the realm of direct experience. Here, the words cannot be regarded as explanation, but rather, an indication or inference that will only be fully understood when it has been experienced. There is an aspect of the dakini which cannot be precisely defined; like a butterfly pinned to the collector's board, she would become a dead relic of something living and free. Vessantara describes her in terms which are evocative but not precise:

> . . . to meet a dakini is not easy. They are not domesticated but wild. To find them you have to leave behind the security of your own views and ideas. You have to abandon the tidy civilised world of mundane concepts. You have to walk out into the unknown, the unexplored, the unimaginable. . . Internally

> the dakini is all those outpourings of something higher and more spontaneous within us that make us feel we are on the right track, that we are making progress on the spiritual path. This does not mean that they are simply comforting. Occasionally they may be shattering, like lightning-flashes of insight that turn our view of ourselves and our world completely upside-down. . . The dakinis, you could say, are the muses of the transcendental.

The more I looked at the meaning and usefulness of apparently far-fetched Eastern myths and beliefs, the more I began to question the validity of those of my own culture. For example, the modern myth of continued growth and productivity as the key to mankind's well-being is regarded by most as being beyond question, but in the context of the planet's finite resources it is completely unrealistic. It is so difficult to become aware of our habitual assumptions and to question them.

I stayed on to see the performance of Tokden, an Indian tantric yogi. Rinpoche himself had referred to this as 'just a joke', and in previous years cold and drowsiness had persuaded me to leave before it took place. This time I wanted to see it for myself, as I heard from the Sherpas that Tokden would bend a steel sword against his bare flesh. Tokden and his two hopeless 'disciples' enacted a kind of spiritual soap opera as they attempted to cope with life, death, love, lust, alcohol, and an assortment of other Samsaric problems. The crowd enjoyed the crudity of the humour as well as, perhaps, the reminder that all does not necessarily go smoothly on the spiritual path.

Although it was dark by now, I was determined to wait for the sword-bending climax to the performance. Western scepticism had returned full force. I knew that Yonden was behind the mask and dreadlocks of the Tokden character, and he seemed too jolly and pragmatic to have developed the kind of mystic powers needed to fall on a heavy steel sword without eviscerating himself. It was bound to be rubber covered with tinfoil, I told myself. If it was, it made some very convincing clanking sounds as Tokden bashed it a few times against the stone steps as a precursor to thrusting it violently against his naked stomach and bending it almost double.

I walked down the hill in mist luminous with moonlight, feeling shaken by what I had seen and wondering if things would ever seem simple and uncomplicated again – the way they seem if we never question or try to look deeper. I had known Yonden for years, and had assumed I *knew* who this person was I called my friend. He was open and cheerful, concerned for the welfare of his fellow monks and the future of Chiwong. His even-tempered concern for others had on the surface seemed uncomplicated enough, but on reflection it was perhaps naive to assume that such consistent altruism came from mere chance rather than deep spiritual practice. That such practices can also produce spectacular side effects and 'magical' powers was generally accepted in this part of the world. It is just unnerving when you suddenly discover it in someone you had thought of for years as a nice, ordinary, uncomplicated friend. I knew it would be useless to try to talk to Yonden about it. He would just dismiss the whole thing with a laugh and a deprecating wave of the hand. 'Just a joke,' he would say, echoing the words of the Rinpoche.

By the following morning almost all the village people had gone home, and the merchants running teashops and soup kitchens were packing up their cookpots and tarpaulins while the ever-present dogs scoured the packed earth floors for leftovers. Even the dogs seemed to be tired. The teashop proprietors looked exhausted after three days and nights of almost non-stop catering. In the monastery courtyard a group of monks were moving the Rinpoche's throne down to the area round the flagpole and building a huge pyre of old roof shingles in preparation for the Fire Puja. I had never understood why so few villagers stayed for this ceremony, but perhaps they, too, were tired as most of them had had nowhere to sleep for three days and had simply stayed up drinking all night instead.

Yonden caught my eye and grinned cheerfully as he heaved the last wooden bench into place, then went back into the darkened temple. I smiled back a little awkwardly, still unable to synthesise my habitual perception of the friendly scholar with the powerful, enigmatic character I had seen last night. The familiar cloak of ordinariness was back in place, but now it no longer quite concealed the inner depths as it had before. I reflected how easily I could have missed the opportunity to recognise someone for what he really was, almost like being given an uncut diamond and hardly noticing it because at first glance it looked like a pebble –

or stumbling on the entrance to a Hidden Valley and seeing only empty desert.

The last flames of the Fire Puja crackled and died, and members of the Patron's family collected ashes to scatter in their gardens. The Rinpoche and the monks began to dismantle the curtained framework that shielded the Sand Mandala. What had been veiled and mysterious was now exposed to view, brilliant colours shimmering in thin sunlight filtering through the open door; a work of art that had taken a whole team more than a painstaking week to create. Now, after mere seconds of glorious public display, it was over, like an ephemeral desert flower. The Rinpoche stooped and with deft movements of his hands brushed the entire masterpiece into a small heap of coloured sand. His attendant leaned forward and scooped the heap into a vase.

After they had gone out, I stood for a while watching the sunlight move the shadow of the small vase as it stood solitary on the wooden base, and smiling as I recalled whispered comments I had heard when seeing the same dissolution being performed in Europe by visiting Tibetan monks. The Western concept of preserving a work of art is so strong that it is often hard for Westerners to cut through it and see the powerful gesture of accepting impermanence that this seemingly wanton act represents. Suggestions of fixative, sprays, other methods of creating the design in permanent colour all bubbled to the surface at the sight of thirty seconds of deliberate destruction.

Early the following morning a small procession filed out, carrying the vase of coloured powder to its destination at the Naga spring in the forest below Chiwong. Morning mist curled soft tendrils through the trees, muting deep maroon robes and lending a ghostly air to the sound of horns and conches drifting through dark branches of pine and rhododendron. The swathed figures settled like great birds around the spring, spreading instruments and texts on mossy banks and heaps of autumn leaves. Slowly, as the ceremony progressed, sand from the Mandala was poured into the spring and the water bubbled and frothed a myriad of colours before swirling and leaping like a liquid rainbow down the mountainside. To pollute a Naga spring in the ordinary way is regarded as almost certain to bring sickness upon the polluter and even the whole surrounding community, yet for those involved in this finely-tuned relationship between environment and humans and their spiritual focus, this offering of compassion-saturated sand is an essential part of maintaining harmony and balance. I had no idea intellectually how it worked. For now, it was enough to sit in the cool moss and rustling leaves beside the Naga pool as the mist-laden trees sprinkled all of us with a fine dew.

It was one year later when I returned for Mani Rimdu and found that Trulzhig Rinpoche's heart-son, Sang Sang Tulku, was making one of his rare visits to Chiwong. He had been educated abroad and spoke fluent English. I mentioned my interest in Shambhala almost casually, assuming his schedule would preclude much time for conversation. To my surprise, he readily agreed to translate any questions I might have for the Rinpoche and within hours I was back in the sunny room overlooking the forested hillside, and the Rinpoche was beaming a welcome as if it were only yesterday I had sat here before. An opportunity like this happens when it is ready to happen, I reflected; it is simply a matter of waiting and staying alert so as not to miss it when it finally arrives.

The Rinpoche had finished speaking and Sang Sang Tulku was translating.

'Shambhala is a Buddha realm – it is a manifestation of the wisdom and compassion of the Kalachakra deity. Shambhala is surrounded by great rivers and high mountains more difficult to climb than Everest. Some practitioners of the Kalachakra Tantra who have gained high realisations and siddhis are able to make a spiritual journey to Shambhala; some can even go in their physical bodies. For others, they can practise in this lifetime and be reborn in Shambhala.

'Khembalung is not a Pure Land; it is one of the thirteen different places which Guru Rinpoche protected for the Tibetan people. He had great compassion for the Tibetans and foresaw that in the future there would be degenerate times, so he saved this refuge for the Tibetans. Because Guru Rinpoche foresaw these times and set aside these *beyul* and hid the *termas*, the texts which are the source of teachings for these times, his power is very great now that we are in the degenerate times that he predicted.

'Khembalung is a Hidden Valley which has an inner secret place within it. This inner place is not accessible to ordinary people until it has been opened by a spiritual master with great siddhis, who can make the spiritual as well as the physical journey to the inner secret place. Khumbu and Rolwaling were both *beyul*, hidden secret valleys of Guru Rinpoche, until they were opened by great spiritual masters. Now they are accessible to everybody and many people live there.'

Trulzhig Rinpoche smiled as the translation ended, and I felt encouraged to ask questions.

'What about ordinary people like me? What would happen if I tried to find Khembalung?'

The Rinpoche was watching me intently, evaluating my question even as I spoke.

'Some people who are good practitioners or who have good luck – good karma from a previous life – can reach the outer levels of places like Khembalung, but the inner secret part is inaccessible until a spiritual master comes and opens it. Just as a building has a management committee, so a beyul has many guardian deities to protect it from intruders. These deities may manifest as tigers or fog on the mountain, which brings danger to anyone who does not have the qualities to open the inner, secret, valleys.'

I did not feel at all confident that my good karma or attempts at meditation practice would come up to standards guaranteeing immunity from irate guardian deities. I said that the Valley was a great inspiration to me, and to other Westerners, and that I hoped to cross the mountains to find at least the outer part of Khembalung, but . . .

I suddenly realised that during his answer the Rinpoche had been weighing up my motivation, evaluating the real reason for my asking these obscure questions. What had he seen? Apart from an insatiable curiosity, why did I want to go there? This sudden absorption in my own mind almost made me miss the next translation.

'The fact that you are naturally interested in this beyul shows that you have a close connection with Guru Rinpoche; this is why you have been able to succeed in many things you have done. If you have a pure motivation, if you are not doing this for money or to be famous, then you will not be in danger – you will have success. You will have to make the journey with your mind focused on Guru Rinpoche, for the inspiration to make this journey to benefit others. Repeat his seven line invocation each day – well, maybe recite Guru Rinpoche's mantra at least.' (I could not help smiling at the thought that Westerners' reputation for being unable to sustain repetitious long pujas had reached even this remote corner of the mountains.) 'You cannot go to Shambhala this way, but maybe you can reach the outer part of Khembalung.'

There was another long pause, as I reflected on the Rinpoche's warnings about right motivation. I tried to analyse what I really hoped to achieve by finding Khembalung. There is a world of difference between finding good justifications for something you want to do and privately figuring out for yourself what really lies at the heart of it all. The Rinpoche could probably see what was there much more clearly than I did. What he had effectively given me was instructions on a practice of studying one's own true motivation; there would be no final evaluation from anyone except my own mind and the guardian deities.

The wail of horns sounded from the temple below. Sang Sang Tulku looked at his watch and stood up to leave with an apologetic smile.

'Excuse me, but the puja is starting, and I'm supposed to be leading it.'

He disappeared through the door with remarkable speed. The Rinpoche's attendant handed me the customary piece of red string and indicated that the interview was over.

The Rinpoche's answer left me with a new set of questions. How would I know if my reasons for going were acceptable? And how would I know when the time would be right? Blundering through the mountains with all the paraphernalia of a fully-fledged expedition was clearly not the way to go about it. The Rinpoche had hinted at the mystical dimension to the search for Khembalung and Shambhala, and it was here I needed to learn more.

15

Within Shambhala

།ཚེ་ཆོས་པར་སྒོམ་ཡང་བྲག་ཕུག་བཞིན།

Dawa Norbu was going on a pilgrimage. He had been meaning to go for some time, he said, but it was not easy with a farm and animals to look after. Still, if he didn't go soon, he would be too old to make the journey. Dawa was a married 'lama' from a remote village in the Khumbu region and looking at his wrinkled, skinny frame and wispy grey beard, I wondered if he might be too old already for the strenuous ten-day march through the largely uninhabited hills and jungle between Khumbu and Maratika. It was not the last time I would discover that the appearance of elderly Sherpas can be very deceptive.

When I heard of Dawa's plans, I managed to invite myself along. The caves of Maratika are regarded by Buddhists and Hindus alike as one of the most significant 'places of power' in the Himalaya, and there perhaps I might begin to understand more about the mystical dimension of the Hidden Valleys that Trulzhig Rinpoche had mentioned. Dawa Norbu's explanations for the significance of the caves were traditional rather than interpretative.

'People have *always* gone there,' he insisted. 'As long as people have been on this land, they have sought the Caves of Long Life. Guru Rinpoche flew there from India with his consort Mandarava to open the Mandala of the Buddha of Long Life. He practised the Yoga of Immortality in the sacred cave, then he flew to the Khumbu to protect it as a Hidden Valley.'

I knew that throughout Asia, these 'places of power' are thought to have special qualities which can enhance one's meditation and bring quicker or more powerful results. It is impossible to prove whether the very expectation helps to focus the mind, or if there is a noticeable external difference at a particular spot due to magnetic fields, subterranean water sources or the 'blessings of the Buddhas'. I had always felt drawn to the stone circles of my homeland, and was disappointed to find that the understanding of their meaning had been lost. The current speculation and romanticising of these places was for me no substitute for a living tradition. Perhaps here in Asia were some clues, even if they were expressed as ancient mythology.

Dawa's wife arrived in the courtyard in front of their farmhouse where we were sitting. She had been supervising the packing, and was followed by an overloaded porter staggering under a doko piled high with blankets, pots and food. Several of Dawa's *peja* were perched on top, carefully double-wrapped in a piece of daphne paper. I thought of the Khumbu porters who had put on an elaborate show of indignation to the sirdar of a tourist group when the thirty-kilo standard load was judged to have been exceeded. In all probability the porters had just completed a local assignment like this when anything up to double the amount might be carried – and often for lower pay. I was glad not to be responsible for the poor fellow's labours as he trundled off down the hill. At least the load would get lighter as we ate the food.

The first two days took us through familiar farming country as we followed the gorge of the Dudh Kosi river south after it plunged from its source at the foot of Everest. Then we took less frequented paths across steep forested hillsides broken by ravines and boulders. Water was scarce. We spent an uncomfortable night in a dilapidated jungle hut whose proprietor charged five rupees a cup for water it had taken him two hours to fetch.

I was glad we were travelling – in traditional Nepalese style – in a group. It was in this area that an American woman working for the Peace Corps had disappeared. Yonden told me he had met her just before she turned off the tourist trail and tried to persuade her not to make the journey alone. She was not safe, he told her, just because she spoke good Nepali. '*I* speak good Nepali and I would not go alone,' he argued – but to no avail. She was never seen again.

By the time we reached the Mahabharat Lekh the land was treeless. Every dusty red hill had been terraced for agriculture, leaving only the steepest slopes covered by a low scrub picked clean by goats. White erosion scars of stones and dust marked gullies ripped out by the monsoon downpour. Only the sacred pipal and banyan trees on the chautaras remained untouched to give shade to resting travellers in this baked and barren land.

Maratika is a forested limestone pinnacle, an oasis of green in the parched red-brown landscape. No one would dare to cut even a bush on the hill that had been a place of power since ancient times. The tree roots twisted like gnarled fingers around the sculptured rocks and cliffs. I stood looking at the hill with a strange sense of deja-vu. As a child I had drawn so many fantasy pictures of a mountain of strangely-shaped rocks, with a road climbing and circling, twisting its way to the top between the outcroppings and tree roots. My road had led to a fortress or temple on the summit, but all I could see here were fluttering prayer flags above the topmost trees.

We followed the spiralling trail up and around the hill through a leafy tunnel of cool green shadow. Near the summit was a cluster of thatched cottages and a newly-built Buddhist temple almost hidden by the trees, completing the synthesis of the present with the visions of my childhood.

The lama of the temple was standing by the gate as if he had been expecting us. We were welcome to stay inside, he said, but as it was already occupied by twenty-two Bhutanese pilgrims we might find it rather crowded. The temple was so small it was hard to see how even the Bhutanese were going to stack themselves in order to fit in.

Outside, a flagged courtyard was lined on three sides by huge heavy bells suspended just above the ground on iron chains. Beyond, stone steps led down into a great arched cave which echoed with the fluttering and squeaking of thousands of tiny bats.

The cave entrance was wide enough to allow a dim light to filter through from above. The rock floor was level but uneven, punctuated with several large smooth rocks, looking like fossilised termite hills. Around the edge the stalactites and stalagmites had fused to form pillars and curtains of gleaming calcite, giving the cave the appearance of a huge temple. A small Shiva shrine bristling with rusty metal *trisul* was among the few man-made embellishments to the cave.

As Dawa squeezed through the narrow space between the limestone pillars and the cave wall, he explained that this was a kind of purification process, like being born again from a womb of rock. Those with bad karma, he assured me, would invariably get stuck. His wife watched his antics but made no attempt to follow. She was probably more worried about her plumpness than her karma. The porter had sensibly remained outside for a well-earned rest. I followed the old man around the circuit, but backed off at the last hole. It looked big enough but, being on the floor, it was full of bat droppings. I decided I had purified enough for one day.

Sita Kumari ran the only restaurant in the village. She shared her tiny premises with two goats and most of the village gossips. Her menu consisted of just one meal – rice, dal, and pickles. This had to be eaten quickly and with some concentration, unless you didn't particularly mind one of the goats licking your plate before you had finished. Dawa was in his element, reciting lengthy prayers before and after his meal, and regaling the villagers with tales of his home region. None of the locals, it seemed, had ever ventured so far north.

We found a small cave in which to camp above a thermal spring on the far side of the hill. It was shallow, tall, and pointed at the top, earning it the local name of 'Guru Rinpoche's hat'. The flat floor was already strewn with a thick layer of dry grass, suggesting that it was a popular camping spot for visiting pilgrims. I spread a sheet of plastic under my sleeping bag in case it was also a favoured spot for fleas and lice. I had only just tracked down the visiting livestock I had inherited from the waterless hut in the jungle.

Sleep was a long time coming. This place defied description. I felt as if I had walked into my own childhood fantasy, yet at the same time there was a contrariness about the experience, like being in a rather perverse dream. The surroundings were as exotic and strange as any fantasy, leading you to expect something extraordinary and magical to happen. I had felt almost surprised when each event had turned out so ordinary. Dawa's traditional rebirthing ritual had been entertaining and good fun, but it seemed to lack any higher dimension the awe-inspiring surroundings had led me to expect. The lama of the Buddhist temple had been welcoming and friendly, but he was more preoccupied with the inadequacy of his kitchen facilities to cater for the twenty-two Bhutanese visitors than with engaging in complex meditation practices. Any attempt to describe how it would feel finally to enter a Hidden Valley while lacking the 'Wisdom Eye' to perceive its true nature would surely be something like this. Or had the real significance of this place been forgotten, as is the case at such sites as Stonehenge in the West?

The stars were just paling into dawn when I awoke. A deep rhythmic humming was coming from within the hill on which we slept. The sound grew until the very rocks seemed to resonate and be part of it. After a while I felt part of it too, as the vibration of the sound soaked into my body from the ground on which I lay. I pinched the back of my hand a couple of times, but the reassurance that I was awake did nothing to dispel the dreamlike feeling. Dawa had no idea what it was that we could hear and feel but accepted it as quite normal in such a magical place as Maratika.

Later, as we walked through the green dappled sunlight of the trees to the foot of the hill, the air seemed to ripple with the vibration of the sound. It was an experience I shall never forget. To know intellectually that all matter, including the earth itself, vibrates with the dance of atoms in its very structure is one thing, but to feel it physically is quite another. Some people believe that the point of stillness between the in-breath and the out-breath is the point at which the body and mind resonate on the same frequency as that of the Earth itself. The great meditators learn to quieten the mind with the power of concentration until it finally abides in complete stillness and clarity. In this state of peace, it is said, they can hear the sound of the vibration of the universe – and that sound is OM. I felt as if I had been privileged to a preview of this experience before I had even started on the prerequisite meditations.

Two Bhutanese nuns were sitting in the entrance to a cave tunnel, reading texts. They looked up and smiled, then continued chanting the verses; homage to Guru Rinpoche.

> In the North-West of the Land of Orgyen
> Born in the pollen heart of a lotus flower
> Endowed with the most miraculous *siddhi*
> You the Lotus Born Guru appeared.

Beyond them, inside the tunnel, a man was standing upright with his face and hands pressed against the rock wall. The humming was louder here, booming and echoing through the darkness. Suddenly I realised that the man was creating the sound, blowing through a fissure in the rock as if it were a ceremonial conch. The resonant notes seemed to disappear into the depths before becoming louder and issuing forth through every crack in the ground.

The tunnel ran horizontally for about twenty yards, then widened into a larger cavern with a level floor and a vaulted roof opening high above at the summit of the hill. Dim green light filtered through the trees that overhung the hole. This was the legendary cave where Guru Rinpoche had completed the meditations which prolong one's lifespan, and then, according to Dawa, flew up to the roof and burst through into the sunlight, making the hole which now lit the cave.

Dawa wanted to read his texts in the cave, so I spent the rest of the day there as well, sitting quietly, listening to the sonorous lilt of his voice, and trying to let go of the preconceptions and expectations I had brought with me. Towards evening we walked back to the great cave at the top of the hill.

Hindu devotees were ringing the huge bells in the courtyard, while the sound of singing rose from the depths together with the sweet smell of burning incense. The great cave was thronged with people. As I descended the steps I could see a group of Bhutanese women lighting butter lamps and singing the Guru Rinpoche mantra while several Hindu families made elaborate preparations with marigolds, rice and red sindura powder at the Shiva shrine. The air was humming with the sound of different mantras and the fluttering and squeaking of the bats, no more than unsteady shadows in the flickering lamplight. Today the atmosphere was quite different, and I suddenly saw that in the midst of all the crowding and jostling and ceremonies there was a common focus, an awareness that went beyond the outer rituals. The sense of timelessness in the ancient rocks of the cave put such superficial considerations as the names and customs of the different religions into their proper context. 'People have *always* come here,' Dawa had said, and now I could feel how this place acted as a kind of doorway between the material and the spiritual worlds, helping the mind to focus and enter that other state of awareness that is common to all spiritual paths once the forms and labels can be seen for what they are and transcended.

I walked up to the top of the hill in the evening sunshine, picking a way between protruding white rocks like pieces of weathered Emmenthal cheese. I sat for a while, watching the light fade to rose and sharing a packet of biscuits with the resident peacock, sacred bird of Tsepagme, the Buddha of Long Life.

How adept did one have to become at meditation before it could really prolong one's life? How would you know, unless a fair sample of yogis lived to a spectacular hundred and fifty or so? I had heard many stories of cancer patients diagnosed as incurable focusing the mind on dissolving the cancer and curing themselves, but mainstream medics are still extremely sceptical. The stories I heard in the East about great meditators were usually so embellished with superlatives that it seemed as if such siddhis were indeed 'miraculous' and only attainable by such legendary characters as Guru Rinpoche, not by ordinary humans like me. Perhaps the only way to find out was to try it.

The plane lurched to a halt on the Paphlu airstrip. I had fondly imagined that the flight would become less terrifying with practice, but this had not proved to be the case. Tapkhey Lama was waiting for me, his exuberant grin and deep red robes setting him apart from the rest of the people waiting by the dirt runway. He had brought a porter to help carry the large amount of luggage I had brought along. Some of it was food and gear for the six-week meditation retreat I was planning to spend at his gompa. The rest comprised glass and other bits and pieces to complete the meditation hut that Tapkhey had prepared for me.

I slowed my pace as the hillside steepened, glad the porter was carrying most of the weight. Three years had passed since I visited Maratika, and my interest in Shambhala had been pushed aside while the travel company grew exponentially. It was as if I had become a victim of my own success. The increasing workload left me no time for the explorations and interests which had inspired me to start it in the first place. By the time I was working fifteen hours a day, seven days a week, I could see that this pace could not last. Too late, I realised how much I had taken for granted my physical fitness and perfect health, as one illness after another left me without enough energy to lead the expeditions. Just to find space for this retreat I had left the office under the care of a manager, hoping he would not be as disastrous as the previous one. The need to take a break was too pressing, however, to contemplate the commercial outcome.

For several years my daily meditation practice had been supported by a few short retreats but I had not been able to take several weeks together. Yet my teacher always emphasised the value of retreat, comparing it to leaving a kettle on the stove to boil instead of constantly taking it off to cool down again before it has even finished heating up.

Tapkhey was chattering away in his usual enthusiastic way, telling me of all the difficulties he'd had with building the retreat hut. I did not have the breath to respond, but Tapkhey didn't seem to notice.

The newly completed temple stood on the crest of a ridge that looked across to the village of Junbesi and the cluster of buildings that was Trulzhig Rinpoche's monastery of Thubten Choeling. Tapkhey had committed his considerable energy to establishing a gompa for the people of his home village, and his constant optimism in the face of huge challenges was infectious. I always looked forward to my brief visits here. The temple courtyard was bright with long streamers of orange nasturtiums in pots which Tapkhey carefully brought inside each night to protect them from frost. From the courtyard I could see the roofs of Chiwong on the forested ridge away to the east, while the Paphlu airstrip was already hidden behind a shoulder of the hill, almost a day's walk behind us now.

The retreat hut was a tiny one-room affair of white-painted stone with wooden windows facing south to catch the sun. It stood on the steep hillside a few dozen yards above the temple, surrounded by juniper trees and rhododendrons. The snow peaks of Shorung Yul Lha, the goddess mountain of Solu, rose above the pine-forested hillside beyond Thubten Choeling. A little stream sparkled and tumbled through the meadow a short distance away. Outside the windows late marigolds and tiny chrysanthemums flowered on in the winter sunshine, while thyme and mint tangled in the grass of the meadow.

Tapkhey plied me with tea in his own kitchen while his brother, the carpenter, put the finishing touches to the hut and set the glass I had brought into the wooden window frames. The kitchen shelves were stacked with dried herbs and jars of pickles and spices. There were also a few jars of Tapkhey's speciality, a deep red fruit cordial made from high-altitude berries which he collected himself from the forest. He gave a jar to me, although I knew he would never divulge the secret of the recipe. A small grey cat appeared from time to time, looking around hopefully for any stray pieces of cheese, then retreating into its nest at the side of the clay oven. Tapkhey had built the oven himself, and fashioned the smooth hole a foot away from the firebox, so that the cat had a warm safe place of its own and no longer needed to singe its whiskers trying to perch close to the fire.

By evening the hammering and chiselling in the hut had ceased and I was able to move in. There was a cramped alcove at one side for cooking, with a few shelves for my provisions and a *chullo* of three stones for a cookpot set in an earth pit. I soon discovered that bending double to reach into the pit to cook was a sure recipe for a backache which became the main physical obstacle I had to contend with during the coming weeks of sitting still. The meditation room itself measured barely eight feet by ten, with a piece of foam on the floor on which to sleep, and a small table. I had brought with me my own meditation cushion and sleeping bag. There was little space for anything else. I arranged my few belongings in the tiny room, set my internal alarm clock for daybreak, and looked forward to six weeks of tranquil meditation.

Tranquillity is an elusive commodity, especially if it is something you are expecting, and dead set on having. The traditional texts speak of *maras*, external or internal 'demons' which do their best to distract practitioners from their purpose. Mine came in the form of Tapkhey's cat, which spent most of its waking hours scrabbling and crashing around in the roof space or under the wooden floor, trying to break in to feast on the cheese it could smell in my kitchen. It didn't seem to sleep much, and for the first few days neither did I. Feeling sure that, in Maratika, Guru Rinpoche could not possibly have suffered anything as mundane as being hassled by a hungry cat, I searched my limited resources for a solution.

I discovered that small air vents had been left in the stonework to allow circulation of air in the roof and floor spaces; these were perfectly cat-size and the source of the problem. Carefully I mixed a small bowlful of sticky mud, collected some pebbles, and spent several hours blocking up all the holes. That night the cat returned, and I listened with satisfaction as its soft footsteps scurried around outside the hut, visiting first one blocked hole and then another. Just as I was slipping into blissful sleep it went into action, scratting and scrabbling at the mud and stones in the hole at floor level barely inches from my head. It was either very determined or simply had nothing better to do, because it kept up its onslaught for most of the night.

Next day I mixed pepper with a bowlful of mud and smeared a new layer of defence on to the blocked holes. Soon after dark the scrabbling started – then suddenly stopped. There was a muffled snort, then a couple of loud feline sneezes. A scurrying away of soft paws into the darkness was the last I heard of the cat for the rest of my stay.

Tapkhey had been coming over most days to see how I was and to bring spinach or fresh milk, and, to his great amusement, I regaled him with tales of my sleepless nights. When I told him the final episode, he laughed till tears rolled down his sunburned cheeks.

'Just look at what you are doing!' he chuckled, wiping the tears from his eyes. 'You sit there all day meditating on Compassion for All Beings and such things, and the minute you stop, you are putting pepper on the nose of the *biralou*!'

I could see his point. 'So you mean that when it wakes me up for the tenth time in one night, if instead of thinking "blasted cat again", I think, "oh poor little thing, it must be *so* hungry, I will get up again and feed it again", then I'll know I'm getting somewhere?'

'That's right,' said Tapkhey. He grinned at me quizzically, and left.

It was a lesson I would always remember. Meditation is every minute of one's life, not just the time sitting still that we usually label 'meditation'. Even so, I was relieved that the cat chose to remain in its centrally-heated nest in Tapkhey's kitchen for the next few weeks.

The internal *mara* – the mind that cannot settle – was a far more complicated matter than the cat. There was a world of difference in being alone in the office, bombarded by information flung at random by phones, files, and fax machines, to being alone with myself and silence, trying to clear out the clutter, chatter and invading thoughts just to make the space to get started. The more I shovelled these intrusions out of the way, the more others – like London drivers – would leap into the space I had just created. The very walls of the room seemed to echo and magnify every mental leap from one subject to another, becoming mirrors that reflected the chaotic patchwork of what I had hitherto regarded as my rational mind. When alone, I have never enjoyed listening to the constant burble of a radio, but I began to understand why so many people do. It drowns out the noise coming from inside your own head. I was visited by thoughts, feelings and ideas I thought I had forgotten years before, but gradually I began to identify with these visitors less closely, observing them for the intruders they were. 'What are *you* doing here?' I would ask them silently.

Eventually they seemed to give up of their own accord and go away, leaving a calm space a hundred times more blissful than that blessed relief you feel when the man operating the pneumatic drill outside your window finally stops and goes home.

Although my current problems of overwork and illness, and the resulting break-up of my marriage to Lhakpa, were still not resolved and reasserted themselves from time to time, I found that when they appeared in a mind that was calm they had less power. Then it became easier to apply Lama Zopa's advice on problems. This was remarkably simple.

'Practise mind transformation. Instead of seeing problems as suffering, develop the habit of recognising them as supportive conditions, the cause of your happiness. Start by trying to see small problems as beneficial, then gradually you will be able to recognise the serious problems as necessary for your happiness.'

When I first heard this, I did not want even to consider it. All I wanted was that the problems would go away. But with space and time to think about it, I could see a basic logic to Rinpoche's words that could not be argued away.

'If a problem can be solved, there is not much point being upset about it. There is no reason to be angry or depressed. And if the problem is something that cannot be changed, there is also no point in being unhappy, in disliking it. No matter what happens, it is useless to become angry or depressed.'

This is easy to understand intellectually, but harder to put into practice when you are right in the middle of a crisis and feeling emotionally upset. At first I found myself thinking it was all very well for Rinpoche to say things like that, because he didn't have any problems. Then I reminded myself that he had fled the Chinese army, crossed the Himalaya on foot, and suffered smallpox and then TB in a refugee camp. He rarely spoke about his early hardships, instead spending every minute being concerned about the needs of others. It was his example, the way he lived his life as much as his actual advice that convinced me. If this was what meditation and Thought Transformation did for you, then it was definitely something worth working on. Although Rinpoche was always pointing out that the only deep, lasting happiness is the happiness of enlightenment, it often seemed a distant goal, the preserve of great *mahasiddhas* and legendary yogis. It is the more immediate things, like Rinpoche's example and the solution of everyday problems, that at first have the most influence.

'It is not that you will be physically protected from enemies or diseases now or in the future. You will simply not be disturbed by them. They will actually help you to develop your mind.'

In a strange way, the despair of illness and exhaustion had brought a sense of openness and space. I had been living with the feeling that I had lost everything, not just the security of all I had worked for, but health, energy and self-confidence as well. Yet somehow, once everything had been stripped away, there was nothing left to lose, nothing to cling to, and in its own way this brought a sense of freedom and the clarity to see everything afresh.

For a long time I had felt uneasy about the way Western culture makes so much effort to deny or suppress our awareness of reality. Now this feeling came into focus as never before. We become conditioned to over-protecting ourselves from every conceivable discomfort or difficulty with insurance policies, safety barriers and liability clauses. There is a whole industry of everything from cosmetics to surgery to help us deny the reality of old age, and a system of homes and hospices to hide the reality of death from those whose turn is not due just yet. We are encouraged to become addicted to consumerism – and the work that feeds it – in order to hide in busyness, to numb our minds so that we no longer even see or care that we are living in a huge charade. We can pretend that we live in a safe, secure world without the dangers and instability that Himalayan farmers must endure. And all the while we are drinking polluted water, eating carcinogenic food, breathing a daily ration of toxic fumes, and living in a climate of greed, racism, armaments, and global manipulation of markets which regularly erupts in violence and instability.

We become so accustomed to living with this denial that we no longer notice the conflict in our own minds. As soon as we are bothered by some inconvenience we feel justified in becoming angry and upset about it because we have succumbed to the myth that everything would be so perfect if only these troublesome *problems* could just be removed once and for all. . . And we lose sight of the truth, which is that each is just an aspect of life, and whether it is good or bad is largely what we make of it.

Taking time out of the mental conflict makes a huge difference. Letting the mind rest in the present moment brings a space to see ourselves more clearly. There is a whole mixture in there: desire and aversion, prejudice and laziness. Our lives are made of ambitions, expectations and projections into the future, and regret or nostalgia for the past. Taking time out, letting the mind rest in the present, is to experience the resonance of our own life once again. It becomes easier to face up to whatever we have been avoiding with a new calm perceptiveness. Instead of always turning away from thoughts that give rise to fear, anxiety or anger, we can find the space just to be with those feelings, feel how they begin, and grow to the point where they can take over our lives completely. By our simply watching them, and being aware of them, they lose their power over us.

This is the beginning of true compassion. Compassion is not a kind of sentimental 'Oh, isn't that just terrible' that we say in response to other people's moans and groans. It means, literally, experiencing feeling, or passion, *with* someone. It means being able to say, 'Yes. I know how that feels, I've been there, and it hurts, doesn't it? But it can change, slowly, if we work on it.'

One of the hardest things to recognise is that to be of any real use to others we need at least to have gone some way in sorting out our own mess. Good intention itself counts for a great deal, but the best results are limited as soon as our own junk starts getting in the way.

It took me a long time to understand fully why giving in to the demands of others and trying to live up to their projections should always cause me so much trouble. Wasn't I abandoning selfishness and instead considering their needs? It was hard to recognise that my motivation was in fact wrong. The problems arose from the occasions when I knew the demands and projections were unreasonable in the circumstances. I lacked the confidence to make this clear without feeling defensive, so would allow myself to be drawn in to trying to fulfil these demands. If demands are unreasonable, there always comes a point at which they can no longer be fulfilled – and at that point those demanding simply become angry because they are no longer getting what you have trained them to expect. Tapkhey's teasing over my escapade with the cat did not imply that I should have let it run riot through my kitchen – he himself would give it a smart reminder on the nose when it overstepped its boundaries in his kitchen – but that the awareness of meditation needs to be carried through into every action. When I could do this I would be able to recognise the right responses to situations and use my energy to give people what they really needed rather than what they thought they wanted.

The great thing about a retreat is that it gives you a clear space to see everything in a wider perspective. It is also one of the greatest pitfalls because there is always the temptation to use it as an escape – and then go back to everyday situations as if nothing had happened. The real test comes when you are back in the fray again and begin to see a real difference in the way you respond to situations. In my case, it has proved to be an ongoing process of thinking I have really got everything well sorted out – until a new crisis appears and all those wonderfully peaceful realisations once more go straight out of the window. And then the metaphorical dust settles and I realise I've just missed another chance to put it all into practice.

Rinpoche often made the point that one of the benefits of experiencing so-called problems is that it can be the final push needed to make the shift in perception necessary to recognise the value of a spiritual path. He would always try to encourage Western practitioners to see this path as being as meaningful to them as it is to Eastern yogis, often lapsing into the colloquial English he had learned from his American students in order to emphasise his point.

'There are many stories of people who, after experiencing some heavy problem, got completely fed up with worldly life, went to find a teacher, received teachings, then did meditation retreat in a solitary place to cut through negative emotions. They practised and achieved the three principal aspects of the Path – the aspiration to engage in spiritual practice, a wish to become enlightened so as to help all beings through compassion and a profound sense of connectedness, and a deep insight into the interdependent reality of things and events. Then, completing this foundation for successful practice, they gained high realisations of tantra.'

It had taken me a long time to recognise that, for the first steps at least, this had been true for me. If I had not been so distraught about the accident on Tashi Lapcha I would probably not have sought an interview with Rinpoche for several years. I would have continued to attend teachings, staying in the background as before, and not made direct contact with someone who could understand the obscure workings of my mind at a very individual level.

Because past and present relationships are often the source of our greatest pain, the first step towards resolving these deep conflicts comes in establishing a committed relationship with a spiritual teacher. Disappointments and betrayals already experienced can leave feelings of isolation and mistrust. With a true teacher we can learn to trust again. When, suddenly, we recognise someone with calm wisdom and clarity who can accept us complete with all our worst aspects, then we begin to feel the confidence to accept those aspects ourselves. That kind of total trust is in many ways a huge leap of faith, because you are laying yourself open to all kinds of possible betrayals and abuse if you project the relationship on to someone who does not from their side recognise the responsibility involved. Traditional texts recommend a twelve-year period of carefully checking out a potential teacher before making that lifelong commitment. I spent only a little over one hour during my first meeting with Rinpoche, and that commitment just seemed to happen at a very deep level without a conscious decision being made. I can only suppose that in Tibetan terms we were simply re-establishing a connection formed in a previous life, or in Western terms I was extremely lucky.

'Any happiness you feel comes from your own mind. From the small pleasure you experience in a cool breeze when you feel hot, all the way to enlightenment, all happiness is manufactured by your own inner factory. If we constantly seek happiness outside ourselves, by pursuing objects of desire, all we experience is pain and dissatisfaction.'

To break free from this, practitioners are taught to become mistrustful of the five senses by which objects of desire and aversion affect the mind. This path is one of extreme self-control, where the individual is constantly mindful not to become attracted or repelled by any object or event. However, Tibetan Buddhism particularly emphasises the path of tantra, which seeks to transform *every* experience into the spiritual path. This uses the transformed energy of all those turbulent desires and emotions, which otherwise get us into all sorts of trouble, to increase the power of our meditation. As Rinpoche would point out, 'We will never attain the happiness of enlightenment by making ourselves more and more miserable.'

Of course, transforming a bundle of chaotic desires and emotions which have up till now been allowed to run riot does not happen overnight. One of the roles of the teacher is to ensure that the student does not make the mistake of simply indulging in a riotous time, thinking it is the same as following a spiritual path.

To begin with, all I knew about tantra were the exotic stories I had heard in the East about flying lamas and great *mahasiddhas*, such as Milarepa who was able to control his body heat to the extent that he could meditate all night in the snow beside a frozen lake, wrapped only in a wet cotton sheet. Rinpoche had greeted my questions along these lines with great amusement. Although he did not deny that such feats were possible, he stressed that this was not the real purpose of the practice. His reasons were more immediate and practical.

'Rather than allowing ourselves to follow habitual patterns of grasping, dissatisfaction, confusion, misery and guilt, we should try to improve our minds by developing deeper and deeper levels of understanding, more skilful control of our mental and physical energies, ever higher forms of happiness and a better life. At first, engaging in spiritual practice takes place at intellectual and emotional levels. However, we need to make changes at a very deep, unconscious level if there is to be any real benefit. Intellectual understanding does not alter our automatic responses. Efforts to suppress negative emotions rather than eradicate them can eventually do more harm than good. We need to change deeply ingrained habits that trap us in a cycle of dissatisfaction and suffering. The use of powerful psychological symbols and the focusing of physiological subtle energy bring about these changes at a very profound level of our psyche. In this way the inner potential that is latent in every one of us can be manifest. This state of complete fulfilment, of full awakening, is characterised by unlimited wisdom, compassion, and skill, or perfect power.'

Listening to this from someone who had clearly attained this state himself was far more inspiring than stories of flying lamas and so forth. At the same time, a modicum of skill in generating *tum-mo*, or inner heat, would not have come amiss in January at eleven thousand feet in the Himalaya. Sometimes the sun would be obscured by snow clouds for days at a time, while flurries of snow dusted the dark pines and the ground froze solid and hard. Tapkhey's potted nasturtiums remained indoors, and so did I. Not that it made a great deal of difference. Without a clay oven I could not keep the fire going once I had finished cooking, and the temperature in the hut soon dropped below freezing. I would sit in meditation swathed in my huge down expedition sleeping bag, sometimes with a hot water bottle tucked inside for good measure. Milarepa would no doubt have been very amused if he had seen the performance.

When at last the watery winter sun reappeared I crept outside and uncurled, lizard-like, in its meagre warmth in a sheltered corner by the frosted chrysanthemums.

Tapkhey arrived, bearing milk and spinach.

'What's this? You are on retreat, so why have you come outside the hut?'

'Ooh, Tapkhey-la, it's so cold inside. I'm just warming up a bit. And I'm reading a *Dharma* book, so it's still retreat.'

Tapkhey's face broke into its familiar grin. 'That's right. You must do what feels comfortable at the beginning. You can be more strict when you get used to it.'

And when it gets a bit warmer, I thought. Tapkhey put down the supplies and sat down on a wooden bench against the wall.

'How is everything going? Are you still all right, and comfortable?'

'Fine thanks, Tapkhey-la. Tell me about some of the things in this book.' I consulted the glossary in the back so that I could splice the appropriate Tibetan term into the Nepali in which Tapkhey and I usually conversed. 'Tell me about *gyu-lu*, the "illusory body".'

Tapkhey laughed out loud. 'Don't you think it would make more sense to discuss some of the basics instead of speculating about the stages just before enlightenment itself? We can worry about all that when we get a little closer to the event, can't we?'

Most of the lamas seemed so sensible and pragmatic. I wondered if any of them bothered to learn to fly these days. Perhaps they didn't now that Nepalese Airlines was increasing its schedules into the mountain areas.

Tapkhey helped me carry the food into the hut. He had also brought some chippings of pine bark dripping with sticky resin to help with lighting the fire. I was finding the pyrotechnics as difficult as the sub-zero temperatures and the long hours of sitting still. There was no paper with which to get the fire started – you had to go straight from the match to the wood, and while Tapkhey made it look so easy, I did not have the same rate of success. Even using what I was sure was a year's supply of his best pine chippings in a few weeks, it was still a laborious process. I never ceased to be surprised, and touched, by Tapkhey's constant concern for my welfare, mixed with a total incredulity at my ineptitude.

It is quite common for students to experience changes in physical sensations when engaging in long retreats, such as feeling as if the physical body has dissolved into light or seeing coloured lights or visions. Working with powerful symbols such as Shambhala can help to channel and integrate these experiences. In this way the different levels, the 'outer, inner, and secret levels' of Shambhala and the Hidden Valleys can also refer to deepening levels of meditation.

Rinpoche had once mentioned the story of the first king of Shambhala.

'He requested the Buddha to teach him a practice that would harmonise with his responsibilities, because as a ruler he could not go off into the forest and follow an ascetic life. The teaching the Buddha gave him was the Kalachakra Tantra, which has been passed down the lineage of Shambhala kings to the present day.'

I was beginning to understand some of the inner meaning of the Shambhala legend. It was as if I had been looking at Shambhala as an image or picture of an actual place that hovered between the material and perceptual worlds, and on one level this was perfectly appropriate. Gradually, it seemed as if this image was becoming less of an opaque picture and more like a window of clear glass, looking out on to the everyday world but in a new way; as if the paradise of the Kalachakra deity lay all the time concealed within everyday reality – concealed until we develop the ability to perceive it. If, using the heightened perception of the essentially clear mind described by Rinpoche, we could see things as they really are, unclouded by delusions, then we would see divinity in everything.

The lotus shape of the kingdom of Shambhala is a symbol to be found throughout the East. Just as the lotus has its roots in the mud and murky waters at the bottom of a pond, yet blooms clean and undefiled in the sunlight far above, so the *Bodhisattva* lives and works in the world, but is uncorrupted and undistracted by it. In the same way, the inner kingdom of Shambhala lies within the ordinary world but is unaffected by it.

This symbolism is also used in connection with the central channel of the psychic energy system, which is visualised as running vertically from the base of the spine to the crown of the head just in front of the backbone of the physical body, with the various *chakras* along its length. Rinpoche's explanation made complex practices sound quite straightforward:

'The most important of these chakras is the heart centre which is the home of the very subtle mind that has been with us from conception – and from lifetimes without beginning. This centre is usually described as having the form of an eight-petalled lotus, the "petals" representing the side channels, or nerves, of the psychic energy system. Just as in basic meditation practices there is much emphasis on concentrating the mind on the physical breath as it enters and leaves the body, so in tantric meditation the practitioner concentrates on subtle "energy winds", or *prana*, which carry the mind through the subtle energy channels of the body.

'As long as the energy winds of the mind are flowing through any of the thousands of channels other than the central one, the gross conceptual minds will be activated. But when these energy winds dissolve into the central channel – as happens naturally at the time of death – these gross minds subside and the very subtle mind of clear light arises instead. Very few people are trained to recognise and take advantage of this subtle consciousness at death, but skilled practitioners learn to awaken it in their meditation. They can use this subtle mind to penetrate the true nature of reality and also gain control over their own death and rebirth.'

The kingdom of Shambhala has the same eight-petalled lotus shape as the heart centre, showing that it is not only the home of the Kalachakra teachings but on a deeper level is a symbol of the actual practice of the Kalachakra meditation itself. It is to this aspect that the old hermit of the story is referring when he tells the young traveller that he need not travel much further 'because the kingdom of Shambhala is in your own heart'.

Rinpoche always emphasised that the purpose of practice is to benefit others. 'Once the gross mind has ceased we can quickly achieve enlightenment with the subtle mind. But stopping there is not enough. The whole purpose of this practice is to free all sentient beings from suffering and lead them to enlightenment as quickly as possible.

'Through continuous practice, we become deeply absorbed in an experience of spaciousness in which the ordinary, concrete appearances normally crowding our vision begin to dissolve. Like summer clouds disappearing back into the clear blue expanse of the sky, dualistic visions cease and we are left with nothing but the clear, empty space of non-duality; the mind feels calm and boundless, free of limitation. This is not a sleepy, dull state; the mind is awake and alert – rejecting nothing, asserting nothing, yet accepting everything. We see the illusory nature of things and recognise that all phenomena are nothing but fleeting appearances arising in the clear space of the mind. As each thought disappears we begin to feel that this disappearance is even more real than the thought's original concrete appearance. Then, when destructive thoughts and emotions such as anger and jealousy arise, we will remain in contact with the deep, peaceful clarity of our essential mind – which is in the nature of love.

'Kalachakra means literally "The Wheel of Time"; the cycle of ceaseless change, creation and destruction, that defines our existence. Through this meditation we become aware that past and future exist only in the mind, and that no object of desire or aversion is permanent. Becoming free from the constraints of time means a growing awareness of the timeless present; an awareness of actual experience instead of becoming lost in thoughts or projections about it.'

These moments of clarity are not the sole preserve of long hours of meditation. They can arise suddenly and spontaneously in a flash of insight and understanding. All too often though, these fresh perceptions degenerate into old habits, so that instead of seeing things directly we recall our preconceptions based on the elusive memory of what was originally fresh and real. Like the hunter who accidentally stumbles on a Hidden Valley, we mark the situation where we experienced the moment of clarity or happiness. Thinking that it comes from somewhere outside ourselves we try to re-create the situation, but find instead only the fading memory of a past experience.

The Tibetan word for meditation literally translates as 'to become familiar with'. Its purpose is to become so familiar with the mind of clear perception that we no longer slip back into old habits clouded by delusion. Like most people, I soon discovered that the most difficult habit to break is the preconception of our own ego or self, with all the limitations this brings to our own potential for development and our ability to help others. Identifying with powerful images like Shambhala and Kalachakra can help us break out of the self-limiting preconceptions of who and what we can become. The practical use of positive symbols is already recognised and used in a more limited way in the West in the archetypal heroes and heroines of our own myths and stories and the role models that children are encouraged to emulate. Once the essential value of a symbol is recognised, the cultural differences that at first seemed so strange and exotic no longer seem important.

I realised to my surprise that I was already familiar with some of these underlying principles. I had intuitively been using similar techniques – at a very basic level – during the years I had been involved with climbing as a sport. If I decided I wanted to try a particularly difficult climb I would spend several days beforehand concentrating on changing my whole mental attitude to it. I would deliberately stop thinking of it as something more difficult or dangerous than anything I had tried before, and start thinking of myself as a person who could complete this particular climb with ease and competence. Then, with this new perception I would visualise climbing the route in minute detail. Of course, the details were largely imaginary, as they were based only on the limited vision I had from the ground, but this did not seem to matter. By the time I actually started the climb it was with a feeling of quiet confidence, as if I were not only familiar with the route but also many others of the same standard.

Of course, excelling at a physical sport is just fun, but it nevertheless offers a taste of the heightened ability achieved by this kind of mental technique – enough to convince me that the meditation Rinpoche described would work in just such an immediate and practical way.

I also noticed some parallels with the concentration aspect of meditation. Rinpoche would often recommend contemplation on the uncertainty of our lifespan in order to increase concentration.

'If you find your mind wandering, contemplate death and impermanence. You may have very little time left in this lifetime to complete your meditation practice.'

In effect, that is exactly what we were doing when rock-climbing. When you are several hundred feet up a vertical cliff you do not have to think consciously about the uncertainty of your lifespan. There is an all-pervading awareness of the vast drop below your feet. This activates our most powerful instinct, that of survival, which in turn focuses the mind in single-pointed concentration on each precise move upwards on the tiny handholds. The knowledge that one moment's distraction would almost certainly mean a dangerous, if not fatal, fall means that the concentration simply does not waver.

There were many times I had reached the top of a particularly hard rock pitch with my hands torn and bleeding from the sharp rocks. I had been concentrating for anything up to two hours on the moves so hard that I had not felt any pain. I was still unable to maintain this level of concentration in meditation for the same length of time – and if someone had meanwhile started scraping at my hands with a piece of sharp granite I would most certainly have noticed it. This presumably was because my motivation to become enlightened and benefit all beings was nowhere near as strong as my basic survival instinct when contemplating a five-hundred-foot drop. However, there was at least the encouragement of knowing that my perfectly ordinary mind had already achieved certain levels of concentration, and so theoretically could do so again, once I had managed to rearrange my levels of motivation.

At one point, about halfway through the retreat, I found I had become irrationally afraid of going outside the hut in the dark. This was as puzzling as it was frightening. Even when I was a child, this had not been one of my fears and I had no previous experience of dealing with it. As a child I had loved to go for long summer walks with my dog, revelling in the mystery of the twilight as much as the warmth of the sunshine; loving the uncertainty of visual perception where anything might be possible, wandering home entranced by the magical softness of the starlight and the moon. Even out here in the Himalaya I could not generate enough fear to keep my torch batteries in order and had several times become involved in rather foolhardy escapades on perched trails by moonlight because the torch had gone dead. I tried to rationalise it by pointing out to myself that, if the cat could smell the cheese, then presumably so could the bears and snow leopards that haunted the forest above the hut. Yes, it was simply a practical wariness that I might step outside the door and tread on the soft furry warmth of a hungry snow leopard in the darkness.

I told Tapkhey of my very rational and reasonable fears. I'm not sure if I expected sympathy instead of the usual peals of hearty laughter, but in any event Tapkhey's response was true to form.

'So what is it you are afraid of?' He grinned cheerfully in the homely morning sunshine. 'There are no bears and leopards left in these forests.'

'So where did that stuffed leopard in the gompa come from? Before it got stuffed it was running around *somewhere*, feeling very hungry.'

'Don't worry! The villagers brought it from miles away. They killed it because it ate their sheep in the high pastures, and then they felt sorry, so they offered it to the gompa as purification.'

I was still too concerned with my own fears to get involved in complicated ethical debate about the efficacy of this as a means of atonement for the negative karma of killing. Tapkhey's reassurances had brushed aside my flimsy rationalisations about wild animals, which I already knew rarely lurk so close to habitation in order to scavenge.

So what was I afraid of? I rearranged my daily routine to avoid the need to go out to complete any chores after dark. This gave a quiet, panic-free space to explore the possibilities in meditation. Gradually I realised that darkness itself is a powerful, intuitive symbol of the unknown. I had touched on some of the deep recesses of my own unconscious and was afraid of taking the next step of confronting those carefully guarded, ego-protecting habits and attitudes. What then? The question brought an almost physical shock. I would be laying myself open to a whole range of possibilities, challenging and exciting but unknown and unpredictable. I would become vulnerable without these carefully arranged defences. This kind of inner unknown was far more terrifying than any mountainous terrain or storm. Small wonder the agile mind twists and turns away from a confrontation and invents any outside threat from wild animals to hungry ghosts in order not to have to deal with it.

Tapkhey was reassuring. 'It is a slow process. You just do the practice and little by little it comes. Don't expect everything to happen at once.'

Like the long, complex way to Shambhala, I thought reflectively. No wonder the great meditators can travel there in an instant of mind, while ordinary mortals have to plod the long road through the mountains and valleys, the rapture and despair, of the journey.

The fear of the dark disappeared as soon as its source was identified. Dealing with the source would prove as long and challenging as the outer search for Shambhala had been. Rinpoche's perceptiveness and advice was always there to wake you up, whether there was an opportunity to see him, or simply to read his books or my notes from his teachings:

'If you have developed direct awareness, then every activity, every event, can be transformed into wisdom. As a human being, you should never set a limit on how much you can accomplish, no matter what your life has been like so far. But it is no use merely reading about the experiences of others; we must cultivate the experiences ourselves.'

Outside the tiny hut, the sparkling frosts of winter melted into spring and primroses opened fragile petals among the scented herbs as I walked to the stream to fetch water.

PART THREE

The Hidden Valley

I believe that to meet the challenge of our times, human beings will have to develop a greater sense of universal responsibility. Each of us must learn to work not just for his or her own self, family, or nation, but for the benefit of all mankind. Universal responsibility is the real key to human survival. It is the best foundation for world peace, the equitable use of natural resources and, through concern for future generations, the proper care for the environment.

His Holiness the Dalai Lama

16

Sky Dancers

།རྒྱུད་བདག་འཛིན་འདུལ་ཐབས་མ་འབད་ན།

Shivaratri. Shiva's night. A rustling throng of pilgrims flowed down narrow cobbled streets to the river and the sacred Shiva temple of Pashupatinath. The reddening sun sank lower behind bat-hung trees surrounding the inner temple, forbidden to non-Hindu outcastes like me who craned their necks at the gate for a glimpse of Nandi, the great golden bull of Shiva standing in the courtyard. His shining rump almost blocked the gateway, so that there was little more to be seen than his great golden testicles.

The pilgrims flowed on towards the burning ghats by the river. A pyre smouldered sulkily in the evening sun, smoke shrouding the stick-like remains of the corpse on the ghat. A smell like scorched hamburger hung in the damp air by the bridge. Beggars sat or lay inches from the trample of passing feet, knowing that today of all days, pious pilgrims would buy merit by giving. Some beggars were lepers, arms and legs ending in mutilated stumps of weeping sores. I felt my mind recoil from this wanton display of ruined bodies; a fear rooted deep in centuries, and overlaid by intellectual indignation now that leprosy can be cured – with care and money. I threw coins and walked on quickly.

May I never be reborn a leper . . .

On the hillside above the river stood a long line of Shiva shrines, carved stone pagodas, each housing a single lingam penetrating a yoni, ancient Hindu phallic symbols of union. In a maze of surrounding temples and courtyards, pilgrim sadhus from India gathered, their flowing white and orange robes and long dark hair a bright patchwork against the white-painted arches and colonnades. In the dappled shade of a tree a young man in faded orange sat upright, one leg wound impossibly up and behind his head, gazing into space.

I settled in a quiet corner by the serpentine form of a stone Naga carved into the parapet. In the flagged courtyard an aged, wrinkled sadhu and his young disciple were preparing an elaborate ritual. Both naked, they smeared themselves with grey ash from the burning ghats, then arranged two small circles of dried sacred cow dung. After many prostrations around the circle and decorative offerings of incense and marigolds, the boy lit the cow dung, then he and his guru sat crosslegged, each in the centre of a smoking circle of dung, to chant mantras counted on their long rosaries. The guru, presumably having reached a more advanced stage than his student, then wound his long matted braid of orange-stained hair around his head, lifted a wok-full of burning dung on to it, swathed himself in his robe and continued to chant amid a cloud of thick acrid smoke.

I moved away, my eyes stinging and watering. Everything I had seen was intriguing but incomprehensible. Perhaps there comes a point when it is no longer necessary to understand it all. Aligning perceptions with those of another culture helps to shake us out of habitual ways of seeing things and enables us to become aware of our own individual and cultural habits. Blindly adopting a different set of ideas and perceptions would be to waste the opportunity to wake up.

As I began to see the meaning and value of the Buddha's teachings, I also saw how essential it is not to become fixed on outer forms or belief systems. I was increasingly aware that the teachings had themselves been a commentary on the habits and illusions of the cultural world view prevailing at the time of the Buddha. The more I saw of Hindu or Shamanic culture, the more I realised how much of what is often presented as 'Buddhism' is an exotic mix of all that. It would take a long time to evolve an understanding of how the essence of these ideas would be relevant to my own situation, in my own culture. There were far more subtleties involved than simply reading translated texts and accepting verbatim what was presented.

Intellectually, perhaps, I had reached the point where I understood the symbolism of Shambhala and the Hidden Valleys and could pursue my interest by studying and continuing with my meditation practice. But, before returning home for good and integrating what I had learned, there was still something inside me that wanted to find just one Hidden Valley, somewhere in these mountains. Just one . . .

I waited by the fountain at Kopan. I came here often now, to see Rinpoche or to spend a few days in retreat. The courtyard and its pipal tree had become familiar, yet still the perception of those first few visits lingered, an unexpected haven of clean air and stillness above the smog and noise of Kathmandu.

I was hoping to learn more about a Hidden Valley, wild and uninhabited, which is said to lie beyond the Ganesh range right up on the Tibetan border near the region of Tsum, one of the few remaining haunts of rare and endangered snow leopards. An old man and his sister take care of a three-tiered pagoda temple and its books and paintings. The name of the Valley is Kyimolung, the 'Valley of Happiness'.

I had heard that one of the teachers at Kopan had spent some time in Tsum after fleeing from Tibet. His knowledge of herbs and healing had earned him the affectionate name of 'Medicine Lama' from people who knew him.

The Medicine Lama received me in his small room beyond Kopan's flower garden.

He did not seem surprised that I should be interested in the remote valley where he had stayed.

'In 1959 I came over the Himalaya from Tibet with several companions. We crossed the passes and came to the high valleys at the head of the Shar Khola. We remained there a short time, and then my companions went on to the monastic universities that were being established by Tibetan refugees in India. There are many caves in Tsum in which Milarepa and other great yogis had made meditation retreats, so I decided I would stay and meditate for a while. . .' He paused. 'After twenty years, I came to Kathmandu, and now, you see, I am teaching at Kopan.'

I sat on my cushion on the Medicine Lama's carpet in silence, trying to imagine the life that had been described so lightly. Twenty years meditating in a cave in a freezing valley at fourteen thousand feet.

The Medicine Lama was writing something in Tibetan script on a scrap of paper.

'This is the name of one of the lamas there. He is a good man, kind, and he knows many people. If you need help, you should visit him.'

Two of the younger Kopan monks who were hoping to visit their families in the high villages of Tsum offered to be my guides for the long haul from the roadhead at Gorkha up the Buri Gandaki valley. Unfortunately for them, the Kopan disciplinarian ruled that studies were more important than taking an extra twelve days at the start of their Losar holidays, and they found themselves firmly grounded. They were disappointed, but promised to contact relatives who would work as porters and local guides.

I rested in the shade of a welcome pipal tree on the outskirts of Arughat. Phunsok and his brother had waited for me as my pace slowed after two days of walking in tropical heat. Although he was the *adarshe*, or mayor, of a village in Tsum, Phunsok still spent much of his time carrying bales of wool over the passes from Tibet to trade in Kathmandu. His younger brother was wearing maroon jeans and yellow sweater – and a very short haircut; the uniform of an off-duty monk earning some subsistence money. He was quiet and a little shy, so I waited a while before asking questions.

'Are you a monk? Do you study at one of the monasteries?'

He was non-committal. 'I like to read *peja* sometimes.'

I changed my mind and decided not to pursue questions about the Hidden Valley. Wait and see, I told myself.

The valley of the Buri Gandaki became a deep gorge bounded on either side by vertical cliffs, and the trail was often no more than a narrow ledge hacked into the precipice. Several tributaries had no bridges, and were crossed by means of a wooden triangle suspended on a rope stretched across the chasm. You are supposed to sit in the triangle and haul yourself cautiously across to the far side. I was relieved to find a suspension bridge across the Buri Gandaki itself, even though much of the planking was missing.

After several days of climbing, the tropical jungle gave way to scattered pine and rhododendron clinging to tiny ledges on the steep slopes. Notched tree trunks led from one level of perched trail to another, an intricate route that crept precariously upwards between massive rock buttresses.

Conversation was not easy on terrain like this, but on occasions when the path was a little wider I managed to glean enough information from Phunsok to realise that Kyimolung probably lay somewhere further west than the area we were heading for, although he was not sure exactly where it was. I wanted to visit the places the Medicine Lama had spoken of and look for signs of snow leopards, so it seemed better to continue as we were than to attempt a vague series of diversions. I tried to alleviate the feeling of disappointment by telling myself that this was the inevitable result of having preconceived ideas. If I had not become so fixed on finding Kyimolung, I knew I would still be happy to explore Tsum. I made a conscious effort to let go of the whole idea.

The Shar Khola flows from the Tibetan border to the east of the Buri Gandaki. Ahead lay the deep valley between the Ganesh and Senge ranges which led to the walled villages of Tsum. Cliffs towered above the valley, with distant trees on the crest still in afternoon sun while green ice-melt rushing through the narrow cleft was already in deep shadow. Forty feet up the vertical face a line of holes had been bored into the rock, all that remained of the original road through the gorge. This had been supported by horizontal stakes driven into the holes and then covered with logs and brushwood – a flimsy and precarious perch which had long since collapsed into the churning race of the Shar Khola. Looking at the only way across now – a series of logs spanning gaps from boulder to boulder in the torrent – I did not like to enquire whether anyone had been on the road when it fell in the river.

Phunsok was sitting with his brother, his finely-chiselled Tibetan features and long slanting eyes almost hidden in the deep shadows below the cliff. He spoke softly, his voice barely audible above the roar of the water.

'Tomorrow we will climb up past the cliffs and we will enter one of the eight *beyul*, the Hidden Valleys of the Himalaya. Many years ago, the great lamas, the men of power, put these cliffs as a gate to protect the Valley from the outside world.'

'But I thought the Hidden Valley was further west?'

Phunsok smiled but offered no more information.

All thought of letting go of preconceived ideas evaporated like spray on the river.

'The Medicine Lama mentioned a gompa on the north side of Ganesh, beyond the Shar Khola. Is that anything to do with the Hidden Valley?'

Phunsok gazed at the river. 'Well, I think there may be a gompa, but there may not be anyone there. People go there sometimes. . .'

'Could we go that way?'

'Well, maybe. I'm not sure if there's any water.'

He was not being unfriendly or overtly secretive and I gave up my questions for the time being. The valley of Tsum itself contained numerous villages, and I had never heard it referred to as a Hidden Valley. Yet hovering on the periphery of thought was a feeling that there was something out of the ordinary up here somewhere, just waiting – if only I knew where to look.

The log bridges over the river were slippery with spray and not particularly well-anchored at either end. The boulders upon which they were wedged were rounded and steep, involving some scrambling and slithering to reach the next set of wobbly logs. Maybe the suspended road had been easier than this. The last boulder gave on to a leap for the shingle bank of the river and the long climb out of the gorge. The deep cleft fell away below, almost hidden in lush green fern and moss clinging to damp ledges on the rock walls. At last the gradient eased and we were in a high valley with the snow peak of Ganesh to the south and the great ridge of Senge Himal, the Lion Mountain, to the north.

The village of Hripche was strung along a low ridge, surrounded by small barley fields. Two full-grown langurs were sitting placidly on a sunny rock, nibbling barley grains, oblivious of the pebbles thrown by a small child on guard duty. Beyond the fields open grassy meadows gave way to pine forests, the air sweet and heavy with resin warming in the sunshine.

I scarcely noticed when we turned south, away from the Shar Khola towards the mountains. Above the pine forests there were patches of snow. I walked slowly, scanning the snow for leopard tracks. Phunsok could not understand my fascination with snow leopards.

'They come down from the hills and eat our baby yaks. And there are bears that eat our potatoes.'

And there are langurs eating the barley, I thought. How ever did these people get enough to eat?

As if he had heard the unspoken question, Phunsok said, 'Many of us go to Tibet. We buy wool there and carry it over the passes, down to Gorkha. Then we sell in Kathmandu, and buy rice to bring back here.'

I said, 'In some places, people kill snow leopards.'

Phunsok shook his head. 'We don't do that. Our lama is always reminding us of our precept not to kill. So it makes life a little harder, but our lives are clean.'

And your valley a sanctuary for one of the most beautiful and endangered species in the world, I thought, wondering why some communities made the decision to kill leopards to protect their food supply while others stayed with their principles and found other ways to live. Was it all because of powerful and charismatic spiritual leaders, or something in the place itself that determined the world that a community would create for itself? I was tempted again to pursue the issue of the Hidden Valley, but Phunsok appeared deep in thought, so I let him walk ahead and continued my search for pug marks.

The trail climbed, then contoured past a stone chorten on a rocky ridge. The steep ice-hung peak of Ganesh stood out sharp against other peaks in the cirque, a plume of spindrift blowing from the summit.

A vicious wind was whipping down from the snowfields, bringing flurries of snow as the sky darkened.

'Is there a sheltered place anywhere?' I asked anxiously.

'Not far. Just past these rocks.' He seemed to have decided already where we were heading.

As I came around the buttress I could see a ridge above, silhouetted dark against the great ice and rock face of the mountain. On the crest of the ridge was a three-tiered pagoda temple and slender white prayer flags whipping in the snow-laden wind.

A group of nuns came to greet us as we approached. They had been clearing some small terraced fields around the huts behind the temple and there were streaks of dust on their faces and their patched and grubby robes. These were not the slender, elegant *anis* I was used to seeing in Kathmandu but strong, solid country girls, still carrying mattocks and hoes from their digging. One of them broke into a gap-toothed smile.

'You look frozen! What are you doing walking about in a snowstorm?' She broke into peals of laughter, and waved me to follow her into the building.

The nuns' kitchen was a small room at the side of the temple itself. A fire of pine logs burned brightly against one wall. Two girls tended pots and kettles on the hearth. It was warm and steamy inside after the blizzard-laden gusts of the hillside, and I wriggled happily nearer the fire. The air steamed visibly as more women crammed into the tiny space. The tea was passed round, and although the nuns' butter had seen better days, it was hot and welcome.

I saw the young porter with the maroon sweater quietly unpacking the tattered bag he always carried with him. He took out a carefully-wrapped Tibetan text and a bundle of maroon robes. Phunsok caught my eye and grinned.

'He is the lama's heart-son. He will take over the teaching when the lama grows old and dies.'

'You all kept this Hidden Valley very hidden, didn't you?'

He gave that subtle, non-committal shake of the head that is so Tibetan. 'It was your karma to come here, so you arrived. Now you are here, you are welcome.'

The following morning the sky cleared and bright sunshine sparkled on six inches of new snow that had fallen during the night. The valley had become a winter paradise, a place of other-worldly loneliness and beauty. The temple stood blanketed in white, shining against the sombre greens of pine forests which covered the lower slopes down to the river. Above the forests rose massive rock and ice walls of the cirque crowned with glittering white peaks.

Some of the nuns were sitting in the snow outside the temple. They had brought out low tables, and laid their *peja* on these. They were happily chanting, oblivious of the cold and great dollops of wet snow slithering off the pine trees to bury themselves in snowdrifts only a few feet away. Khandro, the woman who had invited me in the previous day, was sitting on the stone steps carefully adding another patch to the collection on a worn maroon shirt. She slapped my shoulder in welcome as I sat down, insisting I share her tattered piece of carpet as insulation from the cold stone.

She wanted to know about my journey and I told her of the walk from Gorkha, and what was going on in Kathmandu. She said she had never been to Kathmandu. She had wanted to join the community here since her childhood and her parents finally agreed when she was fifteen. We talked for a while, then were content to sit in silence and gaze at the expanse of space below us, listening to the low hum of chanting coming from the other end of the courtyard.

I had never met people who had chosen such an austere life. It was high, cold, hard work, and they had to grow most of their own food. I could see things were more austere here than in some of the endowed city establishments where everything is provided. Yet she said she was happy and fulfilled, and I could see she meant it. Her meditation and the very simplicity of her life completely sustained her through the long cold months. Far from becoming preoccupied with the hardships, she was content. Whether or not she perceived the other-worldly beauty of this valley as I did was irrelevant. She was in herself a symbol for the antidote to all the problems that arose from having too much wealth, too many material possessions, too much entertainment, too many things to think and worry about. Far from being escapist, her way of life was engaged and balanced. This community was not relying on others to support and care for it; it was acknowledging that so long as we have bodies that need to be fed and sheltered, attending to this needs to be part of the practice. The essence of a Hidden Valley is not an escape to some other-worldly paradise, leaving the whole messy mundane world behind, but a place where the synthesis of the practical and spiritual can become a reality.

Khandro finished her patching and joined her sisters chanting on the edge of the snowdrifts. I sat for a while, listening to the rhythmic rise and fall of their voices, watching the vast expanse of blue sky above the mountains. There was a harmony here, a feeling of spaciousness that, in the quietness, grew into a sense of unity between myself and everything else. Within this clear space everything was in a continuous flow of arising and disappearing, in a perfect balance and completeness. Like the colours in a rainbow, the divisions which had seemed so inherently fixed and definitive – myself and other, this and that – now appeared valid but arbitrary, merely a convenient framework overlaid on a web of subtle relationships reaching out beyond ordinary perception.

I could see why dakinis symbolised that meeting point of inner spaciousness and the outer freedom to dance in the sky. Yet in spite of the stylised poetry and imagery in which they are described, it was no surprise to meet them in other forms, patching shirts and digging snowbound potato fields.

The essence of a dakini is to bring a sense of inspiration, a freedom from all the constraints which we imagine are holding us back from realising our fullest potential and the confidence to stop theorising and get on with it.

Later the women changed out of their patched gardening clothes and into their cleanest robes in preparation for their evening *puja*, or temple ceremony. They settled into their places in two long rows down the centre of the hall and laid out their texts. It was cold now, and there was no heating apart from the rows of butter lamps in front of the Buddha statues. Khandro was clattering in and out with a huge teapot, keeping everyone supplied with hot butter tea. She grinned as she passed me.

'My turn to bring tea today. What, no cup with you? I will bring one.' She headed back to the kitchen for a refill.

The sound of chanting blended with the resonance of the long horns. As the women focused their concentration on their shared meditation, I could scarcely recognise the rough country girls who had greeted me such a short time before. Now their faces mirrored the serene contemplation of the golden Buddhas on the shrine above them, elusive and indefinable as legendary dakinis.

I began to feel that what was happening in here was spreading out beyond the room and filling the valley. I went out on to the porch, stepping over the piles of shoes left by the door. The interwoven syllables of the Kalachakra mantra were painted by the side of the entrance, colours muted in the moonlight streaming into the porch. The valley was filled with silver light. An arch of stars hung over the snow peaks in a cold stillness that had this tiny point of people and energy at its centre.

Khandro returned, still clutching the heavy teapot. She reached the entranceway and stopped, following my gaze into the empty valley. As she turned, I could see her face in the moonlight, and I could see that she was smiling.

Epilogue

།ཆོས་ཟབ་རྒྱས་སྒྲོགས་ཀྱང་བྲག་ཆ་ལགས།

It is six a.m. A small pool of light illuminates a handful of people sitting quietly at one end of a vast empty hall. On a brocade-covered throne a saffron-robed figure sits motionless, deep in meditation. The atmosphere tingles with expectancy, yet there is a perfectly balanced stillness in that great space.

I have been here before. Not in the geographical sense, because this time we are in Barcelona, and before, it was Switzerland. But in the sense that 'here' is the mandala of the Kalachakra, woven by the meditation of His Holiness the Dalai Lama, and that it is also a reunion of participants in this shared meditation even though many have yet to meet in person.

In a few hours, four thousand people will pour into this room for the concluding stages of the Kalachakra initiation. Each has a personal and different perspective and motivation for being here. For me it is an opportunity to re-connect with a source of inspiration which so easily fades in the busyness of living.

This short, silent space before beginning is also an opportunity to reflect. How much of all this do I really integrate with my life, and how much simply gets left behind with the exotic trappings of the ceremony? How many *Bodhisattvas* have I met, working in war-torn Mostar – and not recognised them in this different context? How much does this blissful sense of interdependence with all Beings actually manifest in a way of living that supports and protects them? The questions go on, more series of images than words. Many of the images are those I encountered in the Himalaya, but many now are re-emerging from my own roots, a heritage not lost but sleeping, just beneath the surface.

I do not know if I will go back. Sometimes I receive letters, from my sister or cousins in Lo, or news of the education project from Yonden. For now, it is a process of integration, establishing a meditation retreat centre under the guidance of Zopa Rinpoche, and allowing what I have learned to evolve beyond a fascination with new ideas, into a way of living and being in harmony with my own world.

'Song of the Profound View'

Translated from the Tibetan verses in chapter headings
by Stephen Batchelor

Once more in my small stone hut into which I alone could fit,
A battle was waged between appearance and reasoning.
To distinguish which was true and which was false
I relied upon the host of magical illusions.

When I examined this old monk who previously seemed
so existent,
He turned out to be just like the tracks of a bird in the sky.
The appearance of a bird just turns through the mind,
But if one looks for its tracks they are inexpressible:
emptiness is all there is.

I reflected upon the mode of being of phenomena;
How can they be different from the example of space?
The manifold things that briefly appear in a variety of ways
Are like drawings on water, that cannot stay forever.
Being of the nature of water, they arise from water;
They repeatedly arise from and dissolve back into it.

If one does not understand the way in which the enemy,
the afflictions, exists,
Then in spite of one's lifelong pride of being a spiritual
person, one will be like a cave.
If one makes no effort in the means of controlling the
self-grasping within one's own mind
Then although one proclaims vast and profound
spiritual truths, they will be like echoes.

Acknowledgements

I would like to express my deep gratitude to His Holiness the Dalai Lama, Dilgo Kyentse Rinpoche, and Trulzhig Rinpoche, for their teachings and the inspiration of their example; and to Lama Thubten Zopa Rinpoche for his kindness, inspiration, guidance and enormous patience over the years.

I would also like to extend my warmest thanks to Geshe Thubten Jinpa, translator to H.H. Dalai Lama, for his advice and help, and for checking this manuscript; to Andy Weber for drawing the lotus on page 246; to Tony Colwell for what is possibly a world record in editorial patience; and to Paul, my life partner and fellow-traveller on the spiritual path, for his love and support through the often painful process of transforming an idea into a book.

The Tibetan text under the chapter titles is reproduced with kind permission of Gonsar Tulku and is taken from verses of 'Song of the Profound View' a poem written by Geshe Rabten during a long meditation retreat in the hills above Dharamsala. These verses, translated into English by Stephen Batchelor, appear on page 261.

Select Bibliography

Batchelor, Stephen, *The Awakening of The West*, Aquarian (HarperCollins), London 1994

Bernbaum, Edward, *The Way to Shambhala*, Anchor Books (Doubleday), New York 1980

Brook, Elaine, and Julie Donnelly, *The Windhorse*, Jonathan Cape, London 1986

——, *Chiwong Mani Rimdu, A Guide to the Festival*, Himalayan Travel, Hereford HR2 0TE, 1992

Harvey, Andrew, *A Journey in Ladakh*, Jonathan Cape, London 1983

His Holiness the Dalai Lama and Benson, Gardner, Thurman, Coleman, *Mind Science: An East-West Dialogue*, Wisdom Publications, 361 Newbury St., Boston, MA 02115, USA, 1993

——, *The World of Tibetan Buddhism*, translated by Geshe Thubten Jinpa, Wisdom Publications, Boston 1995

Hunt, Allan (ed.), *Dharma Gaia*, Parallax Press, Berkeley (Calif) 1990

Jackson, David P., *The Mollas of Mustang*, Library of Tibetan Works and Archives, Dharamsala, India 1984

Kornfield, Jack, *A Path with Heart*, Rider, London 1994

Macey, Joanna, *World as Lover, World as Self*, Parallax Press, Berkeley (Calif) 1991

Peissel, Michel, *Mustang: A Lost Tibetan Kingdom*, Collins and Harvill Press, London 1968

Rabten, Geshe, *Song of the Profound View*, Wisdom Publications, Boston 1989

Roerich, Nicholas, *Altai Himalaya*, Jarrolds, London 1924
Salkeld, Audrey, *People in High Places: Approaches to Tibet*, Jonathan Cape, London 1991; (paperback edn. 1993)
Shaw, Miranda, *Passionate Enlightenment: Women in Tantric Buddhism*, Princeton University Press, 1994
Snellgrove, David, *Himalayan Pilgrimage* (second edition), Shambhala Publications, Boston 1981
Thubten Zopa, Rinpoche, *Transforming Problems into Happiness*, Wisdom Publications, Boston 1993
Vessantara, *Meeting the Buddhas*, Windhorse Publications, Birmingham 1993
Yeshe, Lama, *Introduction to Tantra*, Wisdom Publications, Boston 1987
Yeshe, Lama, and Rinpoche Thubten Zopa, *Wisdom Energy: Basic Buddhist Teachings*, Wisdom Publications, Boston 1987